OAKHAM SCHOOL

LIBRARY

Presented by

S. KEATS

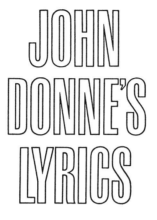

JOHN DONNE'S LYRICS

THE ELOQUENCE OF ACTION

by Arnold Stein

UNIVERSITY OF MINNESOTA PRESS · MINNEAPOLIS

LONDON: OXFORD UNIVERSITY PRESS

To Robert and Ruth Heilman

ACKNOWLEDGMENTS

THE quotations from T. S. Eliot's *Collected Poems, 1909–1935*, and *Four Quartets* are by permission of Harcourt, Brace and World, Inc., and Faber and Faber, Ltd. Passages from Donne's sermons are quoted by permission of the University of California Press from *The Sermons of John Donne*, edited by Evelyn M. Simpson and George R. Potter.

To the published work of Herbert Grierson, Evelyn M. Simpson, Helen White, and Don Cameron Allen I owe debts of long standing. My first apprentice writing on Donne was supervised by Douglas Bush, who, about twenty years ago, suggested that I give my book time to mature. I think I have reasonably satisfied the letter of that advice. The book has wisely dried out in several attics, and this is another book.

For better or worse, I have felt free to borrow from my earlier studies only an occasional point and a few illustrations. The starting place of this book goes back to an essay, "Structures of Sound in Donne's Verse," which the late Charles M. Coffin, friend to all students of Donne, encouraged me to write for the *Kenyon Review*. The material of that essay has been reworked as part of the basis of Chapter I. A few passages from the Introduction are taken from "Donne and the 1920's," which appeared in *ELH*; the opening section of Chapter II appeared as an essay "On Elizabethan Wit" in *Studies in English Literature*. An earlier version of the material on "The Good-morrow" has been published in the proceedings of the

International Conference on Poetics, which took place in Warsaw during August of 1960.

Most of the writing of this book was accomplished under the leisure conferred by the John Simon Guggenheim Memorial Foundation, whose Fellowship I enjoyed for the academic year 1959–60. I am deeply grateful. The Graduate School of the University of Washington has generously helped in the preparation of the manuscript. My colleague, James W. Hall, has listened patiently and borne his burden like a friend. To the University of Minnesota Press, my cordial thanks for much valuable assistance.

Finally, I come to the place where all honest and peace-loving academic authors make the customary declaration. I mean

> *Hesperian* Fables true,
> If true, here only.

I am therefore delighted to say that my most varied obligation is to my wife, Bess D. Stein.

> And if I flatter any, 'tis not you
> But my owne judgement, who did long agoe
> Pronounce, that all these praises should be true.

CONTENTS

John Donne's Lyrics

NOTHING could be plainer than that Donne has been valued for some wrong reasons: for hasty, for unhistorical, for partial reasons; for personal, for self-justifying, or expedient, or obsessive reasons; for reasons more beholden to the interpreted needs of the times than to any principle which presumes to declare its independence of time and interpretation. And what may be said of Donne may be said of every writer interesting enough to endure, or even to endure a vigorous revival.

The history of history does not suggest that the history of literature can be protected from personal distortions. Not that we need be passive toward discovered errors; but it is the nature of what we *call* errors to be discovered after and not before they have been made, and after they have been made some of them at least may prove to have a complicated and stubborn claim or hold on a subsidiary kind of existence. Besides, we must recognize that prime source of literary error: our belief in the present significance of literature written in the past.

I can think of only two alternatives to this predicament. One is impossible, a paper theory: that we abandon all thoughts and feelings of present significance in past literature, that we study it as dead history. (Parts of our study can usefully take this form, I acknowledge, but not the main enterprise.) The second alternative is less obviously impossible, for it embodies a challenging human ideal: that we separate ourselves from the distractions of our immediate interests and concerns in order to think ourselves back to the historical truth-at-the-source. That the effort is ennobling and the results instructive no sane man would deny. It is important to submit ourselves to the discipline of understanding modes of thought and feeling different from our own. But there are difficulties we ought not ignore. Literature intimately involves imagination and feeling and language. Poetry cannot be translated without distortions; nor do we translate ourselves without distortions. As discipline and corrective, the effort is necessary and valuable, but we must remember our own limitations and the native tendency to forget where we started from.

As soon as we begin to exercise a human interest in significance, our efforts are troubled, for better or worse, by our own origins in time, and also by the double motivation that made scholars of us in the first place: the noble human desire to understand the past both for the sake of the past and for the sake of the present. To concentrate on either past or present alone is an incomplete human transaction: the first approaching idolatry, the second approaching robbery.

There is another answer to our predicament, and that is to face the predicament and to wrestle with it as honestly as we can. Then we must accept consciously the struggle with time, the effort to bring past and present into significant relationship — but with no feverish hope for definitive success, with no permanent substitution of a scientific or logical or fixed form of predication for the imaginative predication which the nature and history of literary experience would seem to require. Then we must accept the necessary presence of error and the incompleteness of knowledge. I mean not only incompleteness of the brute information, which can be improved, but the incompleteness of intelligence itself, which may or may not be improved but which can never bring more than a potential part of itself to bear upon the important question. This I take to be a familiar and self-evident fact of individual and historical experience. We are distracted and spasmodic. We concentrate only by excluding other possibilities. Furthermore, part of what intelligence inherits will always prove irrelevant. Most important of all, the literary question is by nature an open one which will not assume its full and latent shape for any intelligence fixed in time. The fact that literature must be experienced individually, must be reperformed, renewed — that is the physical ground for the problem, and anyone can taste the experience of history by consulting the cycles and changes in his own relations with a work of art during one lifetime.

We must believe that it is good to be conscious of problems we cannot solve or dismiss but must work with and against. Donne's modern career requires us to think particularly of the issues always generally present in literary reinterpretations. Donne is a poet of consciousness; in reading him one acquires and begets consciousness. Yet, as this book will endeavor to demonstrate, he is not therefore immune or unresponsive to the familiar claims of the simple. Neither is the writer of this book.

Now I shall speak more specifically about this book and about my sense of its place among modern studies of Donne. I shall begin with the latter and, by way of introduction, review one area of Donne's general appeal to the 1920's.

In Donne the generation after World War I found a frank and direct interest in human experience. To many of these readers Donne must have seemed fresh and authoritative because the experience created by his poems achieved that precious artistic illusion of full immediacy. To a generation shaking off old forms, and suspecting all forms, Donne must have provided an encouraging model for expressing experience apparently freed from the methods and formulations for controlling and understanding experience, although these methods and formulations are, of course, part of the standard equipment of any age, past or present. (Wishing more freedom, we tend to underestimate the subtle controls always present in perception; wishing less freedom, we tend to forget that every effective alteration of thought exhibits the plain inadequacy of those controls which *were* dominating perception. If poets do not deliver any absolutely pure experience, they may still deserve to be forgiven for seeming to do so in the act of enlarging and freshening perception.)

To an age dissatisfied with its own inheritance, and expressing some of its rebellious freedom by shocking comfortable citizens, Donne seemed a kindred spirit — not only by the boldness with which he cut himself loose but by the tortured intensity, the very triumphs and defeats, of his imaginative struggle. His frank interest in the body, in sexual love, and his extraordinary reconciliations of the counterclaims of body and spirit — these passionate experiments attracted a generation discovering its own immediate interest in such problems. If the issue of sex reminds us of Freud, so too ought Donne's remarkable demonstrations of the irrationality as well as the rationality of the human mind. The very old problem of the relations between reason and faith could suddenly present a new fascination as the world began to discover that what had seemed a matter of private conflict for the old-fashioned Christian was a central issue in the new public wars of political ideologies. The fact that there were differences — that men of the new world suffered from the modern infectious dilemma of trying to believe in their own motives while cynically deriding the motives of others — would hardly have diminished interest in a poet who showed how deep and far-reaching the old problem was. Furthermore, Donne was a poet peculiarly able to satisfy the appetite for medieval thought which has been increasingly characteristic of modern culture. And to those who felt, whether consciously or not, the currents of neo-orthodoxy Donne had much to offer. Many no doubt learned from him how relevant even to the modern mind were old lessons from moral theology.

Some final items may help to round out this general catalogue. Donne's poetry illustrates richly the theme of self-division, explored by imaginative consciousness; the theme of death; and the sense of alienation, variously and significantly struggled against. Perhaps we may attribute to Donne much of the same sort of attraction that Hamlet has exerted upon the modern mind.

I review this general range of Donne's appeal because it is so much a part of recent history that we cannot avoid being affected. No one is likely, for a while, to use the old arguments in praise of Donne as if they were still new. Yet we cannot assume that, since the poets and critics of the 1920's made errors, and did not solve the problems they raised, all of the life has gone out of their issues. Some of the items in the above review will make an occasional, recognizable appearance in this book.

Now I turn to a specific matter which has produced a spectacular history. For a couple of decades the existence of a physical immediacy of thought in Donne enjoyed a status rather like that of a dogma of poetic faith — celebrated and invoked, often illustrated and extended by analogy, but seldom examined. Under such circumstances, disciples are likely to discover that their warrants bear the unmistakable style of their own handwriting. A dogma revealed as a mystery is a little embarrassing to those who embraced it as a demonstrable secular truth.

We can easily predict, in retrospect, the efficient work of disengaged historical criticism. Rosemond Tuve will re-create a full pattern of Elizabethan critical commitments and will make clearer for us the discriminating concept of *decorum* and the Renaissance ideal of *wholeness* in literary expression. Leonard Unger will turn a cool eye on the efforts of Eliot and others to understand, to rationalize, to retreat as gracefully as possible from the declared fact of the "fusion of sensibility." René Wellek will demonstrate with full and exacting detail the history of Eliot's parallel efforts in criticism and poetry. Joseph Duncan will produce the immediate background of previous critical efforts to relate thought and feeling. Frank Kermode will undertake a wholesale debunking of the "myth" of man's fall from the undissociated state.[1]

But when all the facts are before us what we are left with, unless we are historical cynics or shortsighted partisans happy in a brief triumph, is the realization that this particular problem may have been explained away, but has not been explained. The answer Eliot produced was in response to a felt question of the times. Perhaps the question is no longer felt; more likely it is no longer felt in ways which can accept the adequacy of the previous official answer. Part of the changes revealed by the unfolding of historical time will always be involved in the discovery that previous answers are no longer adequate. But if we decide that an answer was a pseudo answer, we must not therefore, in our natural enthusiasm to strike off old bonds, conclude that the question was a pseudo question. The solution may have been peremptory, and Donne may not have been a mute inglorious Moses, of rediscovered eloquence and reasserted fame, to lead us forth. But the question of human integration, of integrity, of human wholeness in art or life, remains. It is an old question, so old that we may confidently expect it to be ever new.

Emphasis on the physical immediacy of Donne's thought drew massive attention to the metaphysical conceit. In retrospect we can see that this critical concern was also inspired by certain problems of compelling interest to the new poetics beginning to emerge. An impure or mixed motive, once identified, is likely to provoke suspicious inquiry. Perhaps it is not too skeptical to think that the most effective intellectual motives defy exact identification. And certainly, pure, or at least acceptable, by-products are not infrequently created out of motives that cannot endure too rigorous an examination. Because of insufficient knowledge and historical perspective, and because of an almost obsessive intensity of interest in matters of contemporary concern, modern criticism of Donne made certain historical errors that we shall not want to make again — though it would be rash to assume that new historical errors are not getting ready to be made and discovered.

My present concern, however, is with the critical distortion created by concentrating on Donne's imagery. Leonard Unger and Rosemond Tuve have collected and analyzed the important evidence. No doubt their work has discouraged further applications of the previous critical emphasis. But in addition it may be observed that any cooperative intellectual effort needs to be nourished by the belief that it is continuing to make advances. The dilemma of the program which concentrated on the metaphysical conceit was that it began with a kind of revelation of absolute accomplishment and then found that it had no place really to go. A systematic piety could produce, with scholarly resourcefulness, many parallels and intermediate distinctions that exhibited a practical applicability of the new touchstone. But a certain alchemistical fervor could not long conceal the fact that, if the master knew exactly how, and how far, the new principle was to be applied, and knew its detailed examinable process of derivation, he was no longer about to make an important disclosure. Nor, apparently, was anyone else.

The merits of Donne did not, of course, go unchallenged. Nor were the reliable resources of human reaction rendered inarticulate by the sudden increase in Donne's literary stature. I pass by this interesting history because it has little bearing on the present book. For the same reason, and with a sense of charity and relief, I shall not refer, any further, to the foolish controversy between the admirers of Donne and the admirers of Milton.

I do want, however, to pause for a moment on another item of modern history. The early reception of the revived Donne was inevitably influenced by the early reception of *The Waste Land*. What in Donne most immediately suited the mood of the times was greeted with an excitement which favored the results of imaginative identification and insight more than those of a calm judiciousness. The historian studying Donne's influence cannot, of course, uncritically accept that first excitement, but he must be careful not to discredit it too thoroughly. He should at least recognize and respect its potential value; for immediacy of feeling, whatever its limitations in breadth and balance, must be granted an importance in imaginative understanding and insight. The historian is used to envying the unattainable advantages in immediacy of a first audience; for that very reason, he should not be indifferent to certain related advantages enjoyed by the first audience of a revival. If he has learned the right lessons from his own youthful enthusiasms, he will not try to root them out but to correct and redirect them.

To look back before looking forward, obsession with the conceit may be blamed for hindering the development of critical questions that seemed to promise less ultimate answers. In recent work Helen Gardner, Frank Kermode, and A. Alvarez have expressed attitudes toward Donne which in the past have been neglected. A statement by Miss Gardner is perhaps most central:

It is the fashion today in scholarly circles, in reaction against earlier idolizing of Donne, to exalt his wit at the expense of his artistic and intellectual integrity, and to deny that ideas had any value to him as a poet except as counters to be used in an argument. Donne's greatness needs restating. One element of that greatness is that certain ideas mattered to him intensely and that he made them wholly his own.[2]

Taking Donne's wit seriously has perhaps been more frequent in American than in English criticism. But taking his ideas and images with the right kind of seriousness, which does not confuse the literal and the imaginative, or separate them wrongly, constitutes a problem that is not likely to be solved by any simple formula. For instance, the incremental weight of meaning behind an image, and yet the delicate individuality of its use — both of these are well illustrated by a recent learned demonstration. I refer to the substantial essay by A. B. Chambers on "Goodfriday, 1613. Riding Westward."[3] A formula more often mentioned than satisfactorily followed is that of taking the poem seriously as a whole unit. Though it is easy to deceive oneself and mistake a rather large part for the real whole, Donne's poems demand that we make an uncommon effort to rise above half measures. But many more people would agree to the above statement than would agree to any definition of "wholeness" in poetry.

Let me illustrate the issue by quoting Miss Gardner again, this time in order to disagree with her. In her introduction to *The Metaphysical Poets* and in *The Business of Criticism*, Miss Gardner emphasizes the importance of Donne's critical remark on the Psalms: "And therefore it is easie to observe, that in all Metricall compositions, of which kinde the booke of Psalmes is, the force of the whole piece, is for the most part left to the shutting up; the whole frame of the Poem is a beating out of a piece of gold, but the last clause is as the impression of the stamp, and that is it that makes it currant" (*Sermons*, VI, 41). The statement surely deserves emphasis, but not in isolation. Donne's poems have in the past suffered from critical overresponse to certain brilliant openings, as if Donne did not write whole poems. It is possible also to overemphasize his endings, and Miss Gardner may be encouraging others to do this when she speaks of the "final stamp" as "the point towards which the whole has moved."[4] Some of her difficulty with "Aire and Angels" would seem to derive from the kind of expectation she brings to the ending.

As we shall see in the section "Binary Forms" in Chapter II, Donne can on occasion be rather casual about the end of a poem.

The safest assumption, surely, is that, when Donne seriously thought of the form of anything, he thought of the individual parts and proportions that, in their continuity, composed the whole form. In the sermon from which Miss Gardner quotes, the preacher is at pains to elucidate the sequence and proportion that justify the final brevity of the thanksgiving of Psalm 6. The last clause is not considered except in relation to the rest, and it is a rather long "clause" of three verses, the text of the sermon. Much of the preacher's fine work goes into establishing patterns of relationship and continuity that make allowable the interpretation of the end as bearing "a milder sense then the words seeme at first to present." (This requires hard, close work, not unlike the work Donne certainly put into many of his own poems, with far less evidence of strain; the standard of construction is unmistakably similar, and the reader should mark this well.) It is interesting to note that Donne as a literary man draws inferences, though "only in passing," from the "delicacy, and harmony, and melody of language." We can seldom afford such inferences in analyzing *his* use of affective language.

Insofar as the exegesis demonstrates anything that concerns his own poems, it exhibits Donne's belief in complete structures that may not be immediately visible but that yield themselves to scrupulous analysis and are proved by it. What is condensed, or elliptical, or significantly omitted, justifies itself by reason of the sequence, proportion, and responsible meaning of the whole. In scriptural interpretation ambiguity may mark only the "personal" differences among reasonable interpreters of the text and may yield rather easily to the claims of metaphorical precision. Donne's own dealings with the metaphors of the Holy Ghost, whether satisfactory or not, always exhibit a high standard of metaphorical precision. (The same precision, one may infer, would be expected of metaphors in poems, and of their relations to the whole; the chief difference is that poetic metaphors would not be endowed with so rich and stable a potency of relation to a whole literature of established knowledge and belief.)

Let me quote another of Donne's "literary" comments on Scripture for its relevance to the present discussion. He confesses a "spiritual appetite" for the Psalms and the Epistles of St. Paul, which are

written in such forms, as I have been accustomed to; Saint *Pauls* being Letters, and *Davids* being Poems: for God . . . gives us our instruction in cheerfull forms . . . in *Psalms*, which is also a limited, and a restrained form; Not in an *Oration*, not in *Prose*, but in *Psalms*; which is such a form as is both curious, and requires diligence in the making, and then when it is made, can have nothing, no syllable taken from it, nor added to it: Therefore is Gods will delivered to us in *Psalms*, that we might have it the more cheerfully, and that we might have it the more certainly, because where all the words are numbered, and measured, and weighed, the whole work is the lesse subject to falsification, either by subtraction or addition (*Sermons*, II, 49–50).

Critical problems which concern the relations between Donne's poetry and prose are strenuous and complex; they have not invited enough of the kind of attention they need. But I wish only to insist now on my single point: Donne's intellectual allegiance to an ideal wholeness of form, and to the rational interdependence of parts which alone can create a "certainty" of the whole. Donne wrote his best poems with a diligent regard for wholeness. After conversion he allows himself a "spiritual appetite"; but to his audience he suggests, and to readers of his poems he proves, that before conversion he possessed an appetite for strict forms capable of defending themselves from the challenge of critical addition or subtraction.

Though Donne prized and achieved the effects of spontaneity, both his experience as poet and his experience as orator must have convinced him that the hard work of deliberate thought and precise rhetoric was the indispensable means to the ends of spontaneity. And it is plain that certainty of the whole, whether in poem or sermon, depends upon exactness of the parts. That Donne was deliberate and remarkably conscious in his aims can hardly stand in doubt. Some personal evidence that he expected able readers to recognize and value his efforts may be found in the 1627 letter to Sir Robert Ker: "the King who hath let fall his eye upon some of my Poems, never saw, of mine, a hand, or an eye, or an affection, set down with so much study, and diligence, and labour of syllables, as in this Sermon I expressed those two points." [5]

We may learn something useful from Donne's basic distinction between rhetoric and poetry. When faced with the impossible task of expressing eternity, rhetoric is "empty" and poetry is "weak." What Donne has in mind would seem to be significant. "Rhetorique will make absent and remote things present to your understanding . . . Poetry is a counterfait Creation, and makes things that are not, as though they were" (*Sermons*, IV, 87). If we may infer that Donne's brevity (his remarks are parenthetical) aims at the essential, then we may take seriously the difference between emptiness and weakness. The illusion of poetry, though more complete, in creating the nonexistent rather than re-creating the remote, nevertheless cannot be called "empty." Take away the disabling task of expressing eternity, and the completeness of the poetic illusion must be related to its excellence and profundity. Donne had the same notion in mind when he wrote for Sir Robert Ker the message prefixed to "An Hymne to the Saints, and to Marquesse Hamylton": "you know my uttermost when it was best, and even then I did best when I had least truth for my subjects. In this present case there is so much truth as it defeats all Poetry." Donne may be referring here to his "Anniversaries," the exaggerations of which he defended along similar lines.

I raise this matter because it has some bearing on the wholeness of poems. Not that we are likely to piece together, with any satisfaction, a coherent theory of poetry which Donne may be thought to have held. Nevertheless, we do need to recognize, I am convinced, an element of pure imagination in his poems; for a solid base of his conscious art is the understanding that "Poetry is a counterfait Creation, and makes things that are not, as though they were." Nor is Donne invoking a license for merely frivolous fictions and illusions, like blossoms of artificial truth gaily produced from some abstract nonexistence of untruth. Donne can perform that difficult philosophical feat, and it is not frivolous: "Of the first nothing, the Elixer grown." It is plain that he enjoys the light fictions that play lies into truths and truths into lies. The activity is one important range of his art, but only one. There are also those poems, among his best, in which there is an understood sense that the fiction is a significant one. In these poems the fiction is not to be dismissed because it is a fiction; nor can it be translated directly into the literal; nor can the significance be defined satisfactorily in terms of either the serious or the unserious.

As a matter of fact, if we do not try to reconstruct (or construct) Donne's theory of poetry and imagination, but watch his practice with fictions, we can see that the poem in its *wholeness* may be a "counterfait Creation," but that it is made only in part of "things that are not." The poem is also composed of things remote and things present, as the literal and the imaginative work with and against each other in the unique partnership that creates the individual poem.

It is hard to talk sensibly about the "counterfait Creation" that is the whole poem in its integrity; yet I shall need to make an occasional effort in that direction. But what of the integrity of the poet himself? It is not my opinion that Donne was a brilliant playboy with ideas. And the true poet, as the Renaissance wished to think, may indeed be a true poem himself. But if he wrote lyric poems, the members which compose that personal integrity may be rather widely strewn about, some of them under inscrutable disguise and not quite responsive to a wind instrument that declares the critical day of judgment. I do not promise a direct, sustained, and coherent attack on the subject, but something can be done. This book begins with the premise that Donne's poetic mind aspired, not without success, to integrity. The nature of that integrity will require some explaining, and the process of demonstration cannot be separated from some indirect searching for evidence.

It may be useful to state the kind of mind which Donne did not have. He was, it seems clear, interested in orderly irrationality, and in the disorderly intrusions that make their spontaneous presence felt. But he was not interested in anesthetizing consciousness, or in fragmenting it for the sake of the brilliant (and informative) kaleidoscopes of modern invention. The speakers of his poems may be candidates for modernity in the mobility and inclusiveness of what they see and feel; but they do not fail to possess or discover a focused center of conscious will. Montaigne gives himself seriously to the whims of the mind in a way, and to an extent, which endows him with a modernity that Donne cannot claim. Self-division and self-consciousness in Donne are the unavoidable materials of a conflict which aspires toward resolution. Montaigne would have been interested, but Donne appalled, I think, by the consequences of Hume's analysis:

Our thought is still more variable than our sight; and all our other senses and faculties contribute to this change; nor is there any single power of the soul, which remains unalterably the same, perhaps for one moment. The mind is a kind of theatre, where several perceptions successively make their appearance; pass, re-pass, glide away, and mingle in an infinite variety of postures and situations. There is properly no *simplicity* in it at one time, nor *identity* in different; whatever natural propension we may have to imagine that simplicity and identity.[6]

Though there are passages in Donne that resemble Hume's argument, in Donne such analyses prove to be intellectual and moral maneuvers in a larger campaign — not against the idea of personal identity, but against the evasions within himself.

To mark the difference we need only remind ourselves of the solid structure of continuous rationality in Donne's poems. But we may help ourselves to a more positive distinction by considering Coleridge's admiring comment on "The Canonization": "One of my favorite poems. As late as ten years ago, I used to seek and find out grand lines and fine stanzas; but my delight has been far greater since it has consisted more in tracing the leading thought thro'out the whole. The former is too much like coveting your neighbor's goods; in the latter you merge yourself in the author, you *become He*."[7] We are helped further if we also note a passage from a sermon on which Coleridge simply commented: "Mem. What a beautiful sentence. The eloquence of Inferiors is in words, the eloquence of Superiors is in action!!"[8] Donne has been comparing to music, rhetoric, and logic the kinds of persuasion which "superiors" may present to his soul: "but when I see them actually, really, clearely, constantly do thus, this is a Demonstration to my soule, and Demonstration is the powerfullest proofe: The eloquence of inferiours is in words, the eloquence of superiours is in action" (*Sermons*, VI, 227). When we put these passages together it seems reasonable to say that Coleridge was praising "The Canonization" as a kind of "demonstration to my soul," the complete action of a superior, that powerful proof by means of which "you merge yourself in the author, you *become He.*"

In his best poems Donne aspires to the eloquence of action and never to the eloquence of words. He could have acknowledged the justness, once he had learned the modern idiom, of a remark by another great master of self-imposed difficulties, Paul Valéry:

Man does little else but invent. But he who becomes aware of the facility, fragility, and incoherence of this production will oppose to it the effort of his mind . . . Logic is the best known and most important of all the explicit, formal conventions that the mind sets up against itself. Well-defined poetic rules, methods, canons and proportions, rules of harmony, laws of composition, fixed forms — all these are not (as is generally supposed) formulas of restricted creation. Their fundamental aim is to lead the complete and organized man — *the being made for action, whom, in return, his action perfects* — to bring his whole self to bear upon the production of works of the mind.[9]

To say that Donne aspires to the eloquence of action is to recognize an ideal and to admit some difficulties. The *doing* in a poem by Donne can at best be that of a man trying to become his own superior self "actually, really, clearly, constantly." The action in a poem is perhaps less like a moral or religious action, which may be done clearly and constantly, with a mastered ease of habit, than it is like what Donne calls a holy action: "[we may go] so far, as to bring holy Resolutions into Actions; yet never so far, as to bring holy Actions into Habits" (*Sermons*, IX, 180). In spite of disciplined efforts, an author of "holy Actions," like an author of the actions of poems, cannot reduce to the assurance of habit that indispensable freedom of spontaneity by which the individual shapes and accepts his act.

In Donne's poems we may expect to find significant conflicts between a logic (either serious or playful) and the fiction of a proposition, between the imaginative materials of a "counterfait Creation" *ex nihilo* and the undeniable materials of common experience, between the detachment of wit and the lyric persuasiveness of personal involvement, between the abstractness of ruling ideas and the concreteness of the immediacies of particular experience. We may expect to find ruling ideas which act (for better and worse) as habits of mind, but which may also act as motivating forces toward individually experienced answers. In Donne these answers will not be monumental landmarks, but will be dignified by individual questioning. The answers may be humanized, even, by being made to share in any incidental laughter.

Donne is modern in his full sense of the difficult, in his acceptance of the pressures exerted by a skeptical awareness of diversity, and in his authoritative attention to the immediate details present in the flux of experience. But he is impressively old-fashioned in his tenacious efforts to transform those problems which he discovers in himself into a unity which aspires toward an eloquence of action.

Conscious thought *and* spontaneity together compose the poem, the persuasive wholeness of which we desire to honor by the inferior eloquence of words. *Integrity* is such a word. The *eloquence of action* is another. We assume, because the ideal is necessary, and because we have no other positive choice, that the wholeness of the man is best reflected in the work. But we are not able to transfer the image intact, though we may learn something of Donne's efforts from our own. For example, we may learn to see that Donne's career, as private man, poet, and articulate man of God, deeply honors the ideal eloquence of action, in part, by not dishonoring the freedom of spontaneity which makes an act individual. The oppositions, within man and poem, however hard they strive to achieve order, do not strive to annihilate each other in that order. Words aspire to action. Action aspires to the integrated simplicity of an ultimate eloquence. What is achieved, at best, is an honorable truce, a literary eloquence of action.

The highest purpose of this book is to gain some insight into the integrity of Donne's poetic mind, and this purpose requires taking seriously two propositions: that Donne is a poetic logician endowed with a talent and love for the unity of imaginative form; and that Donne's poetry, though it is not simple, nevertheless deeply and persistently engages important problems which concern "simplicity."

The preceding pages offer a partly detached commentary on this book. These pages are the last ones to be written. They deal abruptly, from the perspective of conclusion, with issues that must justify themselves gradually — by attention to reasonable alternatives, and by due process of evidence, illustration, and argument. The issues I have here discussed, by way of introduction, are ones that I consider most important in the book. And so these remarks, I realize and explain, while intended as introductory, also reflect my final attitudes.

A book on Donne cannot be simple. It certainly cannot be complete. This book has tried to make a number of concessions to the reader: I cite particularly the restricted attention directed toward "The Extasie" and "The Canonization." There are many other silences and brevities. For some of these I might claim conscious courage or experienced cowardice; others merely happen. I have not tried to give all aspects of Donne's lyrics equal emphasis, and I have limited the amount of my reference to his other poems. Many of my observations on the "forms" of Donne's wit were first derived from study of the longer poems, but I have preferred to concentrate the argument. My emphasis on the serious bent of Donne's wit consciously subordinates, as less important for present understanding, his accomplishments in lighter and broader kinds of wit. If on some occasions my efforts may appear too "serious," I offer this defense: there are arguments that cannot be made at all without a disproportionate energy of emphasis, and it is better to rely on the quick good sense of the reader than to burden him with an equal measure of qualification.

CHAPTER I

QUESTIONS OF *Style*

ONE historical introduction to Donne's kind of verse is Ben Jonson's blunt remark to Drummond that verses stand by sense, without "either Colours or accent." [1] In spite of Jonson's personal exaggeration this comment reflects a traditional English approach to the problem of form and content. Sir Philip Sidney is as extreme as Jonson: "any understanding" knows that the skill of the poet is "in that *Idea* or foreconceite of the work, and not in the work it self." [2] Gascoigne, in paraphrasing Horace ("verbaque provisam rem non invita sequentur"), also advised the writer to "grounde [his work] upon some fine invention . . . pleasant woordes will follow well inough and fast inough." [3] Though adding to the original a little schoolmasterly optimism and also the notion of the "pleasant" words, Gascoigne was in the last instance faithfully interpreting a prevailing concept of style. As Quintilian had authoritatively summed up the standard rhetorical position: "words harsh to the ear fittingly describe terrible things, but in general the best words are those that are either most expressive or most pleasant in sound." [4] In theory the secondary laws of decorum would justify minor departures from a prevailing pleasantness, but in practice the primary law that required a poet to be a delightful teacher put a special value on the attractive exterior of his lesson. Fifty years after Gascoigne, Henry Peacham is reaffirming the idea of necessary pleasantness: "A sweete verse is that which, like a dish with a delicate Sauce, invites the Reader to taste, even against his will; the contrarie is harshness." [5]

Looked at from one point of view, the major development of English verse in the sixteenth century might be described as the perfecting of the delicate sauce of the dish. If we think mostly of the five-stress line of the sonnet and other nondramatic verse forms, it is possible to trace this development from Surrey to Spenser. (Surrey may not be the best starting point but there can be little doubt that Spenser marks the peak of the development.) Still maintaining our single point of view, we become aware that after the peak is passed we begin to encounter, both in critical statement and in poetic practice, increasing objections to the concept of the pleasant exterior. We have the testimony of Ben Jonson, whose taste runs more to the dish than to the sauce. We know what he thinks about the kind of verse that "runs and slides, and onely makes a sound." [6] There is George Chapman, who is concerned with matter more important than the tunefulness of his verse. We know what he thinks about poets who can "give a verse smooth feet" but who have no other "tollerable merits." [7] There are other voices but, most important, there is the practice of Donne. His view may be summed up in the line "I sing not, Siren like, to tempt." [8] It is also helpful to know that our perspective is partly shared by Dr. Johnson, who associates Ben Jonson's taste for sound with Donne's: "[his] manner resembled that of Donne more in the ruggedness of his lines than in the cast of his sentiments." Dr. Johnson is aware of the development that leads to Donne's "ruggedness," though he does not try very seriously to explain it: "The poets of Elizabeth had attained an art of modulation, which was afterwards neglected or forgotten." [9]

The great trick that the sixteenth century mastered in the long line (Chaucer was an occasional master, but without colleagues) was that of modulating the rhythm by a deliberate use of the weight implicit in the syllabic structure of the ideal iambic pattern. Note, for instance, Daniel's line, "Paint shadows in imaginary lines." [10] Here the syllabic pattern acts as a kind of ballast to the two feet of the line that are most lightly stressed. The rhythm dips away from the iambic, but is gracefully held from going too far. The effect of the modulation is, relatively speaking, to bring the movement of the line away from the vertical and toward the horizontal, away from a dominantly up-and-down forward motion toward a dominantly forward motion. If the reader did not feel the strong pull of the iambic pattern but had to depend only upon the natural rhetorical emphasis of the line, he would share the difficulty of some resolute antimetrists in finding more than three syllables to stress.

The poets between Chaucer and Wyatt did not use the iambic pattern in this way. I quote two examples, the first from Lydgate, the second from Hawes:

> And to do plesaunce to our lord Iesu,
> He studieth evere to have intelligence;
> Reedyng off bookis bryngith in vertu,
> Vices excludyng, slouthe and necligence,
> Makith a prynce to have experience,
> To knowe hymsilff, in many sundri wise,
> Wher he trespasith his errour to chastise.

> For under a colour, / a truthe may aryse
> As was the guyse / in olde antyquytye
> Of the poetes olde / a tale to surmyse
> To cloke the trouthe / of theyr infyrmyte
> Or yet on Ioye / to have moralyte
> I me excuse / yf by neclygence
> That I do offende / for lacke of scyence.[11]

The iambic pattern in these verses would seem to be most strongly felt as a pattern of stresses. At one extreme the verse approaches the old accentual verse, and does not at all mind admitting an extra unstressed syllable or dropping one. It shows a marked taste for beginning a line or the first foot after the caesura with a stressed syllable, and it sometimes keeps *the effect* of a rough trochaic rhythm going throughout. Most of the metrical variation, the modulating away from the ideal iambic pattern, is in the direction of the accentual. When the syllabic structure is most marked, it coincides (a kind of metrical literalness) almost exactly with the ideal pattern — as in the first, fifth, and sixth lines from Lydgate and the second, fourth, and fifth from Hawes (who, interestingly, carries this regularity through the *b* rhyme of the stanza). But even when the syllabic structure is most marked, the line is still felt as a pattern of stresses, a very regular kind of accentual verse. The movement is dominantly up-

and-down; some of the syllables that are light, and that might potentially flow into each other with more of a forward motion, as the syllables do in Daniel's line, are stiffened by stress and kept distinctly separate. The effect, I believe, cannot entirely be explained in terms of technical skill or its absence. It expresses, whatever else may be involved, a characteristic taste in the rhythms of English.

Let us look at another example, from Barclay's *Ship of Fools*:

> But of *gram*er *knowe* they *lyty*ll or *no* thynge,
> Which is the grounde of *all lybe*rall *cun*nynge;
> Yet many ar besy in logyke *and* in lawe,
> Whan all theyr gramer is skarsly worth a strawe.[12]

They are not elegant lines but they are capable ones. What are we to think when Dr. Tillyard, who certainly does not lack taste, says that the only way to read verses like these "is to gabble them breathlessly with the hopeful intention of lighting on four main accents a line"? May we not think that he is measuring these lines by the standard of a different taste in sound, the one represented by the development from Surrey to Spenser? Another of Ben Jonson's remarks to Drummond provides us with a relevant distinction here: "He said to the King his master M. G. Buchanan had corrupted his eare when young & learned him to sing Verses, when he sould have read them."[13] These are nonsinging verses. In part they use the iambic pattern in what will be one of Donne's ways, to emphasize, to make the rhythm serve the argument as the speaking voice does. That is what happens when the stress falls on "*lyty*ll" and "*no*," on "*all lybe*rall"; even the disproportionate stress of "in logyke *and* in lawe" is the exaggeration of mocking overemphasis. Yet everything in the rhythm cannot be explained in terms of emphasis on the meaning. Back of these lines, and giving them their over-all movement, one may perhaps hear the irritated conviction of the poet. And back of that, still, there is the tradition of verse rhythm to which this example belongs.

We come now to Wyatt, who is the great master before Donne. Wyatt, besides great skill at making a structure of sound work rhetorically and dramatically, has a characteristic taste in rhythm that is closer to the examples quoted above (however more complex and refined) than to the main development from Surrey to Spenser. For instance:

> The *longe love*, that in my thought doeth harbar
> And in myn hert doeth kepe his residence,
> *In*to my *face pres*eth with bolde pretence,
> And therin campeth, *spred*ing *his ban*er.
>
> .   .   .   .
>
> And ther him hideth, *and not* appereth.
> What may I do *when* my *mais*ter fereth.
>
> *Was* I never yet of your love greved,
> Nor never shall while that my liff doeth last;
> *But* of *hat*ing myself that date is past,
> And teeres continuell sore *have* me *wer*ied.
> I will not yet *in* my *grave* be *bur*ied.
>
> *Love* and fortune and my mynde, remembre.
>
> *Like* to these unmeasurable montayns
> *Is* my painfull lyff, the burden of Ire.
>
> *I* have sene theim gentill tame and meke
> That nowe are wyld *and* do *not* remembre
> *That* sometyme they put theimself in daunger.
>
> .   .   .   .
>
> *Bes*ely seking with a continuell chaunge.
>
> .   .   .   .
>
> It was no dreme: I *lay brode wak*ing.[14]

The first and last of these lines may be considered as approaching one extreme — that of a kind of accentual verse in which the metrical structure depends almost entirely upon the stressed syllables, while the unstressed ones fit in where they can or are casually dropped. The last line but one, in the above, adds rather than drops unstressed syllables and thus indicates the expansion that is quite as possible as contraction in this kind of accentual verse.

To my ear these lines from Wyatt are related not only to some of the poetry that preceded his, and to Donne's, but to some twentieth-century poetry — which has also cultivated vertical rhythms and has, indeed, developed a metrical idiom drawing liberally upon patterns of stress. A notable example is the opening passage of T. S. Eliot's

"The Dry Salvages," where unstressed syllables expand the structure:

> The problem once solved, the brown god is
>   almost forgotten
> By the dwellers in cities — ever, however,
>   implacable,
> Keeping his seasons and rages, destroyer,
>   reminder
> Of what men choose to forget. Unhonoured,
>   unpropitiated
> By worshippers of the machine, but waiting,
>   watching and waiting.

When the verse contracts, to range stressed syllable by stressed syllable (as Wyatt's does), the forward motion is tilted even more to the vertical —"The sea is the land's edge also, the granite." Eliot is of course the master of many rhythms, but it is significant how well he likes the stiffened, separated accents natural to spoken English, as in the opening section of "East Coker":

> Now the light falls
> Across the open field, leaving the deep lane
> Shuttered with branches, dark in the afternoon.

The stiffness has much more grace, but is descended from "Vices excludyng, slouthe and necligence." And Eliot's line which opens the last section of *Ash-Wednesday*, "Although I do not hope to turn again," is, for all the difference, in the tradition of Lydgate's "And to do plesaunce to our lord Iesu."

We come finally to Donne. Whether we like the effects or not, his verse characteristically sounds different from the verse of most of his contemporaries. The difference would seem to oppose the Renaissance idea of necessary pleasantness — the dish with a delicate sauce. For Donne is a conscious master of harshness. Although many of his effects have their immediate reference to the dramatic context, these do not concern us for the moment. One becomes aware that, beyond the context, and sometimes even beyond Donne's own dominant taste for metrical sound, there is an attitude that requires harshness — as if it were a kind of necessary unpleasantness, a sauce that does not invite the reader, does not tempt him siren-like, but manages with artistic deliberateness to set his teeth on edge. This attitude may comment on conventional love situations. It may comment on popular verse styles, or on popular social manners. It may cultivate harshness as a comment on those who cultivate grace. It may reflect the wit who is rejecting the unrewarding world, or it may reflect a Christian *contemptus mundi*. This last, we may guess, is back of the harshness in the following verses:

> yet he'will weare
> Taken from thence, flesh, which deaths force may trie.

> And life, by this death abled, shall controule
> Death, whom thy death slue; nor shall to mee
> Feare of first or last death, bring miserie.

The attitude here expressed, like Donne's frequent cultivation of satire, produces a structure of sound that is not contradictory to Donne's basic taste. And to that extent, at least, we are dealing with something that goes beyond the context. We ought perhaps to take a similar view of some of Donne's repetitions of the same sound. We may notice many instances when the repetition drives home a point — as, "Moyst, with one drop of thy blood, my dry soule." But there are many examples where the only discernible point is that Donne likes the effect —"Charity and liberty give me. What is hee?" [15]

When the repetition of a sound is maintained through several lines it becomes increasingly difficult to discover an explanation exclusively in terms of the context. Except that Donne's repetitions seldom contribute to a soothing musical effect, they are not entirely unlike some virtuoso passages in Spenser, where "Birdes, voices, instruments, windes, waters, all agree." Note, for instance, "The Indifferent":

> Oh we are not, be not you so,
> Let mee, and doe you, twenty know.
> Rob mee, but binde me not, and let me goe.
> Must I, who came to travaile thorow you,
> Grow your fixt subject, because you are true?
> . . . .
> But I have told them, since you will be true,
> You shall be true to them, who'are false to you.

There is so much emphasis through repetition that a general effect or mood of emphasis may be thought to go beyond any merely local needs for rhetorical pointing. A device that could in another poet create a mood of sensuous relaxation, here where the rhythm is brisk and vertical, the syllables kept stiffly apart, creates a mood of earnest argument. The same may be said of the following lines from Chaucer; beyond the emphasis on the words there is an emphasis on the dramatic personality, or dramatic pose, of the speaker:

> What? is this al the joye and al the feste?
> Is this youre *reed*, is this my blisful cas?
> Is this the verr*ay mede* of your byheeste?
> Is al this *pay*nted proces *seyd*, allas! [16]

Criseyde's little set speech to Pandarus mostly serves to create a formal attitude that expresses her dramatic role. In Donne's poem the pressure of the repetitions serves the exaggerated pose of the speaker, and so serves the larger dramatic context of the poem. At the same time it expresses one familiar strain, though exaggerated, of Donne's personal poetic voice.

Donne's poetic voice is a subject of permanent interest, but all descriptions must be taken as partial and contributory: there can be no exact definition or final description. We cannot characterize his voice by a line, or a poem, or by studying as many of the technical properties of his verse as we can isolate and describe. Yet the subject is not the less important therefore; nor will it seem illusory to students of literature.

I have indicated thus far Donne's basic taste for a kind of artistic harshness that prefers the varied tones of emphasis to any of the tones of song. This is a view of Donne which has excited less interest than other views, but it has long been recognized, and it illustrates a necessary feature of his character as a poet. De Quincey described Donne's rhetoric in terms which the Renaissance admirer of Donne would have thought correct, as far as they went: "The very first eminent rhetorician in the English literature is Donne. Dr. Johnson inconsiderately classes him in company with Cowley, &c., under the title of *Metaphysical* Poets . . . *Rhetorical* would have been a more accurate designation. In saying *that*, however, we must remind our readers that we revert to the original use of the word

Rhetoric, as laying the principal stress upon the management of the thoughts, and only a secondary one upon the ornaments of style." [17] And Coleridge, no less interested in "the management of the thoughts," went further still in his recognition of the continuous relationship between the *dispositio* and the *elocutio* — further, as he was a better critic, than perhaps any of Donne's contemporaries could have gone. To read Donne, he said, one must read by "the sense of Passion," "with all the force and meaning which are involved in the words"; "the sense must be understood in order to ascertain the metre." [18]

It is now generally agreed that the sensuous qualities of Donne's verse are marshaled primarily for rhetorical and intellectual and dramatic emphasis. But the intricacies of that observation are considerable; nor will the observation itself tell us enough about the sensuous qualities of Donne's verse. Nevertheless, there is an unmistakable soundness in the distinction that sees Donne as interested more in the immediacies of meaning than in the immediacies of grace. And though we must attempt to qualify that distinction if we hope to improve our understanding of Donne's verse, we cannot do better than to begin with it. We may perhaps usefully modify one of Coleridge's points and remind ourselves that the meter is not always to be understood by means of the sense. Coleridge is of course thinking of the many difficult places in Donne. But it is well to notice that the reverse of his statement also is true — that the "sense," and "the force and meaning which are involved in the words," often require our giving proper emphasis to the meter. We cannot neglect the very simple matter of allowing the iambic beat to reinforce rhetorically weak positions in the line and to heighten rhetorically strong positions. [19]

> I Wonder by my troth, what thou, and I
> Did, till we lov'd?

To interpret the weight and the delicate interrelationship of the words, we can use all of Coleridge's formula and more. But at least in the first line Donne gives to an expression that externally differs from spoken prose chiefly by the fact that it is in metered language a precisely designated enunciation beyond the skill of prose to record.

It is what Coleridge calls "passion" that makes that first line just quoted something more than a straightforward example of rhetorical iambics. For the life of the line is not contained by its direct, external emphasis; and the coincidence of rhetorical stress and meter produces only the first stage of the poet's unfolding attitude. But let us, for the time, confine ourselves to simpler examples, as, for instance, when Donne manipulates his argument in order to bring the full weight of the metrical stress on one or two words:

> Natures lay Ideot, *I* taught *thee* to love.
>
> Richly cloath'd Apes, are *call'd* Apes.
>
> Neither desires to *be* spar'd, nor to *spare*.[20]

In longer passages the direct, external emphasis can reproduce the exact inflections of an earnest, reasoning voice:

> Are not heavens joyes as valiant to asswage
> Lusts, as earths honour was to them? Alas,
> As wee do them in meanes, shall they surpasse
> Us in the end, and shall thy fathers spirit
> Meete blinde Philosophers in heaven, whose merit
> Of strict life may be imputed faith, and heare
> Thee, whom hee taught so easie wayes and neare
> To follow, damn'd?

These lines are from the third satire, a poem that Coleridge in a flash of pedagogical insight recognized as a unique test for the literary student's mastery of the flow of sense and verbal values. There may be better lines to quote for justifying Coleridge's enthusiastic praise, but these have the advantage of illustrating how simply Donne can register his main effects. Elsewhere he can use highly developed techniques to catch the precise and fine degrees of emphasis which help create the structure of complex moments and whole poems. But here an absolute mastery of rhythm is concealed under the easy unfolding of syntax. With two[21] striking exceptions ("Lusts" and "Thee"), the most emphatic words coincide with the positions of metrical stress; besides, the peaks of emphasis are manipulated to give certain key words added weight — and all of this is accomplished without halting or forcing the flow of the rhythm.

But what I have just said reveals a characteristic problem: in order to analyze we must separate and arrest component parts of a process, though it is the achievement of integrity by the process, the apparent triumph of simultaneity, which most engages us. It is easier not to put things together again, in order to avoid a task for which we have no adequate language — the only adequate language being that of the artist practicing his craft. The most important thing to say about this passage is that it is simpler than any description of it can be. Donne does not really "manipulate" the emphasis in order to superimpose "added weight"; he does not fix a preconceived enunciation in the more precise and stable form of verse; nor does he increase a predetermined emphasis by translating a prose discourse into the heightened intensities of metered language. The effects may be observed, but this does not render the effects quite detachable. Donne is thinking *in* metered language, and that must mean both *with* and *against* meter, in the creative tension we attribute to art and assume is reconciled in the form which art creates. Donne's verses are not, after all, a translation of an original prose discourse, and certainly not a mere improvement upon one. The verses are the original, and they are characterized by achieving their effects more simply, and inevitably, than prose can — as if the verses did not so much add emphasis as release it, by subtracting everything not essential to the exact emergence of meaning.

To speak in these terms of Donne's lines is to express one traditional ideal of style, according to which the language serves the argument completely and seems assimilated into it, as means into end or matter into form. As an ideal it is capable of inspiring and justifying the claims of more than one style; but its principal associations are with concepts of "classical" style, and its dominant effect is simplicity. The associations and the effect are not often claimed for Donne. But simplicity *is* a feature of his style — and not only the special kind of simplicity admired by Coleridge, the simple diction that conveys out-of-the-way thoughts, nor the colloquial naturalness of word and syntax praised by modern poets and critics. Simplicity is a feature of Donne's style, and it has always had a kind of partial, or translated, or paradoxical, recognition — from the earliest praises of Donne's inspired wit to the most influential modern expressions, Grierson's "passionate ratiocination" and Eliot's "undissociated sensibility." One might put it this way: simplicity is something admired in Donne, but usually along with other qualities. If we exercise our critical skepticism we must also admit that, though these other qualities may perhaps be more attractive or impressive, they have additional advantages that critics are not likely to underestimate: they are easier to see and to name; yet they are an open invitation to critical "originality." It would therefore seem prudent to recognize that simplicity, at least in some special senses, has been, and is, a critical problem that challenges our understanding of Donne.

It is for this reason that I have dwelt so long over the lines quoted from the third satire. They provide us with a convenient opportunity, even while we are thinking of the rhetoric of Donne's verse, to mark for the first time the presence and the problem of simplicity.

And yet, the "very first eminent rhetorician in the English literature" could hardly be thought of as presenting arguments that are always direct and simple. We have no steady alternative but to depend, as far as we can, on our firm sense of these poems as communicating a weighty but often subtle flow of meaning. Many of the best poems are openly conceived as "arguments" in the usual sense of the word. They are also arguments in the sense of having plots, or of undertaking propositions. Nevertheless, we may reasonably decline to approach Donne primarily as rhetorician. The rhetoric of a great wit and true poet is likely to transcend, in the complexities of its imaginative structures, the more useful categories of rhetorical analysis. Besides, Donne is writing poems that are lyrical or dramatic, in which he is personally involved, or plays a role, with varying degrees of engagement or disengagement. Although rhetorical emphases may serve the delicate turns of an argument or serve, by immediate deficiencies and excesses, the larger form of its evolution, we cannot judge Donne's rhetorical intentions by the book. He is a great inventor and a conscious master of imaginative fictions, who can claim to do his best with least truth for subject.

These are matters that, in my judgment, respond less well to a direct, systematic attack than to a gradual and indirect process of clarification. If my aim were a descriptive study of Donne's rhetoric, then of course I should need to reduce, as far as possible, the tendency of parts to overlap. But my aim is more general, and I must exercise critical patience by not fully engaging problems before they have ripened in relationship to each other. An awareness of Donne's rhetoric, then, its general scope and special habits, will provide us with further insights. But I shall not try to follow the rhetoric for its own sake. And even the primary distinction, that Donne is interested more in the immediacies of meaning than in the immediacies of grace, must be considered as a working hypothesis that requires qualification.

We noticed earlier that Donne's metrical tradition tended toward certain kinds of rhetorical emphasis and, in Donne's own practice, toward certain kinds of significant harshness. Now we are to notice, at least in a preliminary way, how the same technical approach can produce its own kind of lyric. The same separateness of syllables, the vertical emphatic movements, the pitch that still seems closer to spoken prose than to song — these can create an unexpected music, restricted in emotional richness, but with power to move and shape. Donne's nearest predecessor would seem to be Sidney, especially in lines like these:

> Not at the first sight, nor with a dribbed shot
> Love gave the wound, which while I breathe will bleed.
>
> For let me but name her whom I do love.[22]

It is Wyatt, however, who is the poet most like Donne in the extraordinary accomplishment of turning rhetorical emphases into the intimate and tender accents of the love lyric. Some of the lines quoted earlier would serve as examples, though none so well perhaps as the famous

> But all is torned thorough my gentilnes
> Into a straunge fasshion of forsaking.

And another line, "Envy theim beyonde all mesure,"[23] provides an excuse for quoting a modern example, some lyric lines from the last section of Eliot's *Ash-Wednesday*:

> And the lost heart stiffens and rejoices
> In the lost lilac and the lost sea voices
> And the weak spirit quickens to rebel
> For the bent golden-rod and the lost sea smell.

In the following lines from Donne the vertical rhythm seems wholly to be serving the emphasis. The movement is held carefully to the meaning, and there seems to be no room for sensuous overtones, for musical effects that go beyond the firm shape of the meaning. But one may become aware of a music that is possible in verse, though one does not hear it often, that sings *within* the precise bounds of meaning.

> Image of her whom I love, more then she,
> > Whose faire impression in my faithfull heart,
> Makes mee her *Medall*, and makes her love mee.
>
> But since my soule, whose child love is,
>
> . . . .
>
> Whilst thus to ballast love, I thought,
>
> My face in thine eye, thine in mine appeares.[24]

The least one may say of these lines is that they are characteristic of Donne and that they have a lyricism of their own. It may be tense and held within the precise movement of the analytic thought, so that it is not capable of performing dainty flourishes, but it is capable of a small pure range. These remarks are summary and detached. To look closely at any examples, as we shall do, is to discover surprises.

There are, it must be admitted, difficulties in making distinctions like those above. For one thing, to speak of the "music" in verse is to acknowledge one of the more discouraging deficiencies of critical vocabulary. But we can try to be tactful in our preferring critical approximation to critical silence — without denying that silence may sometimes be the superior wisdom. For another thing, we cannot draw exact lines between verse music which sings entirely within the bounds of meaning and verse music which does not. The partnership between sound and meaning, in verse as in language, is ancient and obscure; some of the factors involved are hard to name and impossible to measure; but still we can see, not only in different poets, but in the same poet on different occasions, some kinds of shifting and readjustment in the partnership. Another inescapable difficulty is that we must talk of effects, as we experience them, and then try to invent a discourse which will reveal the causes, or point in the direction where they may be presumed to reside. But a measure of cheerful skepticism can be supported.

Some of these remarks are preliminary and anticipate aspects of Donne's lyricism which will be dealt with more fully in later discussions. The problem of simplicity still haunts us, for the partnership of sound and sense may be thought of as representing the union of the poet's individual feeling and understanding. Consider the following lines from "Lovers Infinitenesse":

> If yet I have not all thy love,
> Deare, I shall never have it all,
> I cannot breath one other sigh, to move;
> Nor can intreat one other teare to fall.

Argument and feeling are at one — or so the lyric claims by the intensity and singleness of its first impression. The truth is the lyric truth of the lover's feelings, his unexamined desire for absolute fullness of love opposed by his confession that he has reached his own utmost capacity to feel. Donne's lover may be responding to a universal and therefore familiar desire of love, and he expresses himself in the wholly conventional gestures of the literary lover, but the immediacy of his expressed feeling is authoritative. What the lover says he makes happen, through the simple and faithful movements of the speaking voice he creates. As the voice of love it is entirely persuasive and affecting in its tenderness and longing. And it fully dominates, for the moment, what is *really* incomplete in the lover and his attitudes.

It is not accurate to call the lines simple or direct; yet this is the impression they make — an illusion that here we have no art or fiction. The familiar imaginings of love present themselves as true because here, if only here, they are truly felt. This kind of art in order to succeed must seem simple; its credentials include an apparently unadorned directness of expression. Technically the lines are a special triumph of converting some limited materials of ordinary discourse into artistic form. The balanced period of the first two lines is thrown wonderfully out of balance by that steep island of emphasis, "Deare," which divides the emotional and metrical rhythms of "yet . . . all" from the different rhythms of "never . . . all." "I shall never have it all" descends from the height of aspiration to admit the strain of longing and uncertainty. Furthermore, it is not only the materials of language that are carefully limited; so are the proposition (scrupulously maintained), and the tone, and the bareness of orchestration, the limited sensuousness with which the lyric sings.

But a limited sensuousness in art, though it may restrict the extent of feelings evoked, does not restrict their depth. Besides, what matters most in art is not the size, and certainly not the extensive brilliance, of any one department exercising autonomy. A triumph is a triumph, and whenever we try to see what has really been accomplished, we may expect to find that the simple has not severed all of its normal relations with the difficult. Donne's primary commitment to emphasis and meaning does not make him indifferent to form, to what — if we allow him his own individual sense of music — we may even call musical form. This is one of the firm assumptions of the present study, and some direct demonstration will follow in due course.

Is the simplicity of these lines like that of the lines from the third satire? In precision, and in seeming to release rather than add emphasis — yes. But in the sense that the language serves the argument completely, and is assimilated completely into it as if the language had no other possible justification for being — no. In the sense of a perfect identification between the poet's feelings and what he professes — no. Ordinary notions of sincerity will not do. The poet's tenderness and emotional commitment may go unquestioned, but still the poet is giving form to a dynamic problem of human relationship. As one of the active parties he may have to bear witness against himself, for the sake of the truth of the poem coming into existence. And that truth, though it may not be exactly identical with all other possible forms of truth, nevertheless has its own exacting rules and responsibilities, and its own methods of revealing evasive self-deception and suppression. Or one might merely say that the issue here is more complex than in the satire; it is the exploration of a private truth rather than the formulation of a public argument. For the poet is both inside and outside the issue — like a playwright composing his play by shaping materials from real life, his own emotional life. The simplicity is not one of matter resolved into form; it is a simplicity that projects a voice of love to move us which is authentic both in its immediacy of feeling and in its expression of a permanent human inadequacy. We identify ourselves with the lyric feelings and are charmed, as we should be; but we can also hear something elusive in the voice, something not resolved, that rises from the poetic texture in the partly audible form of a question. It would be easier, and it might be more immediately satisfying, to be charmed by the feelings alone. The least one can say, however, is that the charm would be different.

And so the simplicity, as far as I have analyzed it,[25] would seem to derive less from the achievement or illusion of self-completeness than from the special artistic triumph of working with imaginative richness within narrow limits. The lyric statement both affirms love and implies a problem. Something is not assimilated, is left over, perhaps to be resolved by the completed form of the poem, but perhaps — we may justifiably wonder — to remain as part of the permanent secret of the style.

Here we touch on a concept of style which is different in many of its associations from a classical ideal suggested by the lines from the third satire. Though the mastered ease and grace, the scrupulous working within exact limits, may be related to that ideal, what is different is the something "left over." One of Yeats's definitions of style illustrates the higher claims of what may seem, by ordinary rational examination, to be unassimilated: "Style . . . a still unexpended energy, after all that the argument or the story needs, a still unbroken pleasure after the immediate end has been accomplished . . . after the desire of logic has been satisfied and all that is merely necessary established . . . that leaves one, not in the circling necessity, but caught up into the freedom of self-delight." [26] The most immediate associations of this definition are romantic. We seem invited to think that poetry aspires to the condition of music, that the ideal must be personally, individually experienced, and that it transcends ordinary limits, including those niggardly ones of general necessity and restrictive logic. Energy and freedom would appear to be good for their own sake.

The associations are romantic and modern. Can they be relevant to Donne, or do we respond to their appeal, if we do, only because we are postromantics? Or may we say instead that newer insights do not merely supplant what was valuable in the older views, but may supplement them and help to articulate problems which were always there but which were not perhaps felt as urgent or seen quite in the same perspective? Some problems can use all the cumulative wisdom of human experience, and profit more from the temperate judiciousness of scissors and paste than from the severe judiciousness of scissors alone. Besides, the genuine mysteries of style are of long standing, and they have troubled many perceptive minds in spite of certain useful, if overconfident, efforts either to dismiss them or to solve them peremptorily.

Is not some of the appeal of Yeats's definition due to the presence in it of attitudes which have a long history in Western thought? If we think of Donne's own time, we are reminded of the style associated with the revival of Stoicism, and of its preference for the writer's emphasis on the immediate and individual experience of his thought. It is a style that successfully challenged the old authority of the dominant classical ideal, with its allegiance to stable and universal standards of correctness attainable by the conscious imitation of acknowledged models and methods, through which the writer might then express his own individual mastery. That ideal seemed to some — as to Bacon — an invitation only to persuade all over again, but to say nothing new and undiscovered; and it seemed to deny the possibility that new materials, and a new, individual look at them, might usefully enlarge human truth and its expression. Or to take another example, we may think of the restless originality of baroque styles and of their evident pleasure in energy and in forms that strain beyond "necessity," and beyond the formal resolutions that satisfied earlier artists. We may see in Yeats's "freedom of self-delight" one version of an emphasis traditional in Neoplatonism — the transcending of analogical knowledge by being at the feeling center of what one knows. And we may catch glimpses of long-standing medieval and Renaissance quarrels within the church — between faith and reason, intuition and logic, the affective and the intellectual life.[27]

It does not seem necessary at this date to argue the point that every artist has a voice no less distinctively his than his physical voice. His voice as artist will express the man as an individual, but fully individual and not quirkish, not cut off from source and purpose, from his relationship to the rest of human enterprise. The artist's voice is part of the mystery involved in the old concept that style is, rightly considered, the man. That does not mean the poet limited within his skin — not the poor biography of the man, but the whole man who is most wholly revealed and realized in his style. The modern argument for the impersonality of the artist should not require him to be a dramatic ventriloquist, as if he did not need to have and develop, to acquire and beget, his own individual voice as artist, which will be heard through and above the immediate voices he assumes. For his own private personality, if he is a true artist who can do more than skillfully rearrange what others have created, will not be the defining limits of his expression. Through that expression may be heard the more comprehensive and impersonal voice of poetic tradition, which is an authentic voice of human tradition.

Or so one may think and believe in a metaphorical way that points toward a plausible truth, for which there are positive hints and negative evidence. The oneness of the voice of poetic tradition may not, however, be insisted on; for it can be one voice only in heaven, where the choruses of individual voices are supposedly heard expressing the varied oneness of human experience. But criticism, urging only its present advantages, may surely insist on the individuality of the poet's voice, which will express his own experience as an artist; and this voice will include what he owes deliberately and what he owes unawares to the specific traditions of his art, besides what he owes to the traditions of human experience that make art and are made by art.

Meter and Meaning

The point was made earlier that we should need to qualify the working hypothesis that Donne was interested more in the immediacies of meaning than in the immediacies of grace. The various discussions of sense, of rhetoric and lyric, of simplicity, of the poet's voice – all have indicated that Donne could not properly be said to use the affective resources of metrical language merely to drive home rhetorical points. We come now to a place in the exposition where we must look more closely at the relations between sound and meaning.

We may begin with the simplest kind of example, the familiar use of sound to imitate directly the sense of what is being said. At one extreme the resources of style can be used to convey the effect of a physical state. Pope writes the classic examples of the doctrine that "The sound must seem an echo to the sense" – soft strains for zephyr, or rough, heavy, swift, whichever "echo" is appropriate. The doctrine is based on the power of music, which "all our hearts allow"; but the examples are those of a rather literal, and limited, kind of program music. A less mechanical use of the doctrine may be dramatic on a restricted plane – in giving an external sense of the immediate situation.

Donne delights in the immediate, in the actually moving scene and in the natural, or rehearsed, inflections of the voice speaking the part that is required. As for the more obvious use of sound to imitate the sense, Donne hardly ever plays this game seriously. Even in his two virtuoso pieces describing the storm and the calm, where the opportunities for program music were most inviting, he preferred to create situations almost entirely by other means. He is quite willing to make the sound emphasize the sense, but not imitate it. The one big exception is the comic or satiric context. For example, in Elegy IV, he writes:

> Thy little brethren, which like Faiery Sprights
> Oft skipt into our chamber, those sweet nights.

But the charm of the children and the spontaneous joy of their skipping movement, which we are made to feel and respond to with a natural innocence that matches their own, turn out to be a trap.

The next morning the children are bribed, on the father's knee, to tell what they saw. This same elegy has two other examples of imitative sound: "The grim eight-foot-high iron-bound serving-man," and "I taught my silkes, their whistling to forbeare." These lines have no ironic turn, or counterpoint; they are straight, like Pope's examples. They illustrate something rare in Donne, presumably evoked by the general comic tone of the elegy.

If Donne does not write this way more often, it is not from want of ability. He can exhibit his own mastery of delicate sensuousness:

> As the sweet sweat of roses in a Still,
> As that which from chaf'd muskats pores doth trill,
> . . . .
> And like that slender stalke, at whose end stands
> The wood-bine quivering, are her armes and hands.[28]

But the delicacy is cultivated only for the occasion, that of an enormous joke that Donne is contriving. And in the following example it is for the sake of the ironic turn that the sound imitates the sense:

> So carelesse flowers strow'd on the waters face,
> The curled whirlepooles suck, smack, and embrace,
> Yet drowne them; so, the tapers beamie eye
> Amorously twinkling, beckens the giddie flie,
> Yet burnes his wings.[29]

It is in his satires that Donne makes freest use of imitative sound, though seldom in any literal way. And this qualification is no doubt a commentary on his attitude toward the device. It is not to be taken very seriously, but it can do charming things, particularly if the imitation works through exaggerated emphasis in the manner of the caricaturist.

> He, like to a high stretcht lute string squeakt, O Sir,
> 'Tis sweet to talke of Kings.[30]

When the imitation works in this way, qualities that are presented as external are made to suggest something of the internal as well. So it is not only a mocking version of the fop's voice that we hear; the lines also require us to imagine facial expressions and perhaps bodily movements. This is another way of saying that the sound is less imitative than suggestive and interpretative. In the following lines, which create a whole scene, we sense much of the fop's personality from the way he speaks; and we fill out a picture of his actions partly from the erratic impetuousness with which the verse moves, and then droops:

> Now leaps he upright, Joggs me, & cryes, Do you see
> Yonder well favoured youth? Which? Oh, 'tis hee
> That dances so divinely; Oh, said I,
> Stand still, must you dance here for company?
> Hee droopt.

But the verse that creates a physical situation and suggests a personality requires more than imitative sound if it is to present more than external drama:

> Yet though he cannot skip forth now to greet
> Every fine silken painted foole we meet,
> He them to him with amorous smiles allures,
> And grins, smacks, shrugs, and such an itch endures,
> As prentises, or schoole-boyes which doe know
> Of some gay sport abroad, yet dare not goe.[31]

The third line is delightful physical caricature; one cannot read it aloud without putting the mouth through motions of alluring smiles that feel like grimaces. But only "dare" of the last line really penetrates far below the surface of the fop's personality. The rhythmic arrangement helps, of course, and performs an important role in the psychological drama. But this takes us to our next series of examples, in which the structure of sound does more than echo the sense or convey the immediacy of an external situation.

At one simple extreme we need only remind ourselves of Donne's favorite device of making his sound go along with his meaning for the rhetorical emphasis. The device, even when it is mostly rhythmical, can manage very fine shades of meaning. But we need not pause for simple illustrations of this kind of rhetoric in Donne. Almost any line quoted would serve as example, and we shall soon consider some complex uses which include the simple. Let us instead note another kind of example. A pattern of sound may be used as a kind of musical symbol to evoke a meaning that does not coincide with the formal emphasis. For instance, in the following lines where certain conventional satiric objects are presented for illustration, the verse takes on a roughness that refers less to the immediate objects than to a personal kind of satiric attitude that has been awakened.

> Th'hydroptique drunkard, and night-scouting thiefe,
> The itchy Lecher, and selfe tickling proud
> Have the remembrance of past joyes, for reliefe
> Of comming ills. To (poore) me . . .[32]

Once he has called up the satiric attitude (which is excessive and not strictly relevant to the limited situation), Donne can shift the ready-made contempt where he wants it, to himself.

A pattern of sound can also act as a musical symbol to suggest conflict within the structure of a poem. The line "Tell me, where all past yeares are" is, as I read it, quite different in tone from the lines dealing with the flippant impossibilities of catching a falling star and the like. The incantation evokes a sense of serious magic that is contrary to the dominant tone. The imaginative range of the line is also greater, and not merely because of the potential seriousness. But if one looks at the whole poem from this point of view, the single line may seem to represent a significant disproportion. The lavish imaginative detail, the intense exaggeration that gives the poem its special quality — these too produce a sense of disproportion in a poem that is, formally at least, an epigrammatic joke.

Or consider the more substantial example of these lines from "Loves Growth":

> Gentle love deeds, as blossomes on a bough,
> From loves awakened root do bud out now.

The delicacy of spring's miracle is in the words, along with a rationalistic perception of the source of its power; but the special lyrical qualities of the second line also suggest something of the illusion possible in a sight that is being looked at too closely. The delicate beauty is there, so delicate that it cannot possibly last long, so irrepressible ("do bud out now") that it cannot help returning, every spring.

Our next examples will attempt to demonstrate a more deeply involved relationship between meter and rhetorical emphasis. These examples, though they are intended to exhibit Donne as a consummate rhetorician in verse, do not conclude this part of the argument but are instead transitional. For whenever we try to trace with full detail the exact emergence of metaphorical meaning, we go beyond the useful rhetorical categories. The full case, and the conclusions to be drawn, must wait until the end of the chapter, until we have been able to study the means by which the meaning of a whole poem takes shape.

How shall we read the last three words of this line from Elegy X? [33]

So, if I dreame I have you, I have you.

The first "have," reinforced by the meter, is very emphatic, and so creates a pressure that is felt by the second "have." But the second "have" must resist at least part of that pressure; it cannot coincide with the meter, any more than it can avoid the influence of the rhetorical emphasis. One may imagine that the ear, with a swiftness and sureness which outstrip thought and have been acquired as by second nature, experimentally listens ahead. The trained ear senses in advance that the "I" and the "you" are the regular but unlikely places for stress to fall. The mind informed by such an ear may recognize that a stressed "I" and "you" will mean that out of the dream a real *I* will possess a real *you*, but with far less emphasis on the reality of the possession than on the reality of the identity. However, the deliberate suppression of the "have" would be extreme and unlikely. Yet let us assume that the ingenious ear swiftly tries out the possibility and records it.

Or let us consider that the ear could solve its problem boldly with a stress shift in the fifth foot — like a swift stream encountering an obstacle temporarily too big to flow around. This would throw the weight on the final "I" and especially on the "have." The emphasis would then suggest an egoistic reality of possession, and would suit an assertive, supercilious tone. Or the ear might, at last, attempt its final and most complicated possibility, a spondee in the last foot. It cannot be an exact spondee, with both of the last syllables receiving absolutely equal stress. Of course, we know that this is always true in the transformation of meter into rhythm, but in this particular case we have the privilege of seeing some of the complicating elements openly in action. The "have," because of its rhetorical position, demands a striking emphasis. But then the "you" may be left without enough stress either to make a decent spondee or to satisfy the established expectation of the complex meaning. The result, inevitably influenced also by the obstacle of that egoistic, dominating "I," which resists being suppressed, would then tend toward the assertive tone of the stress shift. The ear, I think, will be sensitive to the imbalance and will compensate in behalf of the "you"— but not too much, lest the reality of the *you* dominate the reality of the possession, or even cancel its effect.

And so, finally, I think one may say that all of the possibilities are contained in the reading the ear at last prefers. The result is a kind of ambiguous hovering that includes (in the pyrrhic-spondee of the last four syllables) both the reality of possession and the reality of identity, and includes them in their dynamic relationship to each other. Needless to say, the voice attempting to register these fine things will require some special effects. It would be naive, however, to assume that all of the potential of a rich line must be heard at each performance. The analogy of musical performance can be instructive here.

The opening lines of the same elegy present us with a similar situation, where the play between meter and rhetorical emphasis holds the key to the metaphorical meaning:

> Image of her whom I love, more then she,
>> Whose faire impression in my faithfull heart,
> Makes mee her *Medall*, and makes her love mee,
>> As Kings do coynes, to which their stamps impart
> The value; goe, and take my heart from hence.

It is the first three lines I am concerned with, and particularly the problem of how we shall read the third. Let us be elementary and inductive. "Makes mee" may be taken as a spondee, and the first syllable of "*Medall*" is plainly stressed. "Makes her," because of the parallel with "Makes mee" and because it follows two unstressed syllables, requires two stresses. So that leaves us with only the last two words seriously in question. (Perhaps I should add that my spondees are relative and are based on a built-up sense of Donne's metrical style. In another style, say Milton's, there is nothing in the line, except the last two words, that could not work within the ample flexibility of the iambic. The "and" would require a little artificial stiffening, but that can always be made available out of the accumulated credit, as it were, of a style.[34] My spondees, I repeat, are not equal in stress, though they would *sound* nearly equivalent in emphasis by means of other resources of vocal intensification. The tension to be expressed is not only within each spondee but in the interrelationship between the two "makes" and between "mee" and "her.")

The metrical possibilities for reading the last two words are again, I think, three. If "love mee" is heard as an iamb, the emphasis will make "mee" more important, as if to assert that the effect is more significant than the cause. One might then say that the coin grants the stamp the favor of reality and makes what was an abstract form into a reality of value. The second possibility is a stress shift that will make "love" clearly dominate "mee," with the resulting changes to the emphasis and the complex of meaning. The third possibility involves a compromise, I think necessary, between the other two. That is, treat "love mee" as another spondee. Hesitating among alternatives, as he must, the reader becomes aware that the metrical uncertainty is a part of the larger ambiguity carefully balanced in the whole complex metaphor of the coining. Unable to decide whether "love" or "mee" is dominant, one hesitates and is forced into the compromise of stressing both. In the hesitation one discovers a buried syntactical ambiguity: "love" may be not a verb but a noun parallel to "Medall." Then we should have something like this: the image that creates her medal (me) also creates her love (me); her love is me and I am her love, brought into being, as a medal, by her image.

Let us try another paraphrase from our present vantage. I love her image more than she does for this reason—that, through her image and its stamp on me, she must love me. Her love of her image gives me (stamped with it) my being in love, so her love is me. And so I love her image more than she does. I also love her image more than I love her (the female She who *has no image or idea*, but is only She —"forget the Hee and Shee"). For it is her image and its effect on me that causes her to love me, that transforms me into her love, that transforms me into an image of her image. But her image is a kind of Platonic idea that (anti-Platonically) depends for its expression, perhaps for its existence, upon me. It may be my idea of her image that makes her love it and so me. If I love her image, then she depends for her existence as a loved object upon my idea of her image, and so *I* am her love as her love is *me*. The identification is established by reciprocal actions, and a philosophical problem is solved by a metaphor to which the metrical structure is an indispensable key.

Our two final examples are brief. They will indicate something of Donne's power to extend imaginative meaning sensuously. First, this familiar line from "The Relique":

A bracelet of bright haire about the bone.

The first effect of "A bracelet of bright haire" is to excite the imagination in a way that always increases the willing expectation of new experience, and therefore seems to open up and extend the potential range of meaning. But "about the bone" imposes a countering sense of limit. "Bone" is absolute and needs no further descriptive designation than "the."

If we narrow our view to the structure of sound we may see a similar pattern of development. The dominating vowels of "A bracelet of bright haire"— at least in reference to the sense of the words, and to the sense and sound of the rest of the line — help convey an effect of warmth and animation. "Haire" is the metrical high point of the line, and it builds upon a vowel and consonant more briefly articulated earlier. At this point, where stress and sound coincide in climax, the imaginative sensuousness of the line is at its furthest extent. But the limit which the second half of the line brings into effect also builds on an earlier sound. The neutral *b* of "bracelet" and "bright" is shaped by the positive *b* of "about" and "bone."

Our final example is the famous last line of this stanza from "A Valediction: Forbidding Mourning":

> Our two soules therefore, which are one,
> Though I must goe, endure not yet
> A breach, but an expansion,
> Like gold to ayery thinnesse beate.

It is possible to remark a certain conflict in the line, though the dominant impression is that of marvelous order and precision. "Ayery," for instance, threatens both rationally and sensuously to break through the limits of the controlling idea, that by which the parting is to avoid material rupture and is to remain instead an admirable connection however extended. "Ayery" is followed by "thinnesse," which is the metrical climax of the line. "Thinnesse" as a word in the mouth suggests a delicacy that carries the magic of airiness a step closer to immateriality. But it is a definite word too, at least more definite than "ayery," and its full ambivalence is defined by the word which follows. The emphatically physical "beate" makes the thinness more definite, even as the thinness becomes beaten materially thinner. And so one may say that gold, the concrete substance, and gold, the symbol of infinite association, together move toward airiness while, with a counter motion, the imaginative limits are fixed and the balance holds firm.

Rhetoric, Rationalism, and Verbal Sensuousness

Let us pause to take a little inventory of our problems and to re-establish our direction. We may not be much closer to defining Donne's poetic voice or simplicity; but these are problems of a kind, not native to literature alone, for which proposed solutions are likely to be less valuable than any increase in our knowledge of the nature of the problems — that is to say, their depth and extent, their inner and outer relationships. The same may be said of the main line of study which has been followed, the partnership between sound and sense in Donne's verse. We have at least learned to distrust the arbitrary assignment of Donne to a school of rhetorical poetry in which verses stand by sense alone and are to be read but never sung. It is not that we have found any reason to reduce the claims of intellectual meaning and rhetorical emphasis in Donne's verse; rather, the most interesting examples analyzed have demonstrated a fuller range of possible meaning which is due to the contribution of imaginative sensuousness — to the "Colours," accents, and song which Ben Jonson, though in a severe moment, and off the record, denied as necessary to verse. Our most complicated examples make it impossible to say, simply, that Donne racked the graces of language into the service of meaning. One can understand the context out of which this kind of critical exaggeration grows, but it needs correcting.

What we must now do, in the interest of balance, is to explore some of the limits of Donne's sensuousness. But we must also try to counter, by looking at a whole poem, some of the inevitable distortions that are caused by intense analysis of individual lines. First, however, we must return to some problems that concern Donne's rhetoric, and here we may try to profit from the advantage of an available historical perspective.

When Coleridge praised Donne's third satire as a test for the literary student's mastery of the flow of sense, he was demonstrating his own individual interest in literary language, as poet and as professional man of letters. The twentieth century has admired this kind of insight in Coleridge; it is what one may expect of a poet who, when he speaks analytically, does so in terms of his familiar experience with the practical inner workings of his craft. The twentieth century has had the advantage of an unusual number of critics who are also poets. Indeed, one of the remarkable characteristics of modern criticism has been the general availability of "inside" knowledge concerning the poet's craft. But Coleridge, we must also recognize, was reflecting not only his individual interest in language but his common education as a schoolboy. It was Coleridge's schoolmaster, James Boyer, who taught his boys to see how every word in the best poetry had its own absolute sense and position, which could not be changed without loss. And he taught them, while rigorously correcting their own imprecise metaphors, that the logic of poetry was "as severe as that of science; and more difficult, because more subtle, more complex, and dependent on more, and more fugitive causes." [35]

The basic lesson, which Coleridge learned with both mind and heart, is worth pausing over for a moment. If we look backward, that schoolmaster was introducing his pupils, one of whom would do him special honor, to the rhetorical standards and traditions which governed the best practice in Renaissance education, as it had the practice in the best schools of classical rhetoric. (Our perspective may conveniently ignore cyclical excesses, and the famous claims and counterclaims of educational competitors.) If we look forward, then we become witnesses to the astonishing enlargement of the interest in language that has characterized the past few decades. The extensions brought about by philosophical, anthropological, and linguistic studies may not seem to have much in common — at least not much more than the parent disciplines themselves. Yet even the casual observer cannot fail to remark that language is now being investigated seriously, not only for its own sake, but for its acknowledged power to illuminate and reveal human nature and the human mind.

Some of the new investigations of language are new in kind as well as in scope, and they are responsive to questions men have recently learned to ask in other fields of learning. But in some respects at least, the new studies of language represent the recovery of an old interest and an old competence. In literary studies the whole range of rhetoric has been at once pushed in further directions and consolidated. A remarkable series of scholarly studies has put our age in better possession of the old rhetoric than any other age since the seventeenth century. At the same time the criticism which received its initial impetus from the early work of T. S. Eliot and I. A. Richards has been busy both with the recovery of old and the discovery of new skills in interpreting literary language. The criticism, at least in some of its extensions, has kept an alert eye on new developments in other fields. But the criticism and the historical studies appear to have influenced each other very little; indeed, in their early stages they seem hardly to have been aware of any similarities in their concern for rhetoric. Yet we can surely make out one line from Richards [36] to Coleridge, and another line from modern literary scholarship to the Renaissance educational traditions that lie behind Coleridge's training and accomplishment.

No single generalization is going to make all the contemporary schools of linguistic thought comfortable with each other's company. And to label them we should have to hyphenate some monstrous combinations drawn from a variety of the influential sources of modern insight. Yet without attempting to satisfy all the schools, we may nevertheless think of one generalization that has a claim to relevance. Coleridge, through his schoolmaster, had available to him an intellectual conviction, elevated to a confident belief, in the stable potentialities of the language of poetry. Though poetry itself cannot without some strain be imagined as the chief prize for which the schools contend, no one who seeks knowledge about language can comfortably ignore the peculiar resources and demonstrated powers of poetic language. But more to the point, no modern practitioner of a special discipline can escape a sense of his own difference when he contemplates the easy possession by Coleridge and his honored schoolmaster of belief in the rightness and reliability of the best poetic language. Many would not want that past belief, and may perhaps be more interested in the peculiarities of language and what it reveals of *unreliability*. The point, however, is less that such old-fashioned belief is rare today than that its possession seems not only difficult but precarious. The faithful may even worry, in their weaker moments, whether they are not perhaps a little odd. If they experience resistance or indifference, even in the classroom, they may justly assign some of the blame to the competitive advantage of newer forms of knowledge that also inspire belief in the rightness and reliability of their predications. But issues like these, involving as they do not only man's social but his individual destiny, do not always respond to the wisdom of short-range competition. When the newer forms of knowledge tend to supplant an old and proved form, they are likely to promise more satisfaction than they can deliver, for they compete for the minds of men.

New disciplines and intellectual attitudes, many of them traceable to the Renaissance, have accelerated in their modern development and have made climactically clear both their claims on the social economy and their cost to the individual economy. It is tempting but futile to blame any single historical period; nor is our society the first to feel that it may have moved too fast and may have demoted some disciplines and values too quickly, on the basis of shallow promises and local hopes. Yet there would seem to be, in spite of the usual disagreements, a genuinely recognized need to try to re-establish or redefine the best of the older educational aims, if only to lend a measure of stability to a changing and divided world of knowledge and values. The nervous and excessive demands made on art are a major symptom of our times. But our concern is limited to the minor symptom of the revived interest in language and rhetoric, and the chief purpose in raising the matter is the opportunity to introduce one aspect of the historical problem involved in the revival of Donne.

It is worth recognizing that the effect of any renewed interest is that it sharpens our imaginative insight, as any sense of historical identification is likely to do. Whenever a past problem seems vital to us, it draws energy from its connection with our own immediate problems. But we must also recognize that such a sense of immediacy may also create its own distortions. Though we cannot escape from this dilemma, we can at least accept it consciously.

If we go back to our modern beginnings in the seventeenth century, and do not make a gloomy leap to present results we dislike, we may see and acknowledge certain intellectual differences between our ancestors and us. Yet we may perhaps conclude quite reasonably that some of these differences are less than absolute. Miss Tuve's admirable study of Renaissance rhetoric (*Elizabethan and Metaphysical Imagery*) would seem to go too far in minimizing the differences between Donne and his predecessors, and, at the same time, in increasing the distance between Donne and his modern "descendants." We can hardly shrug off the general tenor of the imposing evidence she assembles, though we may still remain quite convinced that there are some real advantages in the new approaches modern poets and critics have made to Donne — if we do not mistake these demonstrations for actual historical reconstructions. Some of Miss Tuve's own best work no Elizabethan could have done, partly for lack of historical perspective and scholarly method, partly for lack of critical method and experience.

It is a fact of intellectual life that some things can be studied with fresh intensity only by isolating them, by stopping the stream of time. We must try to keep in mind, however, that the effect may be the self-defeating one of constructing a barrier between past and present. Historical sanity requires that we also try to remember the human conditions that do not change. Artists are tied to their times, and both times and artists are different; even when there are no remarkable discontinuities the language of the past must be relearned in every generation; yet the merit of that language is that it can still speak — of the past, but of and to the present. It is immensely difficult to get the balance right. The literary historian is likely to be tempted by unawarenesses which inspire, or betray, his own insights, or even his objectivity. In his proprietary zeal he may reconstruct a monument which can be entered only by his permission. But we do not therefore need to accept an opposite extreme and make of the past a graven image of ourselves and our own immediate concerns.

Surely there are some recognizable differences between Donne and his predecessors and between Donne and us. In the latter instance the differences may be less radical than some historical criticism would have us believe. As for the differences between Donne and his predecessors, these too may be less radical than modern criticism has declared, and less radical even than some of Donne's contemporaries thought. Contemporaries are always overalert to welcome or lament the new. Their confident judgments, like those of our own contemporaries, may be nearsighted or farsighted; they are not historical judgments but historical evidence and must be weighed.

We should not be surprised if Donne's rhetoric analyzed by itself, or his practice of decorum, or even his famous sensibility, should only *seem* radically new. The original inventions of artists are in part personal rearrangements of emphases available to others. It is the total which is new. Donne's cultivation of immediacy, or the weight he puts on *matter*, on the intellectuality of his discourse, or his flaunting the authorized ideals of "imitation" by turning old themes and attitudes to fresh, individual uses — these are less new taken by themselves than the historical circumstances (which are always new) and the synergism resulting from the genius of new proponents in a new age. The intricate balances by which a genuine style is achieved are always individual and personal, whatever their ultimate or intermediate sources. An artist's perceptions are always conditioned by a multiplicity of environments, but his act of creation makes something new and free, which can never again be wholly accountable to the claims of environment.

Some of these remarks have moved beyond the general historical problem of approaching Donne to suggest a particular answer. In order to justify that answer let us turn to a particular aspect of the historical problem. It seems reasonable to infer that Donne's poetry is influenced by a rationalistic distrust of words — not only the traditional philosophic distrust, but a poetic distrust of the sensuous qualities of words. That distrust was not new; nor is it a direct link with modern attitudes.[37] It was part of an equivocal view of eloquence that was both classical and Christian [38] and that reached its most important historical crossroads in the seventeenth century. Fulke Greville, in *A Treatie of Humane Learning*, makes comments on language that conveniently illustrate the changing viewpoint. Though some of his remarks (not quoted here) may seem to be in the broad tradition that leads back through Erasmus to St. Augustine to Cicero, the spirit and the emphasis are significantly different. The true art of eloquence, says the austere puritan in Greville, is "but to declare / What things in Nature good, or evill are." He reflects an attitude parallel to that of the new science when he calls rhetoric a siren that captures reason with the "painted skinne" of words and misleads with "empty sounds." He would reject (like the founders of the Royal Society) all "termes, distinctions, axioms, lawes" that depend in whole or in part upon "this stained sense of words":

> Onely admitting precepts of such kinde,
> As without words may be conceiv'd in minde.

And of course poetry is "Onely as pleasing sauce to dainty food." [39]

These attitudes, though extreme, were apparently being rather widely considered in Donne's time. and were, in partly different form, to be among the dominant critical attitudes toward the end of the seventeenth century. Greville at his best is of course not limited to the severe gestures against silence authorized by his theoretical pronouncements. And Donne, though certainly influenced by critical attitudes related to Bacon's distrust of the word and to Bacon's rejection of that "magisterial" eloquence which prefers persuasion to demonstration, still is only influenced. His poetry is personal and is not bound to uphold a program. Playing mostly within, but also against, the hard rational control that he maintains, there is great intensity of feeling; and his use of language is metaphorical and generative. There are deliberate limits imposed on sensuousness, but they do not force any radical separation between matter and manner.[40] A greater contemporary, Shakespeare, is even more deeply aware of the duplicities potential in his poetic and human materials. And only a rash judgment would declare that Milton, for all his grandeur and achieved simplicity of expression, is less aware of the deceits of language.

But "rationalistic distrust," whether of words or other instruments of the mind, is always relative — except perhaps in the complete skeptic. The mind that trusts all its operations has graduated from no human school. Let us assume that Donne was a "rationalist" and turn to another aspect of the historical background: the intellectuality of his verse, the emphasis on meaning and consciousness. Here the testimony of contemporaries is unanimous and, however exaggerated, cannot be misunderstood. Donne draws a line "Of masculine expression." His "carelesse houres brought forth / Fancies beyond our studies."

> Thou dost not stoope unto the vulgar sight,
> But, hovering highly in the aire of Wit,
>   Hold'st such a pitch, that few can follow it.

> Indeed so farre above its Reader, good,
> That wee are thought wits, when 'tis understood.

> Donne, the delight of Phoebus, and each Muse,
>   Who, to thy one, all other braines refuse;
> Whose every work, of thy most early wit,
>   Came forth example, and remaines so, yet:
> Longer a knowing, then most wits doe live.[41]

What cannot be misunderstood is that his contemporaries, friends and foes, recognized the intellectual concentration of his verse, the difficult demands he made upon his readers. Those who celebrated him still subscribed to the Renaissance ideal of the poet (or the preacher) as an inspired teacher, one whose works "Came forth example"; but the concept of poet they celebrate is no longer Sidney's "right popular philosopher." Donne's poetry is for the few, to be circulated in manuscript; and he himself expressed regret at having published his "Anniversaries." [42]

How, then, did Donne achieve the intellectual concentration his friends admired? I may remark at once that no claims are made for any absolute originality in Donne. Donne's wit may have accounted for his *deeper* imaginative inventions, and for the lively fitness of his details, but it did not extend to technical invention; for the most part he merely used in his own way, more strenuously, the available techniques and materials. That is what poets usually do, and the results can be distinctive enough to stimulate and defy exact imitation.[43] To a period of rich invention, when the musical sensuousness of verse had been recently brought to its first high development in English poetry, what should have been most startling, what should have seemed most like an original invention, was Donne's example of the kind of poetry that could be written by strictly *limiting* the familiar means of poetic expression. He triumphantly dispensed with many of the conventions of Elizabethan writing; and though conventions may have the power to recuperate, nothing is more likely to make them appear suddenly tired or trite than a demonstration of successful writing that seems to owe nothing to them.

What is most original in Donne, then, derives from the total effect he creates. The qualities that distinguish him from his contemporaries are the individual marks of any genuine poet; but one may also add to those qualities, with reason, the degree of intellectual concentration which so impressed his contemporaries; and, even more important in some ways, one may add the strict limits Donne imposed on the sensuousness, the affective qualities, of his verse.[44]

A modern coincidence invites the introduction of yet another aspect of Donne's rationalism. Donne has been for many modern poets and critics a kind of model for the superior claims of "visual imagery." The term is both too narrow and too vague; besides, the real issues involve larger critical and philosophical considerations. But let us try to keep to one limited side of the theoretical issue. Some remarks by T. E. Hulme may be singled out as a starting place; for whether read, or heard, or repeated by word of mouth, they have unquestionably exerted a striking influence on others. "The great aim is accurate, precise and definite description . . . to see things as they really are." Poetry "is not a counter language, but a visual concrete one . . . It always endeavours to arrest you, and to make you continually see a physical thing, to prevent you gliding through an abstract process . . . Did the poet have an actually realised visual object before him in which he delighted?" [45] There are both ambiguities and errors in these remarks (which of course were never put into final form), but the "visualist fallacy" has proved flexible and persistent; it has, incidentally, contributed to the foolish quarrel between admirers of Donne and admirers of Milton. To make a small point, the modern criticism which has emphasized the cognitive status of poetry would have been much hindered in its development had it not been able to demonstrate the intellectually analyzable content of images. For instance, Allen Tate, in his often-reprinted "Tension in Poetry," candidly admits the advantages of working with Donne's compasses and beaten gold.

Our modern coincidence is not without historical basis. "Sight is the noblest sense of any one," [46] Donne wrote, and certainly believed. Philosophically there was no other choice. The belief is a traditional one, from Plato and Aristotle, to St. Thomas, to the beliefs and practices of modern science. Part of the high prestige of sight must be attributed to the fact that for a wide range of practical human activity sight is an indispensable tool of discrimination and judgment. Furthermore, no sense is more serviceable to the affective needs of education, or more serviceable, one may add, to the rhetoric of political persuasion or commercial promotion. But the most important historical source of prestige is the fact that the sense of sight was long identified with reason; the identification became part of the heritage of Greek rationalism; it also entered the history of religious thought, where it contributed to the already established symbolic meaning of sight.

As a Renaissance rationalist, therefore, and as a poet with a virtuoso command of exact intellectuality, Donne could hardly have escaped thinking of the rational and the visual together. But we are not consequently required to reinterpret his poetic art as an ideal identification of the two. Rather, it is one of the assumptions of this book that excessive concern with Donne's imagery has diverted modern critical attention. Let us take this point of view: the visual imagery is but one aspect of Donne's individual devotion to meaning, one aspect of the tight rational control he maintains. To this extent, then, the visual imagery may serve as a convenient sign of the rationalistic limits he cultivated. I am proposing this formula for a particular purpose — one at best useful, at worst misleading, but one not intended to define a fixed relationship. First, however, let me clarify the problem by quoting the most authoritative statement I know on this subject.

In his *Adventures of Ideas* Whitehead objects to the usual division of experience into appearance and reality; for that division "only concerns the objective content, and omits the subjective form of the immediate occasion in question." In his view, "the foundation of metaphysics should be sought in the understanding of the subject-object structure of experience, and in the respective rôles of the physical and mental functionings." Then this passage follows:

Unfortunately the superior dominance in consciousness of the contrast 'Appearance and Reality' has led metaphysicians from the Greeks onwards to make their start from the more superficial characteristic [i.e., "the objective content"]. This error has warped modern philosophy to a greater extent than ancient or mediaeval philosophy. The warping has taken the form of a consistent reliance upon sensationalist perception as the basis of all experiential activity [reliance, as Whitehead puts it in another place, upon the data "directly provided by the activity of the sense-organs — preferably the eyes"]. It has had the effect of decisively separating 'mind' from 'nature,' a modern separation which found its first exemplification in Cartesian dualism. But it must be remembered that this modern development was only the consistent carrying out of principles already present in the older European philosophy. It required two thousand years for the full implication of those principles to dawn upon men's minds in the seventeenth and the eighteenth centuries after Christ.[47]

This puts our problem in its right perspective. Donne is not a modern "sensationalist." His "visual rationalism"—if I may speak so—is prominent, and is one aspect, perhaps one source, of his great poetic power. But it is only one aspect, and what chiefly justifies our attempting to single out the visual is the critical opportunity to define some of Donne's limitations as a poet. Donne's fullness of perception as a poet, we must recognize, is not tied to the visual; he comes under Whitehead's observation that the warping has affected modern more than ancient or medieval philosophy. Yet if we oppose, though arbitrarily, the visual in Donne to the auditory, then we have one means, and that not negligible, of tracing some effects and characteristics in Donne's poetry of rationalism and consciousness. Perhaps it should be added as warning that our maneuver will permit us to see things in only one prearranged way, to trace a single line as it were. But since the problem of Donne's poetic consciousness will continue to occupy us in many ways, we should be able to afford, and correct, the distortions of a single case.

Donne uses sound, I demonstrated earlier, as an imaginative and generative partner of the meaning—emphasizing the sense in some ways that are most clear; but in other ways, which are more difficult to isolate and define, helping to form and complete the sense. Now I must bring forward and try to relate two further considerations which have been implicit, and occasionally explicit, in the development of this chapter. The first is that, in the partnership of sound and meaning in Donne's verse, sound is not the dominant partner. The second is that, in spite of the prominent bulk and force of rationally determinable meaning in Donne's verse, there are nevertheless qualities of sense and feeling to which we respond, but which our analysis cannot exactly translate or describe.

Let us begin with the second consideration and go back to the old example of Elegy X:

> Image of her whom I love, more then she,
> Whose faire impression in my faithfull heart,
> Makes mee her *Medall*, and makes her love mee.

The alliterative structure of these lines is quite remarkable, and consonants may perhaps be like coins, or medals, capable of being stamped with the pattern of an idea. If we limit our attention to the nasal *m* and to the aspirate, the pattern goes like this:

> m h h m m
> h m m h
> m m h m m h m

There are as many *m*'s in the third line, before the caesura, as in all of the first line, as many after the caesura as in the second line. The alliterative weight of that sound moves toward the final "mee" and receives its stamp of identification with the "mee" (if it does) at that point. If this is an admissible notion, then one may see that the alliteration runs parallel in its development with the expansion of the metaphor that discovers the full activity of the "mee." The alliterative pattern (like the metaphor) is ambiguous. The "her whom" of the first line makes the aspirate dominant through position and emphasis. The same is true in the second line. Only in the third line does the balance begin to shift, with the three alliterations at the beginning which dominate the "her" and lead to the "mee."

This alliterative structure may be oversubtle, especially in its interpretation, and it may well seem exotic. There was no reason to expect it; nor does it force itself upon the reader because he cannot otherwise make reasonable sense out of the passage. But surely the pattern is there, even if I have not interpreted the items correctly. Nor is the pattern there inertly — perhaps just for prettiness. A meaningless pattern in so freighted a passage might be even more miraculous than what we now think we see. Let us then concede the correctness of the interpretation, for if we do we shall have apparently accounted for a pattern of sound which makes a minor contribution, however surprisingly, to a dominant pattern of meaning. But what shall we say of the *l*'s in the passage? They too make a pattern, to which we may respond before discovering that there is a pattern — that of initial *l* in the first line ("love"), final *l* in the second line ("faithfull"), and then the reverse order in the third line ("*Medall* . . . love"). It is difficult to explain what is being specifically accomplished in the immediate context. Yet the device is affecting, and does not distract but seems rather to sharpen the attention and make it more responsive to subtleties which are determinably functional. Perhaps the device is functional too, though on a plane that escapes our power of rational analysis. It would seem appropriate to refer to the old problem of the poet's voice and the self-delight he takes in style; for here something is left over, not quite assimilated into the immediate context, even in a passage so compressed that one would not have thought it could support an extravagance. We have already qualified our working notion of Donne as a rhetorical poet; and though we may not be ready to call him a "musical" poet, we must resign ourselves, unless we can explain the device rhetorically, to accepting it either as adornment or as an imaginative expression of musical form which cannot be assigned a prose meaning. We may reasonably conclude that here is an example of Donne's imagination working through sound, and setting up an unassimilated, if small, crosscurrent in what is a mainstream of rational sense.

If such devices were more frequent in Donne (they are more frequent than might be thought), or if they dominated the imaginative structure of any passages, then we should have to revise our critical attitudes further. For when the imagination is working primarily through sound, as in this minor example, the result is difficult for the expositor (or the poet) to explain very completely in the language of discourse. But since Donne's imagination is more visual than auditory, and ranges, however widely, against the pull of a compelling rationalism, he tends to work out his imaginative vision within the limits that he self-consciously accepts.

If the "something left over" seemed an extravagance in the passage just considered, what are we to think of the brilliant lyricism in the last stanza of "A Valediction: Of Weeping"?

> O more then Moone,
> Draw not up seas to drowne me in thy spheare,
> Weepe me not dead, in thine armes, but forbeare
> To teach the sea, what it may doe too soone.

As a first impression the alliterative structure, which is beautifully woven, may seem to sing almost independently of the meaning. A second look, however, allows us to observe a kind of imaginative structure not unlike that made by the *m-h* in the previous analysis. Not until "seas" does the metaphor begin to focus; not until the alliterative "drowne" and its climactic stress can the force latent in "Draw" be released. The rhythmical parallel at the beginning of the second and third lines helps carry on the relationship between "Draw" and "dead." The "doe" in the next line makes "drowne" and "dead" reverberate. In the structure of lovely sophistries, part of the power of the mistress as symbol lies in the persuasive magic of the consonantal patterns. The *d*'s threaten the finality of death. The *n*'s threaten too, but not without some hint that the final power of decision belongs to the mistress —"then," "Moone," "not," "drowne," "in," "not," "thine," "soone." The *m*'s and *s*'s move back and forth between destruction and safety. The *f* of "spheare," picked up by "forbeare," points toward the saving grace that resides in her magic power over him. Death in the sphere of her arms, though a symbolic death in the ideal world of their love, where she is more than moon, may presage his death in the inferior world of reality. Drawing up seas, drowning, and death — all may be called by actual name in the ideal world where she has complete power. In the physical world, what may be the action of the sea is called "doe"— a thinly disguised euphemism which threatens and persuades, which uses a general and neutral word that cannot be neutral in the context, and particularly since the alliterative pattern of *d*'s has become in the ideal world part of the metaphor of death by drowning.

So much for the second look, and the rationally determinable pattern of sound. But what shall we say of the total effect, and of the rarity in Donne of this kind of singing — its concentrated fullness of emotion, its richness of verbal orchestration? It does not help to say that the fine extravagance of idea is matched appropriately by a fine extravagance of sound. Donne does not give other ideas, which are no less extravagant, so unaccountable a richness of sound, and there is a difference between recognizing, or responding to, a burst of lyric intensity and being able critically to determine the structure of internal relationships. We might let the matter go by saying that the dramatic context requires a piece of thoroughly emotional persuasion, and that the sound must be at least an adequate vehicle for the idea. That may be sufficient for the occasion, particularly since Donne does not write this kind of passage often. But if we regard the structure of sound as doing more than echoing the sense, if it may be essential for completing the sense, then we have reason to feel a little uncomfortable when we cannot determine in some detail what the sound is doing. For instance, here the degree of intensity cannot be determined by the idea alone, and unless we know the degree we cannot understand all of the dramatic situation. Is the speaker turning the emotion on only to persuade? Does he expect that to be understood? Is he persuading himself? Does he know it? Does he expect both of these last to be understood? Even if we ask no more of the sound than this, the difference can be that between a flat and a complex dramatic situation. At the least, we must acknowledge both the rarity of this kind of passage and a total effect of verbal sensuousness that is not accounted for by our analysis of the consonantal structure.

In other poets one is more frequently aware of a reckless excess in the structure of sound. There are, for instance, Yeats's lines, "The uncontrollable mystery on the bestial floor" and "That dolphin-torn, that gong-tormented sea." Though each of these lines, which concludes a poem, has a considerable amount of rationally perceivable meaning, the intensity, and what that intensity means, can be understood only through the force of the sound. That intensity is an important imaginative part of what the poem realizes. The structure of sound is definitely not independent of the meaning, and it is perhaps not accurate to say that it dominates the meaning, but it *is* the chief agent for the emotional release (and the tension maintained within the poetic resolution) that is central to the meaning of each poem. In this excess, even though it works under the larger control of the imagination, there is a kind of letting-go that Donne — it would seem from his practice — prefers to avoid. To cite a different example, it is hard to conceive of Donne's using verbal sensuousness in this way:

> Droop herbs and flowers,
> Fall grief in showers;
> Our beauties are not ours.

And it is not a matter of "softness." These lines of Ben Jonson's, and the poem from which they come, have an impressive discipline.[48] Or Milton can evoke a whole world in a line, principally by using sound to shape metaphor with a full imaginative sensuousness that Donne cannot permit himself—"The haunt of Seals and Orcs, and Sea-mews' clang."[49]

But excess is not the only sign that the auditory imagination is at work. The subordinate importance of visual imagery is another sign. One sees nothing precisely in Yeats's "The Magi," or "Byzantium." States of comprehension are created, but not out of directly perceivable details. This is not to say that the poems are unphysical and abstract. The flame "cannot singe a sleeve." "Blood, imagination, intellect" are all working together, but they are not dependent upon focused pictures, which the imagination might well regard, at least in some states, as the "unpurged images of day." In "Byzantium" ideal states, deliberately ritualized by incantation—as, "Miracle, bird or golden handiwork / More miracle than bird or handiwork" —conflict with states of practical reality, "the mire and blood." These opposing states and their resolution are realized with a minimum of the visual, but still with a maximum of the physical. In "The Magi" this last is also true, and in addition the rhythm is both a more complex and a more directly governing force. In both of these poems many of the effects can be rationally perceived, but the power of reason is at one remove at least—the meaning is felt and understood before the mind realizes that it understands and can check back to discover why. If the demonstrations have been at all reliable, something of this may be said of Donne too. The difference is one of proportion and emphasis—not unlike the differences between Donne and his contemporaries.

Eliot, though his critical remarks on visual imagery may tend to mislead, has many passages where very little is concretely visualized, as in these lines from the first section of "The Dry Salvages":

                                          The sea has many voices,
Many gods and many voices.
                                          The salt is on the briar rose,
The fog is in the fir trees.
                                          The sea howl
And the sea yelp are different voices
Often together heard; the whine in the rigging,
The menace and caress of wave that breaks on water,
The distant rote in the granite teeth,
And the wailing warning from the approaching headland
Are all sea voices, and the heaving groaner
Rounded homewards, and the seagull.

Here it is less a matter of seeing than of being a part of the experience, and of feeling one's way through the presented experience into its timeless pattern of occurrence.

There is nothing in Donne to compare with this. And yet there are lines and small passages that seem to tend in this direction. There is the section of "The Second Anniversary" where the soul is told to get up into the watchtower and see things despoiled of fallacies. Then these lines follow:

> Thou shalt not peepe through lattices of eyes,
> Nor heare through Labyrinths of eares, nor learne
> By circuit, or collections to discerne.[50]

What is most interesting about these lines is the intensity of tone that creeps into the prospect of abandoning the usual human methods of comprehension — through the senses and the rules of rational procedure. One cannot avoid observing that this passage represents, not a chronological development, but one of two sides of Donne's nature. Desire for the release from consciousness is the other side of his poetry of consciousness. In terms of internal drama, within the poet, if Donne's passionately scrupulous intellect maintains a compulsive pressure upon his imagination, then a kind of psychological counterpoint is also true. The soul, when he imagines it released from the body, "carries no desire to know, nor sense."

But the striving for release is one source of his intensity. Note for instance these lines:

> And learn'st thus much by our Anatomy,
> That 'tis in vaine to dew, or mollifie
> It with thy teares, or sweat, or blood: nothing
> Is worth our travaile, griefe, or perishing,
> But those rich joyes, which did possesse her heart,
> Of which she's now partaker, and a part.[51]

There is a sensuousness of phrase and an unashamed directness of feeling that are not uncommon in Donne the preacher, but that one has to look hard to find in the poetry. Or these lines, which are like nothing else in Donne:

> Is the Pacifique Sea my home? Or are
> The Easterne riches? Is *Jerusalem*?
> *Anyan*, and *Magellan*, and *Gibraltare*,
> All streights, and none but streights, are wayes to them,
> Whether where *Japhet* dwelt, or *Cham*, or *Sem*.[52]

The basic conceit is an intellectual and witty one. But the richness of the invocation, the echoing magic of name and place — these are wonderfully in excess of the rational requirements of the idea, and to a degree that is unique in Donne's verse.

The intensity of Donne's drive for consciousness may be a source both of his great imaginative power and of his limitations as poet. The standard that he sets he defines thus: "*Knowledge* cannot save us, but we cannot be saved without Knowledge; Faith is not on this side Knowledge, but beyond it." [53] We feel the force of that attitude even when Donne is wittily destroying the authority of reason, or is flirting with the temptation of abandoning it. Perhaps we may blame on Donne's consciousness the fact that he does not as a poet build separate successes into something that might give him a larger imaginative release, that might give him complete imaginative confidence in the full play of his senses.

Perhaps no poet really can do or does all this. Perhaps he only creates the illusion that he is doing so. Valéry made the proposal, not without some intellectual mischief, that the poet's inspiration might be better understood as his ability to make the reader feel inspired.[54] Certainly we must guard against letting our acquired expectations — the kinds of esthetic satisfaction some poets may have taught us to prize — govern the free individual response which is due any genuine poet.[55] We ought not proceed to judgment too fast, lest we hang, summarily, for "not keeping of accent," "the first poet in the world in some things"; and then allow ourselves to say, in the independent sincerity of another occasion, that verses stand by sense, without "either Colours or accent."[56] To speak, as I have been doing, of the limits of Donne's verbal sensuousness, is to push a legitimate discrimination toward what may be a disabling judgment. It is well to stop short and remember that the announced intention was to trace a single line of direction in order to isolate some effects and characteristics in Donne's poetry of rationalism and consciousness.

Our next task will be to look at a whole poem and try to gauge its effects. This should allow us to revise the distortions that are caused by intense analysis of individual lines. At the same time we should be able to apply, and test, some of the kinds of questions we have learned to ask by means of the study thus far pursued.

"The Good-morrow"

I take this poem as one of several for which Donne deserves Jonson's praise as "the first poet in the world in some things." It is a poem that immediately engages the reader; he is drawn into its action at once, but soon discovers that he must make his own exertions or fall behind. Perhaps it will be helpful first to quote the poem in full.

> I Wonder by my troth, what thou, and I
> Did, till we lov'd? were we not wean'd till then?
> But suck'd on countrey pleasures, childishly?
> Or snorted we in the seaven sleepers den?
> T'was so; But this, all pleasures fancies bee.
> If ever any beauty I did see,
> Which I desir'd, and got, t'was but a dreame of thee.
>
> And now good morrow to our waking soules,
> Which watch not one another out of feare;
> For love, all love of other sights controules,
> And makes one little roome, an every where.
> Let sea-discoverers to new worlds have gone,
> Let Maps to other, worlds on worlds have showne,
> Let us possesse one world, each hath one, and is one.

My face in thine eye, thine in mine appeares,
And true plain hearts doe in the faces rest,
Where can we finde two better hemispheares
Without sharpe North, without declining West?
What ever dyes, was not mixt equally;
If our two loves be one, or, thou and I
Love so alike, that none doe slacken, none can die.

A major initial problem, as in many of Donne's poems, is that we have no given tone, no stable attitude or defined position from which we can follow a clear development. Things appear to be in violent motion from the very beginning, and when the explosive dissonances of the first stanza come to an end, the sustained intensity and the dazzling nimbleness of effects will have imposed an impression on us that cannot end as abruptly as the stanza. The esthetic question, which asks itself, is: will this return, or are we really done with it? To shift, as we must, to an imaginative world of peace in a cozy little room of love is a wrench that we also experience as a kind of violence, even though the subject presented is the peaceful satisfaction of love. And then, though we shall have studied the traditional basis for the metaphysical argument of the final three lines and found the argument "correct"— still, how are we to take it? Not literally? And yet, have we acquired in motion enough sense of the tone of the poem to be able to gauge the degree of the literal in that argument? There may seem to be a kind of intellectual violence in the sudden introduction of an abstruse argument out of nowhere, and perhaps we may feel plunged back into the beginning of the poem, even if on a different plane.

Where tone is a problem, we may be helped by looking for stable elements of structure on which the poem is built. The three stanzas, we may notice at once, correspond to three stages. For instance, in terms of time we have a progression from past to present to future. At least that is the rough division; when we look more closely we can see a finer organization in the basic progression. But the fact of progression is definite, though the stages themselves are not limited only to their correspondence with time. We may also mark a movement from the first world of flesh to that of mind and thence to a world of spirit. The movement also corresponds to a turning from disparate multiplicity to a singleness of identity, with the middle term a kind of unified twoness. Parallel to this, there is a motion from restless change to conscious peace and rest, and thence to an idea of eternal motionlessness. All of these parallel movements refer to a single metaphysical concept expressed by the traditional argument which leads upward from sense and particular experience to a unifying transcendence. But the movements of the argument are not without some enigma and reserve.

The apparent violence of the first stanza is due only in part to the explosive opening and to the startling rhetoric of physical reference. There is also a strenuous intellectual surprise, a play between time-honored idealizing concepts of love and a sensuality which, though dismissed, is given an overemphasis that may seem to dominate imaginatively, by vivid detail and rhythmical energy, the ideal before which it ostensibly makes way. One aspect of the ideal is a common one, a fact in experience and a convention in art: that compelling contrast between the life before and the life after the awakening of love. In retrospect all previous experience is fused into a single, dull dimension of existence, and the awakened lover sees with new eyes that all the objects passionately pursued were unreal phantoms — at worst figures of evil distraction, at best cloudy misrepresentations of the true objects he now sees. If his memory is keen, and the false objects can still be imagined with sensuous immediacy, he is likely to disparage the authority of the senses. The experience is common to lovers, but it may occur whenever there is an awakening in religion, or in philosophy, or in any department of knowledge that aspires to some claim on reality. Donne has united this familiar experience of the lover with its philosophical counterpart, the Platonic contrast between the illusion of sensuous appearances and the truth of the ideal reality. And something of the Platonic movement of love is also incorporated, that turning from the sensuous multiplicity of the individual to a purged love of universal beauty.

But Donne refuses to make the contrast absolute, and there is mischief in his Platonizing. We do not emerge from the cave of the senses, from the sucking and snorting and weaning, with no more of a look backward than is necessary to dismiss the past. That is the apparent effect of the "T'was so"—a summary and a dismissal before the triumphant announcement of the new, exclusive definition of reality. It starts properly enough, by equating pleasures and fancies: "But this, all pleasures fancies bee." However, the verbal form, "bee," is a little ambiguous; we have no ordinary statement of fact. Nor is it clear, logically or syntactically, that the marvelous new "this" is excluded from the definition of pleasures. If we are being awakened to a higher form of pleasure, then we cannot apply the apparent Platonic formula in its usual way. Some of the same embarrassment attends that higher vision of beauty. The earthly examples may have been only anticipations of the true ideal, part of the fancy and the dream from which the lover now awakes; but those muddy particles of beauty intrude themselves with such low, concrete immediacy that they thrust themselves into the very presence of the ideal. Confession and rejection, if wholehearted and single-minded, should have come earlier. One does not re-create, with such imaginative authority, the whole process or cycle of the mistaken past—not as the last step before celebrating the entrance into the new life. And these intimations of the true beauty are not polite, self-rejecting harbingers, as properly they should be; nor are they suffering servants, whose most important service, after adequate self-reproach, is to disappear absolutely, with no afterimpression. Instead, these have been seen, desired, and got—as individual "beauties."

So an intellectual structure of the violence may be discerned in the imaginative disproportion between the immediate prominence of the rejected life and the formal dominance of the heralded ideal. The sensual past advertises itself up to the doorsill of the ideal present. If we solemnly expect a literal use of the Platonic distinctions, then we may be justified in thinking Donne mischievous. But we are not required to take the philosophical part as both central and seriously literal. The structure we feel suggests itself to us, intellectually, as building upon an imaginative disproportion. But this may in part be due to our trained expectations that the ideal will triumph absolutely and erase the past at once. Let us take another view. Is it not possible that we have less an imaginative disproportion, of the sort

I have been describing, than a strenuous tension of interests maintained to the end of the stanza — perhaps beyond? The poem is a witty poem, but the wit, I suggest, does not lie in any intellectual mischief or shocking outrageousness of details; it lies in the sustained imaginative power and imaginative consciousness we experience in the poem. The kind of structure we might expect from such a poem ought not depend too heavily on mere disproportions between elements put into simple contrasting relationship.

We have not tried to *hear* any of the structure yet, for we have been too busy trying to get other matters in their right place. As a matter of fact, the kinds of ambiguities we have been noticing are present whenever we try to read the first stanza aloud. Let us notice a distinguishable voice of some importance which may easily go unremarked.

The opening of the poem is ordinarily felt and described as explosive. Is it? The first question is abrupt, but it differs from the three questions that then follow. These offer three strikingly individual images of physical activity, but they all serve the purpose of presenting possible answers to the first question:

> I Wonder by my troth, what thou, and I
> Did, till we lov'd?

The tone of an oath is difficult to judge. If the speaker is aiming only at the reader's shock over the weaning, sucking, snorting, then we should minimize the difference between the first question and the three that follow. But suppose the oath is not just a casual mouth-filler, but tends toward the serious and swears by a newly discovered faith in love. Suppose the speaker's wonder may be that of genuine personal surprise, not to be translated into anything quite like "what the hell," "who'd have thought."

The chief justification for these remarks, and the first hint, is what must happen when we read the most emphatic word until the last line of the stanza — "Did." "Did" and "dreame" are the two most important words in the stanza; between them they control the imaginative structure and so create an emphasis and resonance which oppose the force generated by the more physically immediate, but more nearly local, images. The noncommittal indefiniteness of

"Did," elevated by rhythmical position, and held up for a long moment of contemplation, creates the possibility of a real wonder, a surprised recognition of something not understood. The "Did" is indefinite and abstract, even though it surely includes the connotations of sexual *doing*. It is an immature abstraction, the summary of a youthful imagination, often bored, incapable of seeing the woods for the trees. What shall we do — what did we ever do with the time? The doing is a summary blank; its abstraction is an unindividualized version of immediate experience. It precedes the account of rejected concrete experience, and then another version of that concrete experience reappears in the more sophisticated abstraction, the philosophical summary of the "dreame of thee." The wonder occurs in the present and looks backward; it produces the insulting items of a sleeping, a preconscious, dream, the "Did" of an *id*, infantile sexuality. But the "dreame of thee" is a waking dream of consciousness; it also occurs in the present. When it looks backward to the past it does not do so with full immediacy; it does not immerse the imagination in the action of the past. Nevertheless, the items produced also impose their pressure upon the ideal state of the waking dream. The items from the past may be thought insulting, and they are not rejected with passionate contempt, as they were earlier. The chief point is that Donne has created a kind of progression familiar in musical structure, and when the items from the past reappear in their second version, they have been imaginatively modified. The first version expressed the full passion of utter rejection. That feeling then can make way for the recognition that the past led to the present, in ways that do not need to be liked but do not need to be hated — once the hate has been expressed, and once a kind of substantial meaning and purpose has been won from the progress. In a sense the development, the form of the progression, is its own justification. It leaves the speaker, as the first question did not, firmly in control of his wonder. The past has been brought into a significant, and subordinate, relationship to the present. The achievement may not be so clean — and the unpublished statistics on the varieties of human temptation might suggest that it is not so generally desired — as a complete and absolute break with the past. But there are compensations too. The honesty is its own reward; and in a poem celebrating the awakening of consciousness in love, imaginative deceptions become progressively harder to conceal.

And so the past is made to serve the present, even if some of the clear and triumphant independence of the present, its pure and underived uniqueness, may be diminished. Instead of uncertainty and reserve concerning Donne's concept of a unifying transcendence, we have a working demonstration of a movement upward that does not cut itself off from the past but imaginatively assimilates the fully recognized crudities of the past into the pattern of progression.

"And now good morrow to our waking soules." The line hails and celebrates an arrival. Its most impressive effect is its newness; for the whole first stanza acts as contrasting background — as if, for the moment, this were the realized purpose, negative and defining, of the first stanza. The imaginative qualities of the line are those of openness and confident approval. In the speaker's voice we seem to hear an unreserved intellectual identification with what he says. We are being invited to believe that this is what he has been moving toward, the unifying idea in the present toward which all the previous images have been progressing.

The first stanza, as first stage, brought the memory of the unconscious past of flesh toward a conscious relationship with the mind of the present. The second stanza makes declarations concerning that present; it prepares for the next stage but also looks back. Fear as a motivation for the lovers' watching each other, however lightly touched, however denied, is an intellectual equivalent of the misdirected activity which characterized the past history of sensual love. So too are those gay injunctions to the explorers, the sea-lovers and map-lovers — let them *have done* what they like to do! Their activities are dismissed from the present, not because they are contemptible or a passionate threat, but because they are inconsequential. In the third stanza the external world enters again, as another intellectual recollection of the past. In a way the reference is even further remote and abstract. The two hemispheres are those of a merely objective world, with which there can be no significant human relationship — that is, subjective interrelationship — except at the one point of contact, the idea of time and change. The "sharpe North" and the "declining West" — these belong to the world of passion and death from which the lovers have awakened. That world, like their preconscious past, has not been annihilated by the poetic imagination; it has been transformed by the lovers' consciousness of purpose; it defines by its cold externality the warm center of a living present.

In the recurring modulations of the poem, its pattern of related and progressive movement, we may see and hear and feel the imaginative form of the poem. The movement itself leads us from a world of misdirected activities toward a lessened sense of their immediacy and relevance. This imaginative form seems to develop from a single principle, but it is a poetic insight and hard to isolate or name. And it was not given at once, or early, for it could reveal itself only in motion as part of the developing form. Let us call that principle a refusal to annihilate the past and the external. But we still must see what this means, this determination to imagine a mastery of present and future while transforming but not annihilating the elements which are excluded from the center of the experience.

"What ever dyes, was not mixt equally." This is the applied conclusion of an abstract argument Donne learned from scholastic philosophy. It introduces the idea of death, not imaginatively immediate or threatening, but not quite abstract either; for it sums up all the rejected images from the external world of change, sums them up as a gentle reminder that they have been defeated and that the triumph of the warm present has been won in spite of them. The end of the poem turns, as the end of each preceding stanza has turned, to a summing up that consolidates the stage attained and looks forward to the next. It is this fact, more than the unexpected introduction of an abstract argument, which accounts for the strange tone at the end. That tone is not triumphant; it is not the tone of an enthusiastic voice proclaiming transcendence. Instead it is quiet, even modest. The argument does not undertake to prove, by any pride in the strength and edge of its logic, the infallible safety of the lovers' final arrival. It restates in other terms what has already been learned by the process of their experience, and it points that wisdom toward the future. It points with the modest tentativeness of *two* possible propositions, both based upon an *if*:

> If our two loves be one, or, thou and I
> Love so alike, that none doe slacken, none can die.

Again we must observe that what seemed violent or disproportionate is rather a tension of interests that carries through to the end, and points beyond the end, of the poem. Not that the poem is unresolved. Its problems are defined and true relationships are established. But its triumph is modest and human; it is a triumph of imaginative consciousness and not of intellectual or spiritual invulnerability. The kind of transcendence toward which the poem develops is not a goal which, once achieved, permits consciousness to surrender itself. That is why the poem both ends and seems to go on, pointing beyond itself. The effect is not a trick of wit; it is rather a proof of the imaginative fidelity of the poem to the nature and form of the experience created by it. That the effect is deeply characteristic of Donne, I may simply note without further comment.

Let me try to demonstrate the reliability of these conclusions by turning to matters I have slighted while following one line of the poem's development. The height of the triumph, at least as declaration, is the most ringing musical statement of the poem: "And now good morrow to our waking soules." But that arresting line does not proceed directly to further assertion. Instead we have the recapitulated items of the external world, lightly but firmly present to give definition to the imaginative scene in which love realizes its inner world. That inner world has a kind of grandeur in its imaginative extent as it moves out to become "an every where." But it is not single and simple either in its materials or in its imaginative reference. For the imagining is a conscious act, and something of the consciousness and the act remain in the effect.

What we have is a metaphor, in which the act and the process of imagining are not completely assimilated into a singleness of identification. It is an imaginative translation that knows it is imagining; the validity lies *both* in the translation (its balanced qualities of precision and fictive power to illuminate and open up just relationships) *and* in the discreet consciousness of the act. The validity lies in both. Although there is a kind of stability in the metaphor itself, which is due to the fact that we recognize the enclosed world of love as having an established form in the human imagination and in human experience, nevertheless it is not a form which is incontrovertible. It is not one of the great and stable symbols presented as lying outside the human mind, and presented so that the mind can merge itself into the symbol without further argument, and with a minimum of consciousness in the act. Let me quote Donne's lines and italicize two words:

> For love, all love of other sights controules,
> And *makes* one little roome, an *every where*.

The everywhere is important to Donne, and not only in this poem. The world of love as it takes shape in the poem defines its pure center both by exclusions and by inclusions. The preconscious dream of sensuality is excluded, but the conscious dream is assimilated into the higher "dreame of thee." The distractions of the external world are rejected; they are disunified and an argument for change and death. Yet here the little world of love does not exclude or quite assimilate the external, but it varies the movement by exhibiting its own imaginative power to move out into the world without suffering the consequences of change. It can enjoy the splendor and variety of the world at home, in the possession of its essential unity.

The unity of love is a unity of having and being. It is not single or mystic. It is not an inner world of inviolable subjectivity. It is a world of twoness united. Its stability depends upon a knowledge of its derivation and present condition. For it is a lyric moment precarious in a world of fact. In order to project its truth of feeling into the future, and its present sense of having escaped from the time-ridden to the timeless, the lovers must know what they feel and feel what they know. But the knowing, it is plain, never achieves a fixed and positive clarity like that of the lyric moment. The knowing is expressed in movement, by the tact and balance of the unfolding form, by the exclusions and inclusions of consciousness, by the intelligence that permeates the whole poem.

The most positive expressions of knowing are those which hail the lovers' waking souls and declare the transforming power of the "one little roome." But the salutation to their waking souls is less positive than it sounds; it creates the feeling of a state of intellectual clarity, but it does nothing to define, to objectify, to demonstrate — nothing, that is, by itself, removed from the demonstration of the form. Of course, it is not removed, except by our analysis. But our power to do this makes possible a negative distinction: that is, we cannot by analysis remove the positive states of feeling. They are defined, objectified, demonstrated, and they exist in positive moments. For instance, the love that "makes one little roome, an every where" expresses a positive and demonstrated state of intellectual clarity, by which love declares its transforming power. The inner reality of love dares project itself into external reality without the usual dangers or consequences elaborately worked out in the philosophy books. But we have a positive intellectual state only because we have an imaginative state based upon a positive truth of the feelings. That truth is not only inaccessible to the arguments of the intellect; it has the sanction of universal psychological experience; furthermore, it is presented as an imaginative metaphor; furthermore, it does not pretend to universal validity, but makes its bold assertion from its private certainty within the moment created by the unity of love.

The distinction I am trying to make is that the *feeling* is projected with a kind of clarity, and positive simplicity, but that the *knowing* is not so projected. To make the distinction is, I suppose, to make a kind of judgment, but it is not one that the poem allows us to press literally. The *knowing* and the *feeling* do not go their separate ways; they are complementary and related; the unity of love depends on their twoness being one, even though they also maintain a tension of interests in the developing form of the poem.

Finally, let us consider these lines:

> My face in thine eye, thine in mine appeares,
> And true plain hearts doe in the faces rest.

The proof of the lovers' identification is in the having and being, in the objective recognition of self in another and the feeling of another in self. In that experience, where the lover sees his own reflected face directly, while he sees directly the other face, but only *feels* its image reflected in his own eye, there exists the most delicate point of contact between the subjective and the objective. The two lovers *are* one in the image, and so fulfill for the moment those propositions that hang over the future. They are one, and they do love alike. They have been mixed equally, and present an ancient proof of human integration, the transparency of the heart in the countenance. It is an ancient proof, mildly modernized and individualized in the context by the play on "plain" and by the special relevance of "rest," which opposes the world of change. But the familiar idea, and the emphasis of the utterance — its "true plain" rhythm, quite lacking in the individuality of the first line — these express a directness of feeling that approaches the trite and the obvious. Out of the context the triteness and obviousness would be unmistakable. In the context they are a remarkable testimony to a kind of simplicity of feeling not usually associated with Donne. It is worth noting and remembering.

The consciousness of metaphor still is present, but it is less emphatic than in the imaginative transformation of the little room. Here the image, as the scene, is more nearly simple and direct, and the quality of the feeling is different. We have moved from the ringing announcement of the good-morrow, to the demonstration of power in the little room, to the climactic warmth of an actual human relationship. Imaginative consciousness, *inside* the little room, is only *outside* the present scene, as part of the form. The scene is completely itself, modest and actual, not needing to define or demonstrate, but doing so in the directness of the statement. In the line "My face in thine eye, thine in mine appeares," the rhetorical emphasis, the meter, and the emphasis of feeling coincide almost exactly. The stress on "thine . . . thine . . . mine," the reinforcement of that single sound by the "my . . . eye" — these draw together in a singleness of effect which is deeply moving here, though the stylistic formula in the abstract sounds unpromising. Only "face" and "appeares," at the beginning and end of the line, express vowels and consonants different from the central interweaving of the *i-m-n-th*.

May we think that this pattern of speech helps project a sense of unity between subject and object, between internal and external world? The line gives us our fullest single expression of the integrity of feelings and action. It is the highest point of feeling in the poem. And when we reconsider the two previous high points, "And now good morrow to our waking soules . . . And makes one little roome, an every where," we must recognize that the highest point is also simplest.

Let us look back to bring some of these observations together. In a world of subjects and objects, the imaginative form of the poem refuses to annihilate the past or the external. Though the poem follows a pattern of transcendence, it does not do so by acts of simple exclusion. It is free of all the familiar assertions of intellectual or spiritual pride, and the fruits of a powerful honesty of consciousness are those of tact and grace. The lovers' unity requires intellectual subtlety and imaginative consciousness; they must be fully awake in order to solve the relationships between past and present, present and future, and between inner and outer reality. The imaginative consciousness never flags; it never forgets relationship. Even at the end of the poem there is no claim for immortality through love; the argument is no literal application of stiff metaphysics, but instead a modest proposal. What is literal, and surprisingly so, is the application of the metaphysical lesson to the real world of love: the alternative to the unity of love is the death of love.

And so the subtlety of the poem ends in intellectual modesty and awakened simplicity. In the partnership between knowing and feeling, the knowing is more obviously active in the poem, though less fixed and positive; but there is a partnership, and the progress is toward simplicity. The wit may lie in imaginative consciousness, but it is not what is usually meant by intellectual wit. In fact, if I have interpreted the movement of the poem correctly, one might prefer an opposing coinage and speak of Donne's emotional wit or the wit of simplicity. When I sum up this chapter in the next section, I shall return to this matter for another look, and Donne's wit is the subject of the following chapter.

Summary and Conclusion

The chapter has been long, the materials diverse, the method to a large extent inductive. It has been my purpose to explore some problems that concern Donne's style. Yet I have had no intention of leading the reader, or myself, on a tour of the critical scenery that did not do some hard map making and finally arrive somewhere. My exposition does not lend itself to summary, but let me try to indicate, in the main, where we have been and come.

The first section introduced some background for discussing the sensuous qualities of Donne's verse; it accepted the distinction that sees Donne as a rhetorical poet interested more in the immediacies of meaning than in the immediacies of grace but warned that the distinction would need to be qualified. In examining his metrical tradition and his rhetoric I noted that on the one side Donne approached a kind of cultivated harshness and on the other side an individual kind of lyric. One aspect of his rhetoric provided the first example (from Satire III) of simplicity in style. The associations with this simplicity are classical; language serves the argument completely and seems to be assimilated into it. In this example, moreover, the feelings are simple, with no tension between the poet's feelings and what he professes. The passage also has a significant bareness; its effects are achieved more simply and inevitably than the effects of prose. The second example of simplicity came from the opening lines of "Lovers Infinitenesse." The bareness here derived from a strict imposition of limits: on the materials of language, the logic of the proposition, the tone, the sensuousness. The simplicity seemed to derive less from the achievement or illusion of self-completeness than from the special artistic triumph of working with imaginative richness within narrow limits. A classical ideal of style did not seem relevant to this example of simplicity, in which the feelings are not simple, but work through tension and raise elusive questions. The section ended with the problem of the "something left over" and the individuality of the poet's voice and style. Most of these topics, here summarized, were further developed later in the chapter, and certain critical attitudes toward the problems became defined, or better defined.

The second section was concerned with a limited analysis of specific examples. The first series illustrated Donne's use of verbal sensuousness to emphasize the meaning of his verse. His practice is deliberately rhetorical, but he does not seriously imitate sense by sound. A further series illustrated a more deeply involved relationship between meter and rhetorical emphasis, upon which the full emergence of metaphorical meaning depends. The final examples were intended to demonstrate some of the musical power in Donne's verse and to qualify the earlier distinction that emphasized his rhetorical bent. But the qualification was not radical, for analysis discovered in certain lines a richer and more complicated meaning created by the imaginative sensuousness.

The third section returned to the rhetoric and some problems which concern historical perspective. It took a middle position and argued that Donne's rhetoric differs not in kind but in degree and individual emphasis from that of his contemporaries. Part of his emphasis may be seen historically as connected with a rationalistic distrust of words and with a kind of "visual rationalism." But again the difference is not radical. What chiefly distinguishes Donne from his contemporaries is the degree of intellectual concentration he achieved, the depth of his imaginative inventions, and what as poet he did without — the strict limits he imposed on the sensuousness, the affective qualities, of his verse.

By letting Donne's emphasis on the visual arbitrarily stand for his rational control, and by opposing to this the auditory, I attempted to explore certain limits of Donne's sensuousness and the significance of those limits. Some examples do illustrate aspects of an auditory imagination and indicate qualities in the style that cannot be explained by ordinary rational analysis; but the correct conclusion seemed to be that Donne's characteristic poetry of consciousness differs from these examples and from other illustrative touchstones of the auditory imagination.

The last section analyzed "The Good-morrow" as a kind of test case. The intention was to apply pressure on the general positions developed by the preceding sections. These positions influenced my critical approach and some of the particular questions I asked of the poem; I tried to keep them in mind while I worked out my immediate interpretation; but I did not thrust them forward to take over the interpretation; nor did I argue directly for or against them during the interpretation. I could not have managed so complicated a piece of expository juggling, and that is one justification for this present section — its opportunity to step out of the argument and take a second look. As much as I can, I shall try not to summarize my analysis of the poem itself, but to look only at the issues that bear on the general critical positions of the chapter.

First, as I expected, the test case does not work out quite as I hoped. It is true that "The Good-morrow" is but one poem of many, and Donne's poems are certainly not all alike. Yet this is no ordinary poem, and though it may not be absolutely central in Donne's accomplishment, it is an undeniable triumph of his art. Any general comments on Donne which do not adequately describe the specific qualities of this accomplishment must be reconsidered. It is a sound principle to think that the burden of proof is always upon general criticism to accommodate itself to the specific qualities of the good poem.

Yet my analysis was partly shaped by, and did grow out of, questions pondered earlier. Specifically, my present interpretation does help confirm the practical value of thinking actively of the problems which concern the partnership of sound and sense in Donne. The poem *is* a musical poem, but the music is more that of form than of song. The music does not depend upon melting phrase or rhythm, nor upon sustained *cantabile* — no more than upon the evident strength of harsh dissonance. But still the imaginative form of the poem is musical in its arrangement, development, and control of theme and texture. To hear and see these results we must be prepared to accept imaginatively the materials and methods of Donne's art — an art in which the affective resources of verbal sensuousness are deliberately limited and approach bareness, in which what is most immediately affective neither is privileged to speak any dominating lyric capsules of truth, nor is yet disqualified from so speaking. Donne thinks in imaginative forms, where part must qualify or justify itself against part, where themes must win their way through an honorable and potent resistance. The resolution is achieved through a progress of transformation and recapitulation, through a system of inner references to what is the past history of any chosen moment in the developing form. By these references and their development such moments build a significant relationship between their past and their future history. It is in his sense of form that Donne must, in these general terms, be considered a musical poet. His refusal to annihilate the past and the external in the progress of his poem can be taken as one sign of his musical imagination.

The poem offers its own individual comment on Donne's rationalism — developing, as it does, by an urgent tension of interests, with the intellectualism suggesting itself less as a limiting rationalism than as a sustained imaginative power which includes the consciousness of itself. The intellectualism of the poem is not located in any single identifiable aspect of the rational — certainly not in any visual immediacy, nor even in the reflected vision of the lovers in each other's eyes. What is most impressive in that scene is the image that expresses the unity of the lovers in an instance where objective and subjective meet, where the emotional high point of the poem is realized with no falsification or neglect of the many issues involved. The intellectual makes itself felt in the poem by its expression in movement — by the tact and balance of the unfolding form, by the exclusions and inclusions of consciousness, by the intelligence that permeates the whole poem. Imaginative consciousness seemed the most comprehensive term.

Perhaps the most surprising development was the recurrence of the problem of simplicity, and the relations between consciousness and simplicity. For the governing ideal of the poem proved itself to be *feeling*, and the poem moved, with the active collaboration of consciousness, toward a resolution in simplicity. In spite of the busy prominence of consciousness, its complicated and pervading activity, it never speaks with the fixed and positive clarity of the poem's chief lyric moment. It is as if consciousness desires to prepare, arrange, and protect an ascendant simplicity of feeling; and so consciousness provides the moving structure which enables the inner certainty within an arrested moment to express itself with full imaginative justification and validity. Perhaps we may say that for Donne consciousness could not do this by itself; nor could lyric feeling be trusted to do this alone. But the two together correspond to the realized unity which is also the experience created by the whole poem. Nor is consciousness to be thought of as merely serving the transcendent moment. It is not dismissed patronizingly. The moving structure must also be able to move beyond the moment and guarantee the validity of the moment both in its process of arriving and in the perspective of its future history. Nor does the consciousness only move, without itself being moved; it gives up some of its brilliant ranging to express, in its own terms, its own kind of simplicity, which is that of a practical, modest, and credible solution. Differences are overcome but they are not swept away. The triumph of unity in love, of awakened simplicity, is firm and imaginatively proved, but it is the achievement of a delicate balance. The poem also leaves open the honest human dilemma; it is modest before time and fate. The destructive worlds without and within, however purged or held at bay, are still there at the end, safely outside the poem but still there.

One final statement seems justified by this example of Donne's musical imagination, his demonstrated sense of form. In this poem there is no deficiency of, or rational hostility toward, the sensuous and affective. Rather, the poet wants the affective to succeed, and he believes in simplicity as a goal. But he imposes hard terms, and rational control — opposition even. Yet it is an opposition that wants to surrender, on honorable terms and not unconditionally, for the desired result is the kind of simplicity achieved by awakened souls. That high standard, described above, is here fully met: "*Knowledge cannot save us, but we cannot be saved without Knowledge; Faith is not on this side Knowledge, but beyond it.*" Of course the poem is not talking about Faith, but it is talking about faith in love. And though we may not be prepared to evaluate the fact, we can hardly miss observing that the high point of the simple unity achieved was that moment of warmth in an actual human relationship. Such an observation ought, at least, to trouble any ordinary concepts of Donne as the athletic wielder of a furious and hypertrophied wit.

CHAPTER II

FORMS OF *Wit*

IN THEIR pioneer study, "Wit, 'Mixt Wit,' and the Bee in Amber," W. L. Ustick and H. H. Hudson[1] cite Pope's objections to Crashaw's lack of "exactness" and "consent" of parts. To Pope "the soul of poetry" resides in "design, form, fable." From our present historical perspective we can understand the just irritation provoked by the worst excesses of the metaphysicals; and we have learned to expect, at least when we examine the past, that toward the end of an age of poetry the worst tendencies of its dominating style will have become both most easily available and most obviously widespread. We also know, by historical experience, that a new age will need to measure its own conscious differences by taking an unsympathetic, or ambivalent, view of the earlier accomplishment. To be unhistorical and unjust would seem to be one necessary stage of all new creative movements before they are organized into their just historical relationships. (Nor is later historical judgment exempt from its own kinds of excess.) When we think of Pope's words now, we can understand both why he should have said them and why he could not have seen that the best of the metaphysicals, Donne, Herbert, and Marvell, might also have said them. The previous century also believed that "the soul of poetry" was in "design, form, fable"; the critical pronouncements were on record and the best poetry offered immortal proof.

The words, it is plain, have altered their meaning during the century between Donne and Pope. In criticism the decisive development seems to have been articulated, though not initiated, by Hobbes, who divided the imagination into fancy and judgment. Fancy was "quick ranging" and perceived similarities between apparently disparate objects; it provided the "ornaments" of a poem. Fancy became the common concept of wit. But "true wit" was judgment, Pope's "the soul of poetry." For judgment provided the "strength and structure"; it perceived the differences in objects apparently similar.[2] That Hobbes's distinction was decisive, and widely recognized as such, can be illustrated in nearly all subsequent criticism. Perhaps the single most authoritative recognition is that by Locke in *An Essay concerning Human Understanding*:

For *wit* lying most in the assemblage of ideas, and putting those together with quickness and variety, wherein can be found any resemblance or congruity, thereby to make up pleasant pictures and agreeable visions in the fancy; *judgment*, on the contrary, lies quite on the other side, in separating carefully, one from another, ideas wherein can be found the least difference, thereby to avoid being misled by similitude, and by affinity to take one thing for another.[3]

One further stage must be noticed. Its appearance is less decisive, for its development is also involved in a complex of social forces and attitudes. But we may take as a convenient landmark D'Avenant's Preface to *Gondibert*, in which he announced his intention to bring truth "home to men's bosoms, to lead her through unfrequented and new ways . . . by representing Nature, though not in an affected, yet in an unusual dress."[4] The "new" may be taken to refer to the operation of fancy, and the restraint in style and the commitment to truth may be assigned to judgment. It is the addition of the "home to men's bosoms" which marks a further stage in the concept of wit — now firmly associated with a prominent sense of moral purpose.

When we turn from D'Avenant's statement to some of the distinctions in Johnson's *Life of Cowley*, the chief differences may perhaps be considered those of a superior articulation by a mind more fully conscious of the implications of its pronouncements. Johnson begins by saying of wit that its expression "is at once natural and new, that which, though not obvious, is, upon its first production, acknowledged to be just." Truth here also is expected to come "home to

men's bosoms," as it is in the less-quoted part of Pope's famous definition of wit, as that which "gives us back the image of our mind."
The criteria of neoclassical decorum are satisfied by Johnson's definition, and fancy is properly subordinated to the true wit of judgment, but there is also an increased sense of moral concern implicit
in his words. A particular obligation to the reader and a serious
commitment to truth — these duties are opposed to the truant flights
or the perverse "industry" of false wit. As J. B. Leishman has con-
vincingly argued, Johnson's grounds for objecting to metaphysical
wit seem as much moral as esthetic. Johnson was also "offended
. . . by its fundamental unseriousness, its detachment, its amorality." Mr. Leishman tellingly quotes the statement by Johnson that
clearly goes beyond any common notion of literary decorum, and
beyond the ordinary debates over fancy and judgment, and beyond
the argument that "the soul of poetry" is in the "design, form, fable."
The "soul" Johnson is moved by as critic is not only intellectual but
moral: "They [the metaphysicals] never inquired what, on any occasion, they should have said or done; but wrote rather as beholders
than partakers of human nature; as Beings looking upon good and
evil, impassive and at leisure." [5]

It is not time to quarrel with his judgment, though eventually we
must — even while acknowledging that there is no critic of English
literature who so wisely makes quarrels profitable (since no critic
can prevent them), or who so advantageously permits the clamber-
ing of dwarfs on his giant shoulders. His is a beautifully turned statement, a feeling judgment; one must be deaf not to be moved. Characteristically, Johnson transcends the local argument over fancy and
judgment to raise other questions of perennial interest. For instance,
one thinks of the common cycle of experience, for both ordinary
men and extraordinary artists: the early unconscious passivity toward accepted models, accompanied by the growing drive to be
different, to exploit individuality, and the opposing need to be like
others and to speak for them. Or one may think of the history of
Eliot's critical attitude toward Donne: the early praise of Donne as
the very type of the poetic, individual amalgamation of experience,
and the later backing away from what, in the religious prose any-

way, seems too individual and personal. One might with reason consider those words which "partakers" are always inclined to apply to "beholders": "unseriousness," "detachment," "amorality." Eliot gives us license to do so when with heavy seriousness he finds Valéry's critical prose unserious.[6] It may be too sharp a line which Johnson has drawn, but the issue is important and we shall need to come back to it.

If we pause for a moment to think of the Elizabethan concept of wit, we are immediately struck with the breadth and flexibility of the term. It means "understanding," and even "wisdom"; it can include the various departments of humor; it means "invention," and can refer either to the depth of "design, form, fable" or to the lesser fertility which animates the minor parts of a design; it means "imagination" and includes both fancy and judgment.

The later seventeenth century had as much reason as any age to feel that it had made some notable progress in discrimination, that it had tightened up an unruly concept and provided clear and workable definitions. There is much to be said still in favor of the definitions that evolved. Besides, they were in some ways historically rooted in larger changes that were occurring throughout a whole society — changes which one may salute or deplore, but which are no longer reversible, except by some theoretical surgery which may be confident enough until faced with the need of inventing subsequent history. The individual duty to resist grinding historical determinism (and its prophets and politicians) is not inconsistent with the humility of accepting the past by trying to understand it. Societies do not stand still, even when some of their achievements are at their highest point. And it is always easier to look back with admiration, or to strive to recover the valuable qualities lost, when one's own age no longer feels the immediate competition of a preceding age. So we are now free to admire, and some of us may even prefer, the superior clarity of neoclassical critical definition. Certainly it made possible a wider currency of critical terms the meanings of which were both more precise and more stable. Besides, we could hardly, now, strip the critical vocabulary of the age from the particular achievement of its literature.

There are always losses to be balanced against gains, and it is difficult not to concentrate on one at the expense of the other. Art engages our intimate feelings, as it must. We cannot respond with diffidence or measured objectivity. Let me express my own judgment and then try to keep it from getting too much in the way. The neoclassical age enjoyed a superior critical vocabulary and the advantages of an advanced technical competence and consciousness; the Renaissance enjoyed a superior concept of wit, characterized by its breadth and flexibility. ("Wit" may have carried too many meanings for the limited purposes of critical utility, but the poets do not seem to have suffered from that handicap.) As a matter of fact, almost everything in the later distinctions can be found in earlier usage, with, I think, two major exceptions. The first is the general agreement to limit and define the term. The second is the seriousness that attaches itself to the intellectual pursuit of wit.

In the later seventeenth century the valuable objects of truth, and the methods of pursuing those objects, gave judgment and the perception of differences a particular advantage not previously advanced. What is involved is less a new claim for the superiority of reason — it is hard for any age to invent a new claim — than a specialized claim. Logic had always had its careful techniques of perceiving differences, and in any argument these might play a dominant part. But in a new age making exact observations not previously made, and excited by the success of its methods, a certain sense of righteous self-confidence attached itself to the perception of differences.[7] (An emancipated scorn of "enthusiasm," and of the syntheses of unexamined similarities, may also be recognized in the historical picture; change the terms and it will fit more than one age.) Righteous self-confidence may not be a very flattering form of moral earnestness, but we do not need to stop here. We can also recognize a marked increase, and a qualitative change, in humanitarian interest. The relief of man's estate proved an attractive part of Bacon's program for the advancement of learning. And when we also add some definite shifts in the structure of society and in its attitudes toward itself, we have the rudiments of a sketch in which we may see why wit should bring the truth "home to men's bosoms" and should behave as "partaker" rather than as "beholder" of human nature. The recovery of "the image of our mind," or Johnson's formula of the "natural," "new," and "just"—these also are to be found in earlier critical theory, which drew on the same sources and knew the same philosophical arguments for "imitation." What is new, again, is the quality of seriousness.

And so we have this addition, the moral earnestness attached to true wit, and we may be willing to consider it a gain. But now we must reckon with a loss. What begins to disappear is the older humanistic concept of wit as an intellectual pleasure befitting the serious but liberal mind. It is the higher part of the concept of wit as humor, itself a large subject still unmastered in the history of thought. One thinks most immediately of Erasmus and More reading Lucian together, and of the candid gifts of laughter that spread their benefits in *Utopia*, and of the magnificent vistas opened up by the structure of *The Praise of Folly*. Wit is the mark of the liberated mind, which enjoys its activity in the world, and can be profoundly serious without being bound as a slave either to the obvious seriousness of the daily task or to the subtler seriousness of "vanity." It is a mark of the perfect courtier. Even Milton, stiffening with age and partisan conflict, and nourished by "sage and serious" doctrine, never quite loses the older humanistic ideal of wit. He may turn it as a sharp instrument to expose error, but he writes as one who not merely uses an instrument but believes in it, as part of the light of reason; and at his best he never forgets that the instrument is double-edged. He also has the older freedom of gaiety, for the most part reserved for private intimacies, but not excluded from his Paradise, nor forbidden the Creator Himself.

One quotation from Ficino may sum up the main point: "When he divided the soul into two parts, namely, mind and sense, Plato attributed joy (*laetitia*) and gladness (*gaudium*) to the mind, and pleasure (*voluptas*) to the senses." [8] We need not go into the accuracy, or historical purity, of Ficino's interpretation. Nor need we consider whether Ficino himself (or even his grand source in the *Philebus*) is the Renaissance fountainhead of this attitude. It is sufficient to note that the attitude is widespread and influential, and entirely at home in England. Considered from this point of view, wit must be understood as giving joy; it is an intellectual pleasure and is quite capable of acting as the soul of poetry.

"Invention" was an important word in the Renaissance; it could stand for the power of a man's mind to conceive, to see likeness and unlikeness — and not merely with an earnest, literal, separative logic. "Invention" also signified the virtuoso's ability to forgo straight performance, and to mix his categories, while he displayed his imaginative skill by the conscious control of what he was doing and by the surprising new lights he cast on his subject. "Invention" was also an ordinary term for the power to recognize the possibilities of a subject and to develop them, to bring out the latencies of a theme while observing the rules, written and unwritten, of propriety, tact, and grace. Mock encomiums, false arguments, paradoxes and problems — these were devices for the student's authorized pleasure in maintaining outrageous propositions, but they were by no means beneath the dignity of mature talent. The standard techniques by which a theme was elevated or depressed, amplified or compressed, in the hands of a master were more than techniques: they were a mark of quality of mind. There was joy in the doing and delight in the recognition. The age practiced the graces of complimentary indirectness, but it also believed that gestures could reflect the soul and style the man. It did not find itself in contradiction. In many ways the Renaissance was more subtle, if less articulate, about separations than the age that followed; it could hold more things in motion together and enjoy closer tolerances. It could value the imaginative for itself, as a communication of intellectual pleasure; or as a double-edged instrument of truth, able to do fine things but needing to be watched; or even, in the case of Giordano Bruno, as the very "principle of infinite fecundity of thought." [9] But the Renaissance had a firm and familiar sense of the imaginative, which was not confused with other things. Wit was prized: its virtues admired, its deceits enjoyed — and marked.

Let us draw upon a literary example.

> Peace, peace, Mercutio, peace!
> Thou talk'st of nothing.

That is Romeo puncturing the magnificent bubble on Queen Mab. Mercutio has the right to grumble a little, by way of letting himself down from the loftiness of a flight interrupted in mid-career. It is a milder version of Falstaff's first outraged "Play out the play."

> True, I talk of dreams,
> Which are the children of an idle brain,
> Begot of nothing but vain fantasy,
> Which is as thin of substance as the air
> And more inconstant than the wind.

The point, of course, is that Mercutio is mildly resenting Romeo's serious literalism. Mercutio knows what he has been saying; his judgment is quite aware that fancy is on a holiday spree. Implicit is the contrast with Romeo's unwitty fantasies, in which the lover dreams himself a true "partaker" of what he says. Mercutio will have his witty revenge when he "conjures" Romeo outside the Capulet orchard; but he will also, with generous relief, welcome Romeo back to the company of the civilized: "Now art thou sociable, now art thou Romeo, now art thou what thou art, by art as well as by nature." To maintain one's place in the peerage of wit both art and nature are necessary. "Can you not conceive?" Mercutio asks impatiently. For, if not, all discourse must be limited to the slow and literal, with no gay leaping of mind to equal mind by flashing indirections. It is a kind of contest, but the pleasure does not lie in the winning or losing, but in the matching of fine faculties, by means of which equal minds may overcome difficulties and meet:

> Take our good meaning, for our judgment sits
> Five times in that ere once in our five wits.

I have been stressing wit as the play of the mind, as an intellectual pleasure. The play of the mind, as the play of the body, could also serve the serious ends of life — both as action and as an educational discipline preparatory to action. For instance, Bacon filled notebooks with false arguments, and this was not merely a lawyer's way of preparing himself for all possible cases. In one sense it was what a dramatist might do, if he took Bacon's own serious, disciplined view of lifelong educational training. That is, a dramatist might practice writing speeches from subtly wrong positions, with a view less to using them than to exercising his imaginative faculties and sharpening his powers of discrimination. As an Elizabethan Bacon is appreciative of this larger value in training the mind, but his personal bent, and influence, tend to the narrower educational view: the practical value in handling error in order to acquire familiarity with its omnipresent, multiple forms, and so to improve immunity. Bertrand Russell once suggested that children be allowed to sample the lures of imaginative description practiced by advertising, in order to protect them from this kind of language. Bacon would have made the process lifelong and more comprehensive. Even in his fictional paradise, the scientific society of *The New Atlantis*, there is a pedagogic place for error in the learned foundation of Salomon's House:

We have also houses of deceits of the senses, where we represent all manner of feats of juggling, false apparitions, impostures and illusions, and their fallacies. And surely you will easily believe that we, that have so many things truly natural which induce admiration, could in a world of particulars deceive the senses if we would disguise those things, and labour to make them seem more miraculous. But we do hate all impostures and lies, insomuch as we have severely forbidden it to all our fellows, under pain of ignomy and fines, that they do not show any natural work or thing adorned or swelling, but only pure as it is, and without all affectation of strangeness.[10]

The last represents advice on style, as if to a "Royal Society." It is more austere in its practical asceticism than the literary compromises which recommend "unusual" but not "affected" dress, and "Nature to advantage dress'd." For Bacon the more desirable arts of imagination and invention lie in the methods by which nature may be made to reveal herself; to this end the arts of language serve best by not interfering. For the most part Bacon was too completely serious to allow much room for intellectual pleasure. There is breadth of imagination in his own writing, and his gravity is lightened by wit; but the wit is usually serving some definite purpose — it seldom exists for its own intellectual sake, or for the sake of anything one would want to call sport. Donne was undoubtedly serious, and involved in his subject, when he wrote *Biathanatos*. But he could send a copy to Sir Edward Herbert with the laughing justification that his book did not need to commit suicide itself: "this book hath enough performed that which it undertook, both by argument and example." There is here a grace of gesture by no means beyond Bacon. But it is doubtful that Bacon would have been as willing as Donne to report, without defensive amplification, one critical response to the book. Donne wrote to Sir Robert Ker that some learned friends had answered "That certainly, there was a false thread in it, but not easily found." [11] This is not to be mistaken as a complete judgment, but it does represent an easy acceptance, at least among equals and connoisseurs, of the principle that the art of error deserves a certain status in human affairs, and ought not be banished from the republic of letters merely because the art of truth is, as everyone admits, more precious.

Let us return to Bacon and his *practical* justification of wit. A claim can be advanced that in its highest form, the "feigned history" of poetic invention, poetry contributes to magnanimity, morality, and delight. Bacon is no advocate; his whole program for the advancement of learning turns away from the older educational values. He is, however, judicious, and his personal skepticism does not meanly pinch off respectable virtues for which he happens to have little use. He is the master of grand intellectual deployments, and can put to useful minor service virtues that a lesser mind would need to destroy. So he can praise the poets without reservation for doing what the philosophers ought to have done:

we may find painted forth with great life, how affections are kindled and incited; and how pacified and refrained; and how again contained from act and further degree; how they disclose themselves; how they work; how they vary; how they gather and fortify; how they are enwrapped one within another; and how they do fight and encounter one with another . . . this last is of special use in moral and civil matters; how (I say) to set affection against affection, and to master one by another; even as we use to hunt beast with beast, and fly bird with bird . . .[12]

It is a view of poetry which has much in common with his interest in false arguments. What is of special concern to us is the serious-

ness with which Bacon, from his chosen position as "beholder," re-
gards these matters and the value of their use.

Another example is even more to the point, for Bacon might very
well be discussing Donne's "The Good-morrow" or "The Canonization." It is a fault attributed to learned men, which renders them
unfit for some activities, that

the largeness of their mind can hardly confine itself to dwell in the
exquisite observation or examination of the nature and customs of
one person: for it is a speech for a lover, and not for a wise man,
Satis magnum alter alteri theatrum sumus.[13]

Bacon's personal dislike is unmistakable. He favors close observation, but he distrusts the "exquisite," and he would set up means to
protect the observer from his own absorption in the subject. He
also distrusts any specialized research (like Gilbert's) that does not
work as part of a grand master plan. But specialized concentration
on a mere person! — the worst thing that can be said is said: "it is
a speech for a lover." And yet Bacon goes on like a true statesman
of learning to do justice to the nature of the mind: "Nevertheless, I
shall yield, that he that cannot contract the sight of his mind as well
as disperse and dilate it, wanteth a great faculty." To "contract the
sight" of the mind is like the invention of false arguments, a valuable exercise of an important intellectual faculty. Even without the
benefit of later critical definition it would not have occurred to Bacon to call this exercise "true wit." But that what he is describing
and approving is "wit" must be clear enough.

There are good reasons for drawing upon Bacon as a chief source
of Elizabethan attitudes toward wit. The first is that, though his interest in literature is casual and ancillary, and fluctuates between
reluctance and hostility, the breadth and authority of his mind endow his pronouncements bearing on the subject with more interest
than those of any contemporary. In addition, he most clearly and
fully anticipates later attitudes toward wit and imagination. Therefore, when he adheres to the more comprehensive and flexible older
view, our distinctions become more significant than if I were to cite
an old-fashioned humanist or merely literary figure. Finally, his attitudes are, though certainly not in all respects, closest to Donne's.

Both occupy positions between the old world of ideas and the new world beginning to take shape. One must add, of course, that Donne does so as a poet; he is therefore committed to ways of language and thought which have little to do with Bacon's program. Nevertheless, there is no single contemporary who can provide us with better historical insight into certain characteristics of Donne's poetry.

The most important single attitude to illustrate is Bacon's firm distrust of the imagination. What distinguishes Bacon's attitude from that of Plato, say, or that of Pico della Mirandola in *De Imaginatione*, or from the general complex of traditional arguments against that valuable but untrustworthy faculty, lies less in the reasons Bacon gives than in the fact that his positive program has little need to come to terms with the imagination. Plato was half poet, and must have both relished and resented this; but at least he did not try to construct an airtight system, in which his own nature was fully immanent, or from which it was fully excluded; rather, he needed both to use and to distrust his imagination, in the ordinary way of a normal man whose calling is also that of a great philosopher. Aristotle did attempt the whole system, and he could place the imagination in small, respectable offices. Bacon has the responsibility of a system, immense in the acknowledged scope of its unfinished business, but philosophically modest, and needing both to clear away and to rehabilitate the clutter of accepted ideas. His reiterated emphasis falls on the world outside man, on matter rather than on forms. Man is to inherit that world, but first he must come perilously close to disinheriting himself. Reality is in nature, and man must purge himself of much of his own nature in order to perceive matter accurately, as it is. The imagination does have minor services to perform, and we note these with interest; in part they are a tribute to the largeness of Bacon's own mind, as the system often is not. But in general Bacon must work toward reducing or eliminating the influence of imagination in order to get the system going. When the day finally comes for propounding the universal theory which is to complete the sixth part of his "Great Instauration," no doubt the system will have produced its own pure and absolute imagination, but Bacon does not expect to live that long.

The basis for Bacon's distrust, then, may be referred to his program, and for our purposes the most useful statements are collected in his *Novum Organum*.[14] First there are his famous Idols, which must be driven out of the laboratory: the innate errors which rise from human nature in general, those of the tribe; and those of the cave, which are the result of the individual man's peculiar constitution. These concern us more immediately than those errors which are not innate but are introduced by the confusions of common language and by the inventions of the received systems of philosophical ideas. The root of all error lies in taking man as the measure of things; for "the human understanding is like a false mirror, which, receiving rays irregularly, distorts and discolors the nature of things by mingling its own nature with it" (XLI). In the individual the passions also interfere, and the formative influences of his own life. When he meditates and searches himself rather than "the greater or common world," he does so with a spirit "variable and full of perturbation, and governed as it were by chance" (XLII). Man is predisposed to believe in "order and regularity." He plays loose with the evidence, and is "moved and excited by affirmatives," and by the unexamined coincidences "which strike and enter the mind simultaneously and suddenly, and so fill the imagination," which then invents fictions that are *similar* "to those few things by which it is surrounded" (XLV–XLVII). Therefore, the rule of the true student of nature should be "that whatever his mind seizes and dwells upon with peculiar satisfaction is to be held in suspicion" (LVIII).

It is not difficult to see in these attitudes the distinctions that later will be made between fancy and judgment. Man's delight in order, in affirmatives, in the petty fragments of similarities upon which he builds his fictions, calls for the stern application of judgment, the disciplined perception of *dissimilarities* where similarities have been complacently supposed or optimistically invented. "And in the plays of this philosophical theatre you may observe the same thing which is found in the theatre of the poets, that stories invented for the stage are more compact and elegant, and more as one would wish them to be, than true stories out of history" (LXII). Aristotle erred in being "solicitous to provide an answer to the question and affirm something positive in words" (LXIII). But "in the establishment of any true axiom, the negative instance is the more forcible of the two" (XLVI). Bacon marks a "radical distinction" between minds: some "are stronger and apter to mark the differences of things, others to mark their resemblances" (LV). Both err in excess, whereas the intellect "ought properly to hold itself indifferently disposed" toward both affirmatives and negatives (XLVI). Yet the negative instance, as we have noted, "is the more forcible of the two."

It is detachment Bacon must advocate, but first he must make detachment possible and profitable by clearing the way and pointing the path. An end must be proposed, a final goal that will sweeten the hard work, and promise full satisfaction to the mind too, when that universal theory will propound itself and embrace the beginning in full bliss. Until that time the system will run smoothly on its own, requiring neither thought nor imagination; for the methods and instruments, once put in motion, will do the most important work, since the system "leaves but little to the acuteness and strength of wits, but places all wits and understanding nearly on a level" (LXI).

Yet in the beginning, plainly enough, the detachment must side with the negative and make party with *difference* against *similarity*. Bacon singles out for attack the traditions of philosophical meditation, chiefly Platonic and Stoic, which have as their basis the belief that man's inner nature and faculties are so constituted that they can apprehend reality, which is made up of the same essential materials. When Bacon cracks and crazes the mirror of the mind, he is deliberately destroying a sacred symbol of meditation, the "glassy essence" in which man can collect and reflect the beams of the essential light. He is attacking a doctrine that presupposes order, and must value the affirmative and the perception of similarities. Dissimilarities are less objects inviting full study than signs that the path has been temporarily lost. Historically the doctrine is hardly that of a spider spinning out of his own substance, as Bacon wittily said. It is a doctrine which must make fuller use of the imagination than Bacon's doctrine, but which must also strive to maintain its own fine controls of the imagination — not stifling it but keeping it active though humble; and quickly taking away from it the credit for any accomplishment, lest the imagination wax proud; and skillfully translating its terms into honorable and safe ones, like "dialectical truths," or "ideas," or, to change the vocabulary, "fact," "proved case," "accepted theory." It is a doctrine that in general has more in common with modern science than much of the abandoned luggage of Bacon's system. But that is another story and not our concern.

Bacon, in spite of the problems of practical application, must advocate detachment. He does manage also to practice it; and the art of detachment, as we have already observed, is related to one of the aspects of wit, the free use of false arguments. In the *Novum Organum* the wit lies in the analysis and exposure of the Idols, the use of error against itself; and though there is not much free play of the mind, and little gaiety, there is an unmistakable pleasure in the activity of the performance. It is in Bacon's intention and effect, however, that he comes closest to that positive play of wit which purges: "now that I have purged and swept and leveled the floor of the mind" (CXV). He is one of the great "beholders" of the human scene, and much of the power of his writing is due to the sharpness with which he can see at a distance. This is a talent he worked at, and it never would have occurred to him that he was therefore less a "partaker" of human nature. As Douglas Bush has pointed out, Bacon could write "On Adversity," after his own disgrace, with not the slightest intrusion of any feelings from his personal disaster.[15] It is not an example of wit but of detachment; yet this personal example may serve to indicate one important aspect of Renaissance wit.

Finally, we may note three brief statements which do not conclude the case neatly, but do let us end with a proper recognition of the scope and complexity of the problem. First, there is Bacon's espousal of the aphoristic method, by which a writer cuts himself off from all the ordinary aids of discourse and strips to the "pith." Bacon's general justification does not concern us, but a single item does; for it is, without intending to be, as good a defense of one kind of wit as we can find. It describes an aspect of Donne's wit as though this were its very purpose. Bacon writes, "And lastly, Aphorisms, representing a knowledge broken, do invite men to inquire farther; whereas Methods, carrying the show of a total, do secure men, as if they were at furthest." [16] Like the false argument, the wit of a deliberate "knowledge broken" opens the mind to further inquiry and serves against complacency.[17] Our second example is a stern piece of positivism which ends with the grudging admission that the old ways of the imagination are still necessary if the case is new enough:

When the inventions and conclusions of human reason . . . were as yet new and strange, the world was full of all kinds of fables, and enigmas, and parables, and similitudes: and these were used not as a device for shadowing and concealing the meaning, but as a method of making it understood. . . . For as hieroglyphics came before letters, so parables came before arguments. And even now if any one wish to let new light on any subject into men's minds . . . he must still go the same way and call in the aid of similitudes.[18]

Here the arts of imagination render an important but subordinate service, like that of an interpreter between mighty principals. But what shall we say of our last example? Bacon is paraphrasing Heraclitus, and he includes his own practical word "means," but does not the sixth aphorism from the *Novum Organum* suddenly give Bacon's whole program the status of a work of the imagination? "It would be an unsound fancy and self-contradictory to expect that things which have never yet been done can be done except by means which have never yet been tried."

Perhaps one should not say "the status," but rather "the secret start"— after which the work will resolutely attempt to erase all the evidence of its origin, and will, with a lesser imagination, invent conditions that require less and less both of man's inherited wisdom and of his full human resources of mind and spirit. The result is an art of detachment quite unlike the art of the poets; and the independence achieved is like that of a resolute, successful offspring, whose ingratitude is both a source and a powerful motive of accomplishment, and yet an inward sign of lingering pain and deficiency.

Let us now, in conclusion, return to the main point. The advantages of the Elizabethan concept of wit lie in its flexibility and comprehensiveness, in the breadth and depth of its tolerance of the imaginative, in its willingness to entertain fictions as an expression of the joyous energy of the serious mind. There was no single definition of wit, nor any general license. There were instead some general

agreements, and the understood obligation that the individual per-
former was to be judged by a peerage of wits and connoisseurs. The
rules were not codified but, as in any art, they were inexorable in
determining failure and graciously yielding in success. Nor did the
lack of definition deprive the judges of authority. As Ben Jonson,
one of the judges, wrote in his commonplace book, *Timber*: it is
custom that determines usage in speech, "But that I call Custome
of speech, which is the consent of the Learned; as Custome of life,
which is the consent of the good." [19] Jonson was not noted for shy
modesty; he would submit his own poems only to a judgment worth
having, as he indicates in an epigram to Donne.

> Who shall doubt, *Donne*, where I a *Poet* bee,
> When I dare send my *Epigrammes* to thee?
> That so alone canst judge, so'alone do'st make:
> And, in thy censures, evenly, dost take
> As free simplicity, to dis-avow,
> As thou hast best authority, t'allow.
> Read all I send: and, if I finde but one
> Mark'd by thy hand, and with the better stone,
> My title's seal'd.

The lack of a single definition of wit, in view of the evident scope
and freedom, surely caused uncertainties in those who were not connoisseurs, and today there are no connoisseurs able to discriminate
without labor of mind. We must labor, and not trust our judgments
too far. Still, we can recognize an extravagant claim for wit, at least
when it is Jaques':

> I must have liberty
> Withal, as large a charter as the wind,
> To blow on whom I please; for so fools have;
> And they that are most galled with my folly,
> They most must laugh. . . .
>
> . . . .
>
> Invest me in my motley. Give me leave
> To speak my mind, and I will through and through
> Cleanse the foul body of th' infected world,
> If they will patiently receive my medicine.

And our suspicions are confirmed by a connoisseur, Duke Senior,
who defines what is wrong with Jaques. One does not command wit,

as Jaques would, without better qualifications than those of a misplaced seriousness.

Elizabethan wit did not need to affect motley; it could accept the risks of a more strenuous freedom. For instance, the inventions of fancy could maintain rich and complex relations with judgment, and these are more challenging than either a simple separation of the two, by indulgence as it were, or a kind of simple congruence of the two, in which fancy has little more distinctness of character than what is required to see that it *is* assimilated to judgment. Elizabethan wit could walk a finer line, and part of its pleasure lay in that fact. It was an exacting art, at best requiring a man to be both beholder and partaker — in ways not charted and defined in advance, but demanding individual definition every time. The lack of rules, in this sense, was part of the freedom, and the difficulty, and the intellectual value of the best achievements.

Epigrammatic Reversal

First a few words on the sections that are to follow, and on the methods and purpose of this attempt to describe Donne's wit. The classifications that are to be used have, I believe, some descriptive and organizational merit, but they are by no means complete and self-justifying. Many of Donne's poems fall between categories, or embrace more than one. For instance, later sections not only will exhibit some different characteristics but will incorporate some of those from the earlier sections. Furthermore, though most of my attention will be directed toward the structures of poems, it is impossible to separate these entirely from certain qualities — for example, the character of the texture or the tone, the kind and degree of imaginative deceptions, the kind and degree of detachment, the nature of the gaps left in an argument, etc. These qualities may be more characteristic of certain structures than of others, but they are too free in their ability to combine and to attach themselves to other things for any profitable effort to locate them in specific categories. If my purpose were entirely descriptive, these qualities, and others, might challenge and embarrass my method beyond endurance. But the purpose, for better or worse, is not to describe in any final way the external forms made by Donne's wit. Rather, I shall follow these external forms not only for their own sake but for the help and external evidence they may provide for perceiving the "internal" forms — those characteristic movements of Donne's mind in creation, the forms it takes and makes.

The first classification, that of epigrammatic reversal, is an arbitrary one. It does not include those poems titled epigrams, poems which were admired by Donne's contemporaries and not always distinguished from his elegies. My interest, however, does not lie in the swift pithiness, in the single trickshot at the odd subject, but in form. As the main criterion of the epigram I shall take that characteristic reversal, the sudden surprising point at the end. One may note that this criterion was not admired, or even accepted, by connoisseurs like Ben Jonson. Yet the popular notion of epigram, and the frequency with which later imitators of Donne cultivated the final witty turn, may justify this partial abuse of the term.

Actually, not much is at stake in this category; the *Songs and Sonets* yield few examples of poems that depend on their concluding point. Yet many do end with a kind of epigrammatic point, and therefore one can make some useful distinctions in terms of the amount of weight placed upon the final resolution. The rare kind of poem I shall call epigram (by this criterion) will seem directed entirely toward its conclusion. The body of the poem may be considered as a sort of bubble expanding only to be punctured; or it may be regarded as an elaborate and entertaining pretext which conceals the surprise about to spring; or it may seem a sustained feint and deceptive flourish which gets the reader into position to receive the real thrust. The epigram is in part a test of the writer's ability to invent an apparent relevance that turns out to be irrelevant, or vice versa. The greatest master was Martial, whom Donne knew and certainly admired. The justification for this kind of writing I have discussed in the preceding section: such epigrammatic wit involved the pleasure of an intellectual game, and at its best could purge the mind of some lightly rooted pretentiousness. But it is not a very serious game in Donne; the tone is likely to be gay, detached, and even cynical, fitting a poem that is clearly occasional and does not pretend to be anything but a pure fiction.

What I have been describing as epigram is a more significant and frequent characteristic of Donne's wit when it appears as a quality of texture. Then it can suggest an unmistakably serious game. At other times this texture seems a masked quality of the tone, an integral part of the developing imaginative structure, to be understood only in terms of its contribution to the whole poem. Epigrammatic texture works through local deception and defeat of expectation — as part of the sudden dead end of an argument which reveals the necessity of a new start or a new direction, or as the kind of reversal which opens up a further possibility of solution, one that was perhaps concealed by the surface argument or could emerge only when that surface had worn itself out. Donne's poems abound in such surprises. We cannot understand his kind of poetry without taking into account this aspect of his wit. Though general and pervasive, epigrammatic texture could be isolated as a subject for study; however, I have chosen to approach Donne's wit through the study of structures, and the qualities of texture will be fitted in as best they can. Nevertheless, I may note in advance that the category of epigrammatic structure is important chiefly as an introduction to more complex forms and as a means of alerting us to the more flexible ways of epigrammatic texture.

There are only two poems in the *Songs and Sonets* that by our definition seem to qualify as epigrams. Even these two, we must admit, are better examples if we do not look at them too closely. The poems are "Womans Constancy" and the song "Goe, and catche a falling starre."

The first poem proposes a set problem: what the woman will say when, tomorrow, she breaks off the affair. The development is not in terms of whimsical and farfetched fancies, but is drawn from the subtle resources of the deceptive heart, which produces a train of ingenious arguments not unfamiliar to human experience, though these arguments have an individual freshness and precision. When the woman rises to her most extravagant point, the lover takes over and undercuts her efforts with insulting ease:

> Vaine lunatique, against these scapes I could
> Dispute, and conquer, if I would,
> Which I abstaine to doe,
> For by to morrow, I may thinke so too.

The body of the poem would seem to be a pretext preparing for the joke at the end. It is reasonable to interpret the poem this way and to call it an epigram.

But when we look more closely that reasonable interpretation seems a little less than satisfactory, and then we begin to see why so few of Donne's poems are simple epigrams. The joke at the end is most obvious and draws the loudest laugh, but there are other jokes which deserve our attention. The mistress' little speech, for instance, has a kind of dramatic charm and delicacy. It *is* a feminine speech, and opens with a fine mimicry of affected emphasis. Of course the whole speech is a mimicry by the poet, who speaks in his own voice only during the first two lines and the concluding four. In the lines quoted below, the first is transitional, with the poet beginning to shift from his own voice in order to express the feminine mind:

> Wilt thou then Antedate some new made vow?
> Or say that now
> We are not just those persons, which we were?

By the second line he has the tone and manner, which are mincing and affected. All of the advantages of female impersonation are realized in the third line by the emphasis which falls on "just." But the mistress moves from a feminine manner of speech to more ambitious and paradoxical reasonings — at which point she is cut off. The mimicry of style is funny, but so in another way is the progression of the speech, that psychological mimicry of the woman whose mind has masculine ambitions. Another effect of the speech is a kind of comic excess, but it is difficult to know in exactly what direction to laugh. For that extravagant display of duplicity and reserve in love quite exceeds the minimal decencies of polite lying. It is unquestionably a display, but of whom and for what reason? After all, it is the lover who is inventing the whole scene in advance, enough in advance to be somewhat provocative; and then, after the rationalizations anticipated on the morrow, he demolishes the argument he has imagined by anticipating his possible agreement.

One begins to see that the broad and obvious joke which is the epigram contains details perhaps a little too fine and individual for the apparent point. One begins to suspect the presence of a real woman; and if it is an actual mind and personality which are being mimicked, then the speaker and the situation itself are deprived of a certain sterility usual in the gay and heartless detachment of the epigrammatic joke. For instance, the apparent reversal may conceal a deeper reversal, by which the speaker invents an obviously false speech in order to prevent an actual speech that might be quite decently plausible, but could hardly hope to escape an embarrassing comparison with the speech already on record. In other words, the speaker, while pretending to "abstain," may instead be disputing and conquering. That would be a more subtle joke and a more complicated situation. We cannot be sure, for there are latencies in the situation that are not developed but that may be part of a private and personal poem which only pretends or threatens to be an epigram.

"Goe, and catche a falling starre" creates a situation that depends on its exaggerated fictional unreality, for all the invented implausibilities accrue to that major invention of fantasy, the woman who is both true and fair. We begin with random and remote imperatives; and then the imperatives, while still pretending to be random, suddenly look homeward, to the impossibility of preventing envy and the impossibility of discovering what undevious wind will "advance an honest minde." Then the Elizabethan traveler is commissioned to journey in search of "strange wonders." The only part of his report which is quoted is the negative item, the nonexistence of that ideal woman. It is this impossibility which the speaker perversely elects to consider possible, with an innocence that disowns the elaborate rhetorical preparation and ignores the sworn testimony of her nonexistence, doubly attested since all travelers are professional liars bound to report the existence of the impossible:

> If thou findst one, let mee know,
> Such a Pilgrimage were sweet.

But this homely innocence is another pose, like the perverseness, to which the speaker again reverts, in order to clinch the pattern of impossibilities:

> Though shee were true, when you met her,
> And last, till you write your letter,
> Yet shee
> Will bee
> False, ere I come, to two, or three.

The poem is a structure of surprise moving toward a point which is clinched by a sudden reversal. The preparation is prodigal, but the poem moves toward a single point, and there are no complexities of situation or personal involvement to trouble that point. Yet the distinctive qualities of the poem are not in the basic scheme, and certainly not in the assumed attitude, though these were most available for imitation by the cavalier poets. What we tend to admire more is the inventive power of the details, their freshness, and surprise, and range. We may admire also both the casual ease of the general control, the apparent looseness underneath which the organization maneuvers, and the masterly control of the parts: the balances, manipulated pauses, the skillful metrical emphasis. But the most distinctive quality of all is one which produces an elusive and haunting effect of the whole poem — the disproportion between the lavish imaginative details and the basic scheme of the epigrammatic joke. The creative energy released serves the form, but is not wholly contained by it; details are not deliberately matched and restricted to purpose, as, for instance, in the perfect architecture of Ben Jonson's "Still to be neat." Though the example is a minor one, it is interesting for setting a characteristic problem; what is here done simply is typical of Donne's art in more complicated examples.

Inversions

We come now to a form of wit in which the element of surprise does not turn on a point but extends throughout the whole poem. The most familiar examples resemble paradoxes and problems; that is, they maintain an unexpected or improbable proposition, one which consistently inverts the normal way of looking at things. But other examples are characterized by their dealing with a theme which is less improbable than unusual, or with a theme approached from an unusual angle, or with a theme which is provocatively difficult to maintain in the chosen context. The kind of wit displayed is that which the Renaissance would have recognized as the self-justifying play of the mind, the immediate purpose of which was to provide intellectual pleasure. Whatever the variety in scope or in degree of concentration, one constant requirement was that difficulties be cultivated and surmounted. It would be possible to illustrate this kind of wit from nearly all of Donne's poetry and from much of the prose. Except for differences in concentration, and consequently in form, many of the verse letters and the elegies closely resemble examples in the *Songs and Sonets*. But my major concern is with the lyric poems, which are, after all, both most challenging and most revealing, though they do not demonstrate to the fullest degree Donne's power to sustain and extend a theme.

The poems I shall deal with, then, are characterized by the cultivation of difficulties, and one may expect them to be rigorously disciplined in spite of any intrinsic levity or implausibility. They are not lyrics in any usual sense. That is, though wit and the lyric are not opposed, nevertheless this form of wit does exclude personal involvement and some kinds of imaginative complexity. It will be plain that in these poems Donne treats his themes with clear detachment; his own intimate feelings do not actively affect the development of the poems, even though the effects and implications of the poems may be relevant to his, or our, feelings. One further prefatory note. The present classification is both larger and firmer than the preceding one; nevertheless, I shall need a little room to mark gradations and degrees. Some of these examples have much in common with the epigrammatic reversals of the earlier section, and I shall begin with these. Later it will be convenient to discuss examples that seem to fall between the main body of inversions and the forms of the following section.

"Loves Usury" ends with a flamboyant flourish, but it is one that does not alter what has already been set up in the poem; rather, the ending confirms and caps the inversion of attitude which characterizes the theme. The theme itself owes little to the epigrammatic twist, which serves mostly as a means of ending with a bang. The poem is a gay compact with the devil, called the "Usurious God of Love," but the Faustian bargain is as unserious in nature and details as the flaunting anti-Platonism of love during the body's period of triumph. When in the poet's old age the god collects his conventional (Platonic) profit, the poet will submit and pay:

> Spare mee till then, I'll beare it, though she bee
> One that loves mee.

Perhaps one new thing is added or implied: there will be no usual recantation, but the defiant rebelliousness will continue to the last moment. Nevertheless, the surprising final turn is less novel than it may at first appear, and this is to the benefit of the sustained inversion of attitude.

"The Baite" ends with a gentler, more conventionally lyric, turn:

> That fish, that is not catch'd thereby,
> Alas, is wiser farre then I.

But the effect is chiefly to keep up the lovely game to the end. The correct exaggerations of pastoral love are maintained, a little too correctly, by pushing the extensions of fanciful flattery a little too close to their literal and physical meanings. To friends who knew his style the cool sensuousness which Donne adopted must have provided one kind of delightful surprise. And no contemporary wit would have missed the peculiar fish imagery, or that outrageous compliment to the lady swimmer threatened by "Each fish, which every channell hath." But the mockery is never allowed to extrude, and the epigrammatic ending plays out the play with a gracious gesture and a straight face.

Our next group of poems will include "The Curse," "Confined Love," and "The Undertaking."

"The Curse" takes as its theme the heaping of maledictions upon anyone who presumes knowledge or surmise concerning the identity of the poet's mistress. The immediate occasion seems to be a pretext in order to get the poem started, and then it whimsically disappears. The ending is a witty turn, of the sort one might expect if the body of the poem were a sustained feint to draw the attention away from the real point of the poem: "For if it be a shee / Nature before hand hath out-cursed mee." Yet the ending does not seem significant enough to justify regarding the structure as merely a device for setting up the final thrust. In fact, the ending may be thought to be quite as occasional as the beginning; one is a device for starting, and the other is a device for cutting off, smartly and at the right moment, a string of individual inventions which do not develop though they do rise to a kind of climax of intensity. This type of theme is difficult chiefly because it is too easy, and it threatens to be boring because it is extremely limited and cannot conceal an inevitable repetitiveness. At their best the variations may manage some immediate surprise and a certain degree of individual freshness, but there can be no real surprise in the structure and no inner development — only an arbitrary external structure to give some show of movement. At their worst variations on such a theme tend to be strained and farfetched, as it were in compensation for not having anywhere to go.

Yet Donne does achieve a certain success in overcoming the difficulties of easiness.[20] He invents abuse which is characteristically psychological rather than physical, and he creates a kind of narrative circumstantiality. A reader aware of the native tradition of "flyting," and of the examples left by Catullus, Horace, and Martial, might well think that Donne's wit had accepted and met the challenge. One may conclude, therefore, that the poem is a witty inversion, the deliberate acceptance of a limited theme. Its aim is a display of individual inventions; its most noteworthy triumph is its power to escape normal exhaustion and to rise in the last stanza to its liveliest abuse:

> The venom of all stepdames, gamsters gall,
> What Tyrans, and their subjects interwish,
> What Plants, Mynes, Beasts, Foule, Fish,
> Can contribute, all ill which all
> Prophets, or Poets spake; And all which shall
> Be annex'd in schedules unto this by mee,
> Fall on that man; For if it be a shee
> Nature before hand hath out-cursed mee.

Some sort of last trick is necessary to end a poem which has no real beginning; and this is a good trick, for it cuts off the flow sharply with a fine rhetorical flourish, while it laughingly acknowledges the implausibility of the game which has been played. In the competition between wit and nature art must lose: if the unknown object of the poet's inventions is a woman, then he has been wasting his time. But he has been wasting his time anyway, if he has *not* been playing a game. And nothing could be a clearer admission of the game than the final attitude toward women revealed in a poem which, ostensibly, is retaliating against any effort to pry into the precious identity of one woman, the poet's mistress. Some of nature's curse cannot escape falling upon that darling, in spite of the fiercely protective cover of art's curse.

Once we perceive a relationship between the ending and the beginning of the poem, we are forced to question the "reasonable" perspective which allowed us to conclude that the wit lies in the individual inventions and in the overcoming of the formidable difficulties of too easy a theme. If the final turn of the poem does point back to the beginning, then it is not adequate to consider the opening a pretext to get started or the final turn a rhetorical device for stopping. Instead we must admit that Donne has managed to produce, if not a development, at least a structure — though we had assumed that this kind of theme needed to proceed by variations, with no more than a slight illusion of structure. We are then left with two reasonable interpretations. The first has already been presented; the second is that the main body of the poem, while fulfilling the special requirements of the theme, is also undertaking a further inversion, by which the artificial extremes energetically cultivated are turned back on the ultimate source of the poem, the woman presumably being defended.

Neither interpretation would regard the ending as the epigrammatic point toward which the whole poem was directed. The choice lies between a simple inversion (the treatment of theme) and a double inversion (the treatment of theme plus its final reapplication). In either case we are left with a strong sense of disproportion between the actual texture of the poem and the apparent structure. This was also true of our experience with "Womans Constancy" and "Song," but in both of those poems, in spite of their cultivated deceptions, there was a firmer continuity to the logical structure. Here we have an unmistakable gap. If we take the second interpretation seriously, we must reckon with a deliberate omission and sustained concealment. The final turn of the poem points the reader in the direction of the beginning, but he must bridge the gap by himself, with his own wit. The example is, though a minor one, an illustration of the contemporary remark that Donne's readers were thought wits by the mere act of understanding his wit.

"Confined Love" is in tone, manner, and form a witty inversion. It is a kind of writing best illustrated by the major achievement of "The Indifferent." Although the turn at the end is not epigrammatic in the sense I have been using, the poem does practice a kind of concealment, and a holding back of the best point until the end in order to release implications and strengthen the astonishing plausibility of the argument. The fact that the theme is limited, and the argument perforce restricted, increases the difficulty of the poet's reserving any final surprise. That Donne achieves this surprise is a mark both of his epigrammatic art and of his commitment to this particular form of wit. But one must also note that his delight in the unexpected and in disproportion is more deeply and more frequently committed to the difficult surprises of a concealed continuity of structure than to those of either a concealed or an open discontinuity.

The poem limits and loads the argument immediately:

> Some man unworthy to be possessor
> Of old or new love, himselfe being false or weake,
> Thought his paine and shame would be lesser,
> If on womankind he might his anger wreake.

And so, disabled by nature he revenges himself with law, and is the anonymous author of the monogamist imposition on nature. The stanza ends with the inevitable challenge of Renaissance naturalism: "But are other creatures so?" The second stanza produces the traditional analogies to support such an argument, but they are charmingly fresh. The rhetorical skill depends far less on the analogies themselves than on the sly attribution of human characteristics to nonhuman nature, and on the imaginative quality of those attributions. Are the heavenly bodies forbidden

To smile where they list, or lend away their light?
Are birds divorc'd, or are they chidden
If they leave their mate, or lie abroad a night?
Beasts doe no joyntures lose
Though they new lovers choose.

The stanza ends with another challenge: "But we are made worse than those." It is a challenge not only to the attitude being opposed but, quite plainly, to the argument being advanced. It must be made good, and it sounds difficult to maintain; the effect is to stimulate the intellectual pleasure of anticipation.

Donne has inconspicuously placed at least one item in support of the proposition he now must uphold. The heavenly bodies which "lend away their light" not only defend the unconfined activities of nature, but they imply in those activities a positive benefit conferred. Donne's readers would have expected the freedom of the birds and beasts to be defended; only the fanciful aptness and charm are new. But a positive benefit conferred, and lost — that moves the argument to the offensive, and from a surprising direction. Donne advances his proposition in the last stanza with another series of analogies, drawn this time from the public and private activities of human existence. The "faire ship" is intended to "seeke new lands" and deal with them; it is not "rigg'd" to remain in harbors.[21] And private creative activities, for which men stay at home to build and plant — when they have done so, they do not "lock up" or let fall in ruin what they have made. The analogies are partly masked; they convince us of their immediate human naturalness and rightness, but the link that joins the analogies, and advances the positive proposition, is allowed to remain latent until the final triplet:

Good is not good, unlesse
A thousand it possesse,
But doth wast with greedinesse.

"Good" is the positive term withheld, the concealed attribute, now released, of the "light" which the heavenly bodies "lend," of the fruits of human intercourse or the shared pleasure of private creativity. Greediness, like the vices of the first monogamist, attempts to confine good and is a negative evil opposed to the happy energies of life. We may well be surprised, but less by a sudden novelty than by an unexpected inevitability now dropping into place.[22]

"The Undertaking" is a poem with a surface of disarming simplicity. It argues for concealing the true vision of love, the "lovelinesse within," which, once discovered, requires the composite brave deed: to love "Vertue'attir'd in woman," to "say so too, / And forget the Hee and Shee." But the brave deed requires a still braver one, to hide this love from "prophane men." That will make the composite brave deed, now augmented, braver than all the deeds of the Worthies. The poem starts here, with its announcement of accomplishment, and with a concealed term:

> I have done one braver thing
> Then all the *Worthies* did,
> And yet a braver thence doth spring,
> Which is, to keepe that hid.

We are led to believe that the braver "thing" has been done, and the keeping it hidden is a still braver accomplishment, a further stage beyond the vaunted deeds of the Worthies. The next two stanzas playfully explain why what is hidden cannot be disclosed. They do not explain what is really being concealed, but only claim that it is useless to reveal what no longer exists. This is a way of emphasizing the mystery by suspense; and we are teased, but not enlightened, to learn that as things now stand other men "Would love but as before." Then we have the disclosure concerning "lovelinesse within," and we re-enter that circle of bravery.

There has also been a shift from the experience of an "I" to that of a "you," never identified. The argument has also made an inscrutable turn, for what was claimed no longer to exist is now discovered, without apologies, as quite available to the qualified beholder. Then suddenly the secret is shared with the "you." There is no transition into the sanctum; we slip into it and only mark the exit when the "you" is encouraged to carry on and to be secret. He will do so because there is no other prudent course, the argument indicates. But once he has practiced the truth and kept it hidden, *then* he will have done a braver thing than those famous heroes, and will be qualified to accept the necessity of the higher bravery, "Which is, to keepe that hid." What? Nothing else than the fact that he has bravely kept his truth hidden, and if it is braver to conceal bravery, and still braver to conceal the fact of one's concealment, then he is caught in an awful embrace of the beginning and the end, riding on a merry-go-round of perpetual motion.

There can be no doubt of the presence of witty mischief, but it too practices an art of concealment. A play on words presents a thin disguise, yet never lets the disguise drop. "Brave" means "courageous," and the enlightened lover must "dare love," even though his prudent course of concealment may seem a strange part of valor. But "brave" also means "showy," and is connected with notions of brag and boastful exhibition. To conceal one's extraordinary deed is braver than to have done it, and it will be braver yet to conceal that one has concealed it. Courage and bragging have ancient and primitive associations; warriors bragged themselves into courage. Donne's wit also discovers a modern and sophisticated relationship. There is a kind of pride and invisible ostentation in concealing high accomplishment, and that pride is perversely increased by the thought that the unworthy do not know, and that they would be still further impressed by such a gesture of heroic silence.²³

The key to the invisible ostentation is consciousness, which is capable of contemplating a succession of gestures of silence. The rareness of this mystery may have some playful acquaintance with that high mystery of sexless love, which is not invulnerable to the claims of both kinds of bravery. The play on words is disguised; but the natural human need to share and communicate is *unstated*, though it underlies both kinds of bravery. It is courageous to be silent, because one wants to tell. What cannot be mistaken in the imaginative argument is that, once courage becomes conscious of itself, it loses its character as a simple act and enters a train of necessity by which it multiplies itself, as it were, in a fertile succession of self-contemplations. We may perhaps guess that Donne is having some philosophical fun, and demonstrating that human thought leads to no transcendent unmoved mover, but heads the other way, toward the immersion of self in the generation of inferior images. Donne certainly is having some psychological fun and inventing a genre of "one-upmanship," in which pride uses the infinite resources of humility.

The human need to share and communicate is unstated; it is a gap which the wit of the reader must bridge when he recognizes the disguised doubleness of bravery. That the revelation of true love requires the courage to "say so too" is an obstacle, and a perplexing requirement which leads back into the heroism of silence. Even more mischievous is the fact that the "I" suddenly drops his evasiveness and confides, on the pivot of a mere "if," both the brave deed and the braver secrecy to the "you." A still deeper secrecy shrouds the whole scene of communication and transference; but this is only acted out and never discussed, unlike the advertised deed of hieratic secrecy which is the formal subject of the poem. If the "I" has contrived to eat his cake and have it too, while passing the burden of bravery and consciousness to stronger hands, the "you" may be expected to digest that lesson. But it is the consciousness of the "I" which acts, controls, and reveals, by the wit of the poem, more than as actor he could formally subscribe to. There is a kind of gap and omission between what the "I" says and what the whole poem reveals, but this is a familiar gap in drama or in a dramatic poem. The omission is more subtle and important than the deliberate, *fixed* gaps of the poem, though it is more convenient to emphasize the latter now, as a preparation for omissions that will concern us in later analyses.

Nevertheless, the imaginative complexity of the poem is admittedly greater than our classification needs to consider. The present usefulness of the poem lies in its resemblances to "The Curse," and to "Confined Love." Again we see the wit operating through deliberate omissions and concealments, with the final turn of the poem pointing the reader toward the beginning, and his own task of exercising wit. "The Undertaking" is of course a superior poem. It manages a deeper and richer basic design. The final surprise is no mere epigrammatic trick, no thump on the back to accompany the explosion of a witticism. It is a delicate final touch that is part of an imaginative structure which has been taking its full shape before our eyes. The fineness of grain, the firmness, and the scope of the poem's imaginative form are at the furthest possible remove from the kind of joke which depends on one final pulling out of a rug. Such jokes require long intervals of rest between applications. The design of "The Undertaking" engages our thoughts more fully; it is not an ingenious but stationary trap: it is an imaginative design in motion, and we must put ourselves in motion in order to participate.

We have been looking at witty inversions which, even while developing a set theme with a fine show of discipline and continuity, have indicated Donne's willingness and imaginative ability to bring into play certain fixed gaps and omissions latent in the development of the theme. In "The Undertaking" we may observe a still more ambitious development, the inclusion of the speaker's own implicit experience. The imaginative richness and complexity achieved through this new dimension perhaps transcend the expected range of the witty inversion, and the poem seems rather to belong in the more elevated company of Donne's best poems. Yet the example is a useful one for reminding us how many of Donne's poems are related to a form of inversion, the acceptance of an implausible or difficult theme. Now let us turn back to look at one of Donne's most successful examples of this kind of writing.

We must note in advance that "The Indifferent" does employ one fixed, and necessary, omission. "Indifferent" is a technical term in philosophy and religion, but the word also has other areas of use and meaning. In "The Undertaking" some of the wit turns on a concealed meaning of "brave," but in "The Indifferent" the whole development of the poem is closely related to the explication of its key term. The development is tied, as frequently in Donne, to a little narrative movement; but the narrator's participation is minimal, and consists mostly in a rather heavy acting out of a few bits of the speech he is delivering; he is the confidently indifferent man who, far from concealing, will reveal all as fast as art will permit.

The poem is a defiant address to the ladies by the indifferent man, who stands apart from the hurly-burly of love and constructs his witty argument from the privilege of his indifference. At first the indifferent man is the impartial man, unprejudiced, and so fit to testify in a case.[24] And a case is drawn up, with Venus as the judge who "examines" and pronounces sentence. The speaker himself has managed a kind of preliminary hearing. The long catalogue of female types, paired in opposites, presents his evidence of impartiality. The manner is gay and boisterous, the energetic overflowing of a clear conscience, delighting in the record of its acts, and ready to perform more of the same and only the same.

> I can love her, and her, and you and you,
> I can love any, so she be not true.

The word "true," though delivered by the speaker as if lightly and casually, marks an apparent shift in attitude. "Will no other vice content you?" he begins. Now he has dropped the cheerful recital of his own qualifications, and he acts as if the word "true" were either a personal reproach against which he must defend himself or an external enemy which he must attack. He defends himself by advancing countercharges which are witty inversions; they pretend to explain the perverted motives of fidelity in a normal world of vice:

> Wil it not serve your turn to do, as did your mothers?
> Or have you all old vices spent, and now would finde
>   out others?
> Or doth a feare, that men are true, torment you?

The speaker's defense becomes less extravagant and more earnest — as if the enemy fidelity were too determined to be put off by jests, and threatened nothing less than the speaker's loss of liberty. The line of wit is also maintained as the psychological and physiological surfaces of love are turned to catch the light, while the norm of love is irreverent, old-fashioned sensuality, to "serve your turn to do" ("For the best turn i'th'bed," as the incautious messenger says to Shakespeare's Cleopatra). There are bawdy jokes, both verbal and syntactical, in

> Must I, who came to travaile, thorow you,
>   Grow your fixt subject, because you are true?

But there is a pretended earnestness also maintained, as mockery of a serious tenaciousness attributed to the enemy. Then in the last stanza the speaker shifts his role and tone again. As plaintiff he "sighs," having assumed without warning an attribute of the naive traditional lover; and he is vindicated by an unexpected act of grace as Venus, the divine judge, overhears and intervenes in his behalf.

Only at this point do the further implications of "indifferent" emerge. As in other instances we have noted, the wit of the reader is required to bridge a gap and to recognize that the preceding argument has prepared the shadowy sketch of a deeper argument, which is abstract but relevant, and which exhibits the local fiction in a universal aspect. In "The Undertaking" we saw how Donne's wit had discovered a correspondence between primitive and sophisticated behavior latent in the meanings of the word "brave." In "The Indifferent" his wit has made the same initial discovery of a correspondence between word and human deed. The vindication of the indifferent man turns out to be less an act of whimsical grace, or arbitrary epigrammatic reversal, than a mocking parody of established and authoritative religious and philosophical arguments.

In the religious disputes of the Reformation the point was frequently made, especially by Protestants, that certain matters had been left for the individual conscience to decide. They were scripturally neutral, neither required nor forbidden by God; they were also, as debate demonstrated, unprovable. The stubborn could not be convinced, and those who considered themselves rational and open-minded saw a Protestant virtue to be gained from necessity. Since the Scriptures were clear on all points necessary to salvation, the dubious and indeterminable points were not necessary at all but indifferent. An earlier history and version of the doctrine may also have some minor relevance to Donne's poem. Indifferentism offered a possible solution to the medieval conflict between realism and nominalism; for one's point of view, that is, whether one mark the differences or the similarities, helps determine whether the individual remains individual or joins the species. Donne may be glancing at this distinction in his first stanza, where the differences among individual women are all resolved by the indifferent man, who sees only one species: lovable woman.

A still earlier history of the argument is to be found in Stoic doctrine, which Donne's poem closely parodies. In "Communitie" he makes an open game of the Stoic distinction. We must love good and hate evil,

> But there are things indifferent,
> Which wee may neither hate, nor love,
> But one, and then another prove,
> As wee shall finde our fancy bent.

He is referring to the Stoic adiaphora, which in the strictest interpretation comprehended all things that did not concern the rational man's good (true virtue) or his evil (the wickedness which might destroy him). Everything else was indifferent — including what was desirable but not "good," and what was better avoided but not "evil."

Let us consider Donne's implied argument. In "The Indifferent" love is a pleasure and indifferent to the true concerns of the moral life or to the salvation of the soul. Those who treat love seriously treat the affections seriously; their rational control becomes perturbed and their judgment perverted. The truth of the affections becomes the vice of the soul. Such people lose that original freedom of indifferency, as Adam did when he transgressed. They open the *tabula rasa* of their minds; and they do not receive images of good or evil equally, indifferently, but they show a bias toward evil. What is forbidden fruit becomes more pleasurable. They seek the ultimate refinements of vice, like a jaded Roman emperor, and their last desperate invention is fidelity. They not only reject the basic law which is in accordance with nature; they turn away from fixed custom, the secondary law of habit ("vice-nature") — what their mothers practiced. They are tormented by fear, one of the basic affections that disturb recreants. And they would spread their evil habit as a disease, according to the kind of progression familiar to Stoic and Christian philosophers.

When Venus intervenes the heretics are punished as they deserve. The institution of love, we are given to understand, will be returned by divine fiat (like a primitive church restored) to its original state of indifference. Thrown in for good measure are the political overtones of establishing dangerous constancy. When a resolute "two or three" heretics manage to impose their false views and get them established, then we may expect the secondary laws of custom and habit to tyrannize over the primary law of right reason, which is in accord with nature. The punishment is fit: the heretics become the fixed subjects, and are bound to their vice, the evil of their affections, like Stoic or Christian sinners hopelessly contemplating impossible good.

But the indifferent man is not disturbed by his affections. He demonstrates, whether cheerfully, earnestly, or wittily, his freedom from any of the progressive symptoms described in the handbooks. To him love is an indifferent pleasure, in accord with the law of nature and the true church of Venus. His soul is not engaged. Love, he proves, has no *felt* importance to him, and in his promiscuousness he is essentially impartial and moderate. In contrast to the passionate heretics he maintains a kind of golden mean, or a Stoic apathy, in what might seem licentiousness if not practiced by the indifferent man.

Some of these details may seem strained. But clearly Donne's poem demands an effort not unlike the one just demonstrated. We are not dealing with tricky verbal ambiguities or associative connotations; the ideas which Donne evokes are, or were, familiar ones, with a history. Though they do not begin to focus until late in the poem, this would seem to be Donne's conscious purpose. He requires the reader to make the necessary conjunction, and to fill out the argument by a process of extrapolation as he thinks back on its concealed relevances and thinks anew on its implied consequences. Technically the poem is a mock encomium, a false argument, carried out with superb flexibility and control of the inventions. It is not just an argument, however, but an imaginative argument, one which controls extraordinarily close tolerances and employs not only logical but psychological turns — those which reflect the minds of the participants in the poem, and those which engage the mind of the reader. Though the challenge is a mocking one, and a highly conscious fiction, it goes far in its chosen direction, and for this reason alone would attract the mind. But the mind is not allowed to dwell at leisure upon the implications; instead, it is actively involved, not only in solving the argument and discovering the inner continuity underneath the apparently casual and spontaneous movements, but also in discovering something of its own intimate nature as it is worked upon and as it responds.

The reader is involved, but not the speaker. This is a distinction that helps us clarify the limits of the poem. As a witty inversion it goes far, but in a single direction. The imaginative form is more subtle than one would have expected, but the fiction never seriously tempts us to try it out as potential truth.

Binary Forms

With the exception of "The Undertaking," which was introduced early for its value as a standard of comparison, all the poems I have been discussing may be considered as having either a unitary or a simple binary form. The poems based upon a unitary form develop a single statement which, in spite of some precalculated surprise, or indirection, or final reversal, does not depend on any inner conflict; everything finally drops into its appointed place and the effect turns out to be single. In the simpler binary forms we find some tension or disproportion, or even a second argument or form emerging from the first, but as a kind of connate shadow or subdued reservation. The poems which carry their themes as far as possible in one limited direction always have an implied point of opposition; the normal human views which have been brilliantly controverted are pushed back, as it were, by a powerful beam of artificial light, but they gather and exert their pressure on the borders of the poem. Indeed, if the pressure were not there and felt, the poems would lack their occasion and would be deprived of a necessary dimension of meaning.

My distinction between the rudimentary and the more fully developed binary forms is for the most part quantitative. It follows that, whenever the opposition is more than a stationary pressure which suggests movement only by its implied reaction to the monologue of the poem, whenever the opposition can move by itself and can therefore develop, this movement must occur *within* the poem. Donne can invest implied movement with surprising significance, and one cannot impose this distinction without some care. Still, the degree of conflicting movement and development within a poem provides the best way of recognizing the characteristics of binary form.

A distinctive movement of Donne's mind is the vigorous pursuit of a limited theme, or the single-minded exploration of some emblem or symbol, or some pattern of human relationship that yields an abstract and analyzable significance. The very titles of Donne's poems suggest his preferring to seek imaginative intensity through concentration and depth rather than through range. But a theme carried far, even in jest, or a theme followed into its deeper meanings, inevitably meets an opposition real or implied. Besides, Donne's profound and nimble wit cannot long suppress its awareness of inadequacies in the momentary argument and of other alternatives. In some of the best poems the consciousness of what is being created may be felt as a distinct pressure on the creation, or may even act as a direct participant. We have studied one such example in another connection — "The Good-morrow." But we do not need to consider such complex examples now. It is enough to remember that consciousness can act as a countering force within a poem. And to this must be added another limited observation, one we shall need to study further in a different context. It is not only in the religious poems that Donne exhibits the need to

> Be covetous of Crosses, let none fall.
> Crosse no man else, but crosse thy selfe in all.

In a profound sense which takes many forms it is an inner truth of his mind that "No Crosse is so extreme, as to have none." [25] Whether he is using himself in jest, or inventing and practicing on a theme, or striving to unite himself with a position in which he may wholly believe, he finds it natural and necessary to cultivate opposing forces. We must follow some of these matters further; however, though it is useful to mention them now, we have for the moment gone beyond our immediate concerns.

It is instructive to consider "The Sunne Rising" soon after "The Indifferent." In tone they seem to resemble each other, and in structure both may be considered witty inversions of a normal perspective carried through with surprising liveliness and consistency. It is the differences, however, which tell us more. "The Sunne Rising" develops through progressive stages which move in a single ascending motion, but then the poem turns back on itself and makes a gesture of reconciliation. We cannot take the gesture seriously, as we shall need to in other poems, but neither can we disregard it quite. Furthermore, the gaps in the argument are not related to any time scheme; instead, certain reservations in the argument are maintained as part of the continuous play of consciousness in the poem. The poem opens with an absurd scolding of the "unruly" sun, which has presumed to intrude on lovers who are still in bed. Then, not at all absurdly, but with hard, masterful control, the sun is redirected toward its proper subjects, the timeservers of low or high station. But love is declared independent of time. The second stanza opens with a surprising recourse to arguments from the conventions of the sonneteers:

> Thy beames, so reverend, and strong
> Why shouldst thou thinke?
> I could eclipse and cloud them with a winke,
> But that I would not lose her sight so long:
> If her eyes have not blinded thine . . .

We suspect a certain mockery in the use of these familiar exaggerations, and before long we find that they are used as a bridge to even more extreme claims for the power of the mistress.

What is most immediately surprising is the radical shifting of attitudes in the poem. From the solipsistic whimsy of scolding the sun, the speaker turns a hard view outward and produces that shrewd, commanding rhetoric which defines and dismisses the timeservers. Then the speaker turns to a different kind of whimsy, this time a publicly authorized but transparent fiction for indulging in certain amatory sentiments. The organization and major voice of the poem express views of reality which derive mostly from *interior* experience; so that even the demonstrated mastery of external experience is used to reject or subdue the kind of world in which external experiences occur. The effect is remarkable and produces a deep and continuing surprise; for the external demonstration not only supports the internal view directly, and indirectly guarantees by its presence that fancy has not run wild; it also keeps up a certain unofficial but inevitable sense of conflict.

> Looke, and to morrow late, tell mee,
> Whether both the 'India's of spice and Myne
> Be where thou leftst them, or lie here with mee.

It is the little word "late" which complicates the exaggeration – by its fidelity to the literal world in which chronology and geography are subject to exact and reliable laws that are external to the confident constructions of individual desire. One expects the lover to have good store of images and to charge certain far-off places famous for their beauty and worth with signifying his beloved, but one does not expect the lover to have much interest in geographical locations – even when a shrewd sense of longitudinal relationships favors a preposterously late day in bed with the beloved.

It is a charmingly dissonant, small note, serving the purposes of love's imagination but retaining some of the strangeness of its origin in recognitions which lie outside the closed world of love. At this point we may mark a shift in the attitude toward the sun, a midway stage between the initial abuse and the final patronizing. Then the kings of the world are invoked as witnesses, by means of the sun's daily survey:

> Aske for those Kings whom thou saw'st yesterday,
> And thou shalt heare, All here in one bed lay.

The Indies, as images of the earthly paradise, fall within the allowable scope of exaggeration by literary lovers. But the kings are appropriated without quite the same sanction of custom. They are not real kings, we know, and they could not all fit in that private English bed; but what they represent imagistically is not a distillation of all that is precious and delightful on earth to the imagination of a lover who does not feel himself quite on earth. The kings are being used to contribute to the process by which the world is being contracted into a Neoplatonic world soul residing in this one bedroom. The lovers possess in their bed what does not seem to incommode them as an idea and image, a composite token of the material possession of that gross external world.

The process of contraction continues in the final stanza:

> She'is all States, and all Princes, I,
> Nothing else is.
> Princes doe but play us; compar'd to this,
> All honor's mimique; All wealth alchimie.

The lovers are the soul, the form, not only of states and princes, of which they are the perfect model, but of earthly reality: "Nothing else is." Then we have the reconciling joke on space and time, the easier task which the aging sun will have in warming the lovers' small material world:

> Shine here to us, and thou art every where;
> This bed thy center is, these walls, thy spheare.

The mocking tone is directed formally at the sun and at the parts of the world subservient to the rule of time and the business of getting on. But the world of love, through the office of wit, does not turn its back on the material world and insist on its own transcendent superiority — as we might well have expected. Platonic concepts are used, not to remove love from the world, but to establish the superior reality of love *in* the world. And so the world is not thoroughly rejected; instead, it is put in its place by the assertion that the lovers are the perfect reality imperfectly represented by the world's body. They are above time, and their enclosed room is the center, the heart, of reality in the world. That part of the development which rests lightly on conventional metaphysics may be thought quite as playful as the borrowing of conventional assertions from the love creed — the power of the mistress' eyes and the value of her beauty. Both kinds of assertion are used arbitrarily, as if they were unanswerable proof, and much of the wit lies in using them so confidently and in such sly juxtapositions. Besides, there is a sort of incongruity in producing the metaphysical argument to prove the reality of the lovers' little world in terms of this world rather than in terms of a transcendent world. The intellectual extravagance seems to be as deliberate as the physical one at the end, by which the sun is advised on its new orbit.

Are the extreme claims of love mocked, and the habits of the abstracting intellect? To some degree this must be so. But a balance is held in favor of the natural pleasures of love in enjoying its office and in enjoying its familiar illusion that it is superior to time and that it is composed of the very best moments and materials of the outside world. It can afford to renounce and patronize what it essentially possesses; it is, or believes itself to be and in its moments of belief is, self-sufficient. Nor are the lovers entirely static in their "illusion," though that is modeled on a concept of unified changelessness. The movement of the poem endows them with a subtle motion, that of a living progress toward the ideal they represent. We are first made to see them as two lovers — he looking at her and contemplating the exalted privilege of his possession. We then see them, after the intermediate image of the kings, in an image of complete unity, as all states and princes. This is followed by the highest declaration, that "Nothing else is." Immaterial honor is a shadow imitating their reality; material wealth is counterfeit, the preposterous product of alchemy; the princes of the world play-act what the lovers *are*.

But the lovers are also playing, and from their privileged and ancient illusion mocking other illusions. The question of time is vigorously raised and quietly dropped, or at least the initial terms are allowed to lapse. They may be assimilated into the higher argument; but a poem, even when it is an imaginative argument, is likely to create a desire that like be answered by like. One must admit, however, that the vigor of the initial terms is answered by the vigor of the higher argument, and that the motion to exclude the outer world is completed by the final inclusion. There is, nevertheless, one gap or omission. It is an untouched center of the poem — that privileged and unexamined illusion from which the lovers look out on other illusions.

Some lines from stanza 76 of Marvell's "Upon Appleton House" may serve as commentary:

> How safe, methinks, and strong, behind
> These trees have I incamp'd my Mind.
> . . . .
> And where the World no certain Shot
> Can make, or me it toucheth not.
> But I on it securely play,
> And gaul its Horsemen all the Day.

It is the word "methinks" that governs the stanza. Like Marvell's, Donne's mind is both engaged in its imagining and detached; it is active, and it contemplates itself acting. There is evident pleasure in playing out the illusion, in calling the turns, in speaking first and fast — and in doing all this knowingly, in holding the initiative and the control by wit. It is a game, but serious, and it has strict rules.

The fiction is one that must be conscious of itself and that gives joy, not by asserting or trying to authorize an illusion, but by the imaginative energy which the skill releases for those who can participate, and by the excitement of balancing on the delicate line, and by the dividends of any fiction powerfully and accurately pursued: the new lights and shadows it raises for contemplating the truths of ordinary experience.

If the fiction were not presented with a competence which owes important credentials to the demonstrated knowledge of the ordinary external world; if the fiction did not have its own persuasive plausibility, based upon the authoritative experiences of the interior world of love and contemplation; if the fiction were not able to combine and balance both worlds with sure mastery of them and of its own form and status as fiction: then we should have at worst an absurdity, at best a light entertainment to be enjoyed and dismissed. Formally, the interior world dominates and the issues are resolved in its favor, but the wit has also imposed its formal counterbalance. And so the poem, though it is a witty inversion, and though it makes a gesture of reconciliation, may be regarded as a complex binary form, in which nothing is fully resolved.

"Loves Exchange" has never attracted much critical attention, though it is a major achievement of Donne's wit — a superb inversion that crosses itself by an internal irony, so that the form turns back on itself, intricately balanced against its counterpulls, yet pointing toward a resolution. It begins at top speed, and the pace of the whole poem is not only a brilliant technical accomplishment which delights; it is a means of exerting significant pressure as it makes close turns and reversals, and as it contributes a kind of personality or voice to the developing debate.

> *Love*, any devill else but you,
> Would for a given Soule give something too.
> At Court your fellowes every day,
> Give th'art of Riming, Huntsmanship, or Play,
> For them which were their owne before.

We begin with a peremptory inversion: Love is a devil, but one who does not honor the usual compact. The prized accomplishments at court, which seem to derive from such a bargain, are more nearly an act of infernal grace – at least that is what the timing, so shrewdly held back, suggests.

> Onely I have nothing which gave more,
> But am, alas, by being lowly, lower.

This is the pathetic lover speaking, opposing the speed of his brilliant indictment with the slow statement of his own sad case.

He develops his own pathetic situation in the same deliberate tempo of ironic acceptance:

> I aske no dispensation now
> To falsifie a teare, or sigh, or vow.

These are the "prerogatives" of Love and Love's minions; no one else can have the right to "forsweare." But the lover does have one plea to make, in the course of which he is carried away, as it were, by a fervent lyrical prayer to Love. He is carried away at a speed which recalls the earlier tempo, and does not inhibit a clever nimbleness and a cunning rhetoric of metrical management:

> Give mee thy weaknesse, make mee blinde,
> Both wayes, as thou and thine, in eies and minde;
> Love, let me never know that this
> Is love, or, that love childish is;
> Let me not know that others know
> That she knowes my paines, least that so
> A tender shame make me mine owne new woe.

This phase of the irony is completed by another change of pace, in which the speaker confesses the justice of Love and the nature of his guilt. He did not trust the "first motions" of Love; and, like the small towns which do not surrender until after "great shot" has broken their resistance, he may not "article for grace" but must surrender unconditionally.

Only now does the underlying issue emerge. We cannot expect to strike a bargain with so powerful a devil, and to be a candidate for grace requires a kind of prevenient grace. The first motions of love must be trusted; we may not seek to know even that what we feel *is* love, for consciousness and love are enemies. If one does not as a child renounce knowledge, knowledge when applied to love will make one childish. The specific items the speaker desires *not* to know make an amusing sequence, as if the trick were done with mirrors. ("Tender" and "new" suggest the child again, and a wordplay helps multiply the knowledge: *my known* "new woe.") And so the speaker has taken two ironical tacks. He has renounced knowledge in a defiantly ostentatious way that is overprecise and that consciously exhibits in its flourish of triviality a ridiculousness in the power before which he is helpless. By submission and laughter he gains, not a victory, but some compensatory share of power in the force which is destroying him. He can see and acknowledge his crime of consciousness and, by that same consciousness, exhibit the ways of love.

The speaker was forced into submission by the "great shot," "Having put Love at last to shew this face":

> This face, by which he could command
> And change the Idolatrie of any land,
> This face, which wheresoe'r it comes,
> Can call vow'd men from cloisters, dead from tombes,
> And melt both Poles at once, and store
> Deserts with cities, and make more
> Mynes in the earth, then Quarries were before.

The preceding stanza was moderate in movement, but the last lines leaned, as transition, toward this burst of sustained speed. It is the only stanza in which a single tempo prevails; for Donne has, with the ear of a fine musician, varied his tempos, but never with simple alternations. The movement of this stanza is lyrical, and turns back on itself only to renew its forward drive again. As lyric it sings the praise of love's power, and is carried away by its own rapt motion, leaving neither interval nor breath for any dissidence. Yet the effect is not single, but resembles that of the earlier fervent prayer to Love — though this lyric is a more difficult technical achievement, with the style more at odds with the substance, but the overtones of defiance harder to separate from the singing rush of the enthusiastic praise.

The manner is ironic of course, but it is not the simple irony of overpraise or even of mixed praise. The song is a tribute to the power of love by the helpless victim, but it is not one of recantation; for it both justifies his defeat and emphasizes the special distinction of his punishment. That face of Love is not merely the "big shot" that de-molishes small towns; it is the reward of a true rebel, which dignifies as well as crushes the solitary protagonist. He has had his vision of the face, even if it is an unbeatific one of a devil. He suffers, but he has seen it, while the mere "minions" enjoy their petty grace of suc-cess — in blindness. The great power of the face of Love is a power that commands men to act out their drives in blindness. The hero's weakness as a lover is the strength of his consciousness, but out of that weakness comes an unexpected strength, the ambiguous reward of his vision. Finally, he has one humble last request to make, that he be killed and dissected (as a specimen of consciousness?), for torture will defeat Love's purpose: "Rack't carcasses make ill Anatomies." Then, and then only, we may infer, will that gift of blindness descend. He calls himself a rebel, but in the drama of his defeat the part he has cunningly written for himself suggests a tragic martyr.

The poem is, we can see, no simple inversion, though it is beauti-fully turned and carried through. The consciousness deftly implied in "The Sunne Rising" is explicit in "Loves Exchange," but the reso-lution is advanced in the limited terms of a special assignment of wit. We are allowed to see the relations between love and consciousness only from a controlled angle. The poem limits a large problem, one that often worked more richly in Donne's imagination; what we get here is a brilliantly focused view which triumphs by virtue of its focus. The drama between love and consciousness does not try to convince us that it is a real drama. It is a kind of benefit performance, an origi-nal play wonderfully produced but deliberately denying itself that special and precious dimension: the desire to make the audience be-lieve in its reality.

An audience expecting a play instead of the play of wit may well be puzzled. For one thing it is tempting to seek satisfactions that wit, as the play of the mind and the creator of intellectual pleasure, the wit which Donne's contemporaries prized, never promised. It is easy to share in Dr. Johnson's historical error of misapplied seriousness. If we are left puzzled and with a sense of incomplete satisfaction, it is because Donne's art succeeds almost too well in carrying a jest toward truth and makes us want either less or more satisfaction.

Even the sympathetic reader of Donne, justly uncomfortable by so stolid a reaction to a dazzling poetic performance, may acknowledge that elsewhere Donne more fully engages and resolves the difficulties he creates. The limited and "categorical" point I am making is that here, as in some other examples we have noted, the major creative energy of the poem goes into developing the predicament.

Nevertheless, to step back from this concern with analytical categories, the poem is manifestly triumphant in its own difficult terms. Tragedy is a form hard to mock successfully without gross exaggerations; yet Donne has managed to create and stay wonderfully close to a genuine inner pattern of tragedy, and to unite that pattern with an ironic, triumphant humility, and to make authentic religious feelings bear on a pagan and secular theme.

"The Will" seems to be a performance of great virtuosity, the surface studded with brilliant and surprising effects. Virtuosity in this sense implies a concentrated mastery of the surface, or of qualities just below the surface, which can be made to seem profound but are not so. The poem would appear to be an excellent example of Miss Tuve's general thesis that metaphysical style fulfills the requirements of genre and decorum, for here Donne seems to keep the incongruities, the satiric and other overtones, carefully adjusted to his witty arguments against love. Yet there is a chafing quality to the imaginative details which might open the way to a distinction between wit that merely fills out a preconceived pattern, however unexpectedly, and wit that pushes and pulls at a pattern. More to the point of the discussion, though, is the fact that the poem is not a witty inversion, for that form of wit is included in a larger form which evolves.

The first four stanzas are organized as epigrams, in which the key to the meaning is held back until the final turn, when everything snaps into place. The point of the bizarre bequests hinges on a characteristically unpleasant lesson taught the poet by love. In the first stanza he gives to ambassadors his ears, "To women or the sea, my teares"; for love has taught,

> By making mee serve her who'had twenty more,
> That I should give to none, but such, as had too
> much before.

Then he gives his truth to courtiers, his candor to Jesuits, his thoughtfulness to clowns and silence to travelers. The inappropriateness of each gift is obvious and funny; but the exact terms of the incongruity are reserved until we learn that, since he has been required to love where love cannot be received, he is giving only "to such as have an incapacitie." The incongruities continue, but controlled by a new definition. Faith goes to Roman Catholics, good works to the Dutch "Schismaticks," modesty to soldiers, patience to gamblers:

> Thou Love taughtst mee, by making mee
> Love her that holds my love disparity,
> Onely to give to those that count my gifts indignity.

By now the reader will have learned the formula for the epigram, and will be testing his wit against the poet's, trying to outguess him by anticipating the special term which defines all the incongruities of the stanza. The crux of the poem comes now, in the fourth stanza; the reader has become experienced, the easiest organizations have been used up, and the poet's wit is challenged by its most difficult task.

> I give my reputation to those
> Which were my friends; Mine industrie to foes;
> To Schoolemen I bequeath my doubtfulnesse;
> My sicknesse to Physitians, or excesse;
> To Nature, all that I in Ryme have writ;
>   And to my company my wit.
> Thou Love, by making mee adore
> Her, who begot this love in mee before,
> Taughtst me to make, as though I gave, when I did
>   but restore.

The triumph is brilliant and conclusive. Donne's wit wins, yet not because he produces with ingenious virtuosity still another variation from an unexpected corner, or practices any deceptive feints of prestidigitation, but because he reveals in what has seemed to be no more than a cleverly superficial formula a profound imaginative truth. The items themselves are presented with a certain deception and ambiguity, so that the immediate, serial experience of the reader may resemble that of the preceding stanzas, except that the incongruities now are denser. The gifts are also to a less extent external, detachable qualities and attitudes which a man might pretend to strip off and hand out — like tears or candor, or even faith and good works. Reputation and health, perhaps even one's poems, may be detachable in this sense; but industry, skepticism, and wit have a kind of inwardness and relatedness; they are harder to imagine, even in jokes, as autonomous. The basic conceit of the last disposition of property now comes under sudden pressure. In what sense does a man really possess the important gifts he would bestow? They are not free and unencumbered if they have been lent him, or if he is revealed as an agent less acting than reacting, as much worked upon as working.

The surface perversities of love now give way to a similar and more authoritative irony. First the matter of chronology. The mistress "begot" love in him, and then Love exerted its ready force and made him "adore" her. But he did not understand either the timing or the source of his feelings. Love taught him to "make" love as though he "gave," to act as though he were creating instead of responding. By extension, all of the bequests in this stanza are tainted with the same defective title. By the excesses of "adoring" he has been misled into acting as though he could give, as though the gifts were really his. But all he really did, and is doing, is to "restore." Nor are the gifts themselves quite free of dubiousness. And so the fiction of the last will and testament is called into court and challenged. So is the personal will of the speaker himself, who reveals that he has not had the clear possession of *himself* that he has assumed he had.

The fifth stanza gives up the effort to outwit the reader, or to make the basic formula yield either new surprises or further discoveries. The discoveries of the fourth stanza turned out to be radical, challenging both the basic fiction and the speaker's privilege to direct that fiction only against others. The immediate implications, it seems, are allowed to rest for a stanza, but the fiction itself has been as good as killed off. The impetus which continues the invention is not listless; the incongruities are apt, but they are all general; they lack the concentrated, biting individuality they have previously had. They are for the first time quite understandable without the key at the end, for they are merely incongruous, the matched extremes of inappropriateness. At the same time the applied lesson of love sounds more like true history; it has the flatness of a factual account. Since the mistress prefers younger lovers, the speaker, who still loves, turns the responsibility over to Love, which "dost my gifts thus disproportion." This defines the incongruities well enough, and there has been some surprise after all: the real author of these items was not the witty poet but Love.

The last stanza buries the fiction but immediately revives it in another form. The poet will give no more of his bitter gifts but will "undoe" the world by dying. There may be some surface bravado intended, but the cooler and more stable meaning seems to be that he will undo himself: when he is dead the world might as well be dead, for all the difference to him. He is going to die (though this has been a long last gasp) "because love dies too." It has taken a long time to discover the fatal cause. We have been made too busy with the effects. He is dying for love because his love is dying, and the last testament has been reviewing the major symptoms and progress of that death. The adoration caused by Love may have blinded him to the fact that love was begotten in him, that he had no real power to *give* in love, but only to respond and to restore. But now he will "undoe" the world, or at least the hold which the world has on him, by dying; and he has been rehearsing his death in the approved manner by stripping off his possessions and giving them away as bitter gifts. The undoing of the world is a manner of speaking and thinking, but the undoing of love, though expressed only in images, is literal and actual. He has learned the lessons of rejection and dependence. He may not have the power to give, but he has the power not to give; love may be begotten *in* him, but he can die *to* love.

Until the fourth stanza his witty inventions are too clever and external to look at themselves. But then they do, and the energetic fiction is surrendered. The inventions of the next stanza are turned over to Love, which is less witty than the speaker. Love needs proportion and response; the useless gifts of the fifth stanza, though less bright and lively than the bitter ones, are useless in some basic ways that do not depend on carefully matched timing. I have called these inventions "general." They also suggest finality, for instead of the individual figures of social satire Donne now demonstrates incongruity by using such figures as those of the dead, the mad, and the starving. The last stanza continues in the same imaginative vein. The poet's mistress (like the world) will live on, but unloved. Her beauties will be as worthless as unmined gold, her graces as proportionate and relevant as "a Sun dyall in a grave." A living death is the final portion of the mistress who neglects both Love and him.

The poem has been an invention and a practice in annihilation. But until the fourth stanza, when wit broke through the set form of its fiction, all of the energy was directed outward, against the mistress, Love, and an external world. The discovery of his own complicity, and of the true order in the relationship of love, allowed the speaker to suspend his fiction and redirect it toward the conclusion he perhaps ought to have wanted, but away from which his wit threatened to carry him. The death which served as an initial opportunity for fiction now achieves a richer imaginative state. Even the satiric purposes of the death, when they give up their varied exercises, gain in concentration. The real mistress, if it is she who prefers younger men, may be less interesting than the fictional lady, but the death is more purposeful, and her fate more successfully arranged.

The ostensible form of the poem is a witty inversion, an implausible theme accepted and carried through with great power of invention. Donne triumphantly fulfills the expected requirements. Yet the real form seems to underlie the ostensible one. Its action is dramatic, for the speaker discovers himself personally participating in what is, or has pretended to be, a tongue-in-cheek exhibition. The set theme is fulfilled, but almost everything necessary for that might have been accomplished in the first three stanzas. After that the poem deepens, though it manages to complete with unfaltering energy the form it has begun, while it also goes on to reveal a form that includes the first one.

The form within a form seems less like the binary forms I have been discussing than like those poems in which the latencies of an issue surprise the reader by their delayed emergence and cause him to revise or supplement the pattern of his response. We have noted such effects in "Womans Constancy," "The Curse," "Confined

Love," "The Undertaking," and "The Indifferent." Nevertheless, "The Will" is a binary form in the sense that it is resolved arbitrarily, as a practice in annihilation, and in the sense that it breaks through its set form to a deeper imaginative recognition, but not to a deeper imaginative resolution. Its form resembles that of "Loves Exchange," in that the predicament underneath the surface resists the explicit resolution. The stanza by stanza development of the poem employs deliberate gaps and omissions. The result is an established texture of surprise. But the chief surprise of the poem is an authentic imaginative discovery that seems neither prearranged nor camouflaged. Instead we must reckon with a form that develops through the discovery of its own further potential.

Consciousness, which was given an explicit role, but carefully limited, in "Loves Exchange," and an implicit role in "The Undertaking" and "The Sunne Rising," here seems to create its own part with a kind of lyric spontaneity. The lyric springs from an insight of consciousness; that insight is inward and simple; it cuts through that equilibrium of external complexity which the poem has been brilliantly balancing, and it points toward a virtual solution which influences the actual one.

The poem provides a convenient opportunity for declaring that Donne is a master of binary forms, but a dissatisfied master. His deepest desire, which can make itself felt even in a rigorously disciplined form of wit, is to take another step. What we must at least acknowledge concerning the form of this poem is that Donne backs away from the witty inventions which face outward in their ironies, and that he turns toward an irony which is inward, and simpler, and more profound. This is an internal form of the poem which compels our interest. The descriptive classification is expendable, and has served its chief purpose in bringing us to this point, from which we can now proceed to poems in which Donne takes a more certain further step.[26]

Ternary Forms and the Wit of Simplicity

The major examples of this section will be the following poems: "Aire and Angels," "Loves Growth," and "Lovers Infinitenesse."

The list could easily be extended, but my purpose being to explore and substantiate certain critical perceptions, what I cannot accomplish with these poems is not likely to be accomplished by a survey that aims at exhaustiveness. Before turning to the major examples, however, it will be useful to glance, by way of introduction, at some minor examples.

First a statistical item. Twenty-one poems of the *Songs and Sonets*, more than one-third of the collection, are composed of three stanzas each.[27] The number of stanzas, we know, does not always correspond to the inner divisions of a poem. Some poems with three stanzas do not develop a significant ternary form, whereas poems with fewer or more stanzas may. But it is at least plain that Donne liked the division. By nature, or by second nature, he found it useful as a logical form; and it pleased him, as it has pleased other lyric poets, as an esthetic form.

> Send home my long strayd eyes to mee,
> Which (Oh) too long have dwelt on thee.

"The Message" begins with these proper credentials of the lyric but then turns, as any song is likely to do, to consider the lyric possibilities of an alternative. "Yet since" then holds the stage and reaches the firm conclusion that the mistress should instead continue to keep his eyes.

> Send home my harmlesse heart againe,
> Which no unworthy thought could staine.

"But if" then raises its opposing voice and tends to the conclusion already reached in the first stanza.

> Yet send me back my heart and eyes,
> That I may know, and see thy lyes.

Two objections have been raised, but now they melt away as the poet combines the two negatives into one positive purpose: the organs in question, which have been much abused, will be necessary for what somehow is going to happen; instead of merely reflecting her perfidy, they will witness and enjoy the consequences of her own failure in love.

"Take heed of loving mee," begins "The Prohibition." The poem does not sing, and the dominant voice is the vehicle of a subtle and pressing argument, by which the conclusion of the first stanza confirms and supplements the opening: "If thou love me, take heed of loving mee." The opposing voice gets its chance in the second stanza: "Take heed of hating mee." There is no inner opposition, and the argument arrives at a similar conclusion: "If thou hate mee, take heed of hating mee." We may now anticipate a busy third stanza, the first line of which is "Yet, love and hate mee too." In reconciling its extremes, which have been cultivated for that purpose, the stanza cleverly reworks arguments of the two preceding stanzas and triumphantly concludes:

> Lest thou thy love and hate and mee undoe,
> *To let mee live, O love and hate mee too.*

One may regard "The Prohibition" as a slight performance, but the opposing and reconciling of extremes by Donne is more than a casual exercise. The witty inversions, as I have suggested, are a means of exploring and carrying through an extreme — with the opposition implied, and either just outside the poem or gathered upon its borders. In the binary forms extremes are opposed, either without reconciliation or with an implied, or arbitrary, or trivial, or incomplete, reconciliation. It is useful now to remind ourselves of this design in Donne, and to note the reconciliation of extremes as a method suitable for both lyrical and logical forms. If the pattern is basic, we may expect our most significant evidence to be found in those poems which most fully and most deeply engage, and therefore reveal, Donne's mind. Yet it is worth observing the casual presence of the pattern in poems which are clearly occasional, where he cannot be thought deeply involved, but seems rather to be working in what he found to be a natural and useful way. Two other brief examples may suffice.

"The Relique" contemplates the meaning of the symbolic "bracelet of bright haire about the bone." Two fanciful conjectures are advanced. The first is what the gravedigger will think when he discovers it. His response is individual and private as he imagines two lovers contriving an assignation "at the last busie day" of doom. The second conjecture is public: what will happen if a superstitious age, on the lookout for miracles, discovers the relic. This provides the opportunity for a third and true account, not of the relic but of what it represents — the miracle of the couple's relations, which are private but have something to teach the public of love. The exposition of this third stanza is triple in its development. Like the gravedigger and the superstitious age, the lovers too are characterized by ignorance. But theirs is not accidental or willful. It is a true, essential ignorance of the nature of their faithful love: "Yet knew not what wee lov'd, nor why." Then their external behavior is described, but this too is mostly in terms of negatives, what they did not do, what limits they naturally accepted. The two of them may make an anonymous "loving couple," and they may call themselves "harmlesse lovers," but when it comes to expressing "what a miracle shee was," the lover must invoke ignorance again. It is neither the specific ignorance which might call her "a Mary Magdalen," nor even the essential ignorance of the nature of their love. It is rather a courteous and disciplined assuming of ignorance which will not attempt to go beyond human limits and language to describe the nature of the miraculous.

> but now alas,
> All measure, and all language, I should passe,
> Should I tell what a miracle shee was.

The poem does not produce extremes which ache for reconciliation, but simply two fanciful propositions answered by a declaration. The answer deals imaginatively with some actual circumstances of love and personal relations; it suggests a scope and form of love; but it neither answers directly, as a method of reconciliation, nor exempts itself from its play of fancy. Yet the triple form has its esthetic and rhetorical value. It provides a graceful way of balancing the witty and the serious, of complimenting and amusing a lady while expressing a literal and imaginative truth about their relations, a truth of the kind for which it is difficult to create a context that can be touched upon lightly and with tact. If the lady is Magdalen Herbert, we may guess that the poem does reconcile some extremes, emotional and social, more apparent to Donne and Mrs. Herbert than to us.

Our second example is even simpler, a problem in rhetorical and logical organization imposing no imaginable pressure on Donne beyond the intellectual one of working out his poetic proposition. "The Dissolution" is written as one free, impromptu stanza, with internal variations both in the pattern of rhyme and in the length of line. It begins with an unmistakable unit of eight lines, which rhymes *abcd / bacd*; the stresses which correspond evolve in this pattern: 3453 / 4553. Then Donne departs from that pattern, though more in the rhyme than in the beat. The next unit is one of seven lines; it is clearly recognizable as a unit, though less by rhyme and meter than by its logical distinctness. The rhyme pattern is *eeffe / gg*, the metrical pattern, 45355 / 45. The final unit, marked by one extended simile and completed by another, is of nine lines. The rhyme pattern is a variation on that of the second unit: *hhi / ijk / kjj*. The metrical pattern is 345 / 532 / 557.

These details are fussy; what do they show? Donne has a single notion to demonstrate: namely, that though his mistress has died before him the nature and force of his love will cause his soul to overtake hers. It is an improbable proposition which requires a process of preparation before it can be made good. The first unit begins with the statement of her death and the return in death of all things to their first elements. But the lovers were made of one another; and since his body involves hers, he is now burdened and smothered, but no longer nourished, by those elements of which he consists. The second unit opens with a statement which translates the four elements into terms of love (fire of passion, sighs of air, tears of water, and earthly despair). These are the elements by which he is smothered, for they are not worn out by love; instead, her death has "repaired" them. In fact, he might live a long and wretched life, "But that my fire doth with my fuell grow." These two units, then, both consist of an opening statement which is carried two further stages. The last stage of the second unit is the pivotal point toward which the argument has moved and on which it can turn for its final solution. The argument has a kind of overlapping, soritical movement; there are two compressed propositions in the first unit, while the second unit carefully elaborates and imposes a specific direction on the second proposition of the first unit. Incidentally, each of these units is divided into two distinct periods which are reinforced by the rhyme and the meter, as a glance at the details in the preceding paragraph will indicate.

The last unit departs from the established logical method and concentrates on demonstrating the relevant validity of the pivotal point by developing its consequences. If the two lovers are one, and the incomplete syllogism of the first statement holds, then she will return to her first elements and so will he. But the initial effect has been to overwhelm him with a double share of those elements, which now have no egress or reciprocal flow; subject and predicate are baffled and turn back into each other. It is the active element of fire which provides the key to escape, and the apparent smothering was instead an interval for collecting force. All that Donne needs from the previous demonstration is the pivotal point; he can drop his logical method, which he does, and can gain both surprise and precision by an apparent indirectness. Two images, lightly connected with death, but drawn from areas of discourse and experience entirely different from the close, private language of love and its exotic though familiar idiom — these two images demonstrate how he can both accumulate fuel and expend it all at once. The development is threefold. "Active" kings bring in foreign treasure, but the more they bring in the more they spend: they are the kings who "soonest breake." Similarly, and he is amazed that he can speak — amazed as the intuition spontaneously takes shape, and amazed as he playfully contemplates the fiction he is perpetrating —

> This death, hath with my store
> My use encreas'd.
> And so my soule more earnestly releas'd,
> Will outstrip hers; As bullets flowen before
> A latter bullet may o'rtake, the pouder being more.

The poem is a wonderful trifle, a witty inversion that accepts a difficult theme and follows it through with remarkable invention and aptness. Our present interest in examining the poem, however, is to note that its structure is threefold, even though there are no formal divisions, and though there are no opposite extremes to reconcile. We may fall back, here at least, on a more general notion of Donne's finding the form logically natural, rhetorically useful, and esthetically satisfying. We must regard it as significant that this one impromptu stanza assumes three inner divisions, and that each division has a triple development.[28]

We come now to the first major example of this section. The ostensible subject of "Aire and Angels" is a familiar masculine dilemma of love, the tendency to spiritualize crossed by the opposing tendency to materialize. In "A Valediction: Of the Booke" Donne describes these extremes, but he does so gaily and in passing:

> Here Loves Divines, (since all Divinity
> Is love or wonder) may finde all they seeke,
> Whether abstract spirituall love they like,
> Their Soules exhal'd with what they do not see,
>   Or, loth so to amuze
>   Faiths infirmitie, they chuse
>   Something which they may see and use;
> For, though minde be the heaven, where love doth sit,
> Beauty a convenient type may be to figure it.

"Aire and Angels" has its own gaiety of wit, but the dilemma is accepted as a serious one which the poem will try to resolve.

The stanza of the poem is apparently a free variation of the sonnet; a sestet comes first and then an octave. In the opening stanza the sestet presents as narrative the poet's first experience with the beloved. He had loved her before he knew her face or name, affected as men are when they sense the mysterious presence of an angel. Even when he came into her presence he responded as if he were actually seeing an angel and were being dazzled by the brilliance of the sight:

> Still when, to where thou wert, I came,
> Some lovely glorious nothing I did see.

The octave has a double development; first an argument counters the nonsensuous apprehension of love, and so makes way for the opposing action.

The argument participates in a delicate intellectual comedy by opposing the extreme of abstract spiritual love with reasons drawn from the same high atmosphere. Since the soul, in order to act, requires a body; and since love is, in the order of being, inferior to the soul, because it is created later and is indeed derived from the soul: therefore, it follows that love must also take a body and not usurp an existence belonging to a higher stage of being. There is nothing extraordinary in this philosophical argument — except its application to these circumstances, and the stylistic ease with which that is managed. Once the argument against the extreme of abstract love has been made, the opposing movement can begin:

> And therefore what thou wert, and who,
>   I bid Love aske, and now
> That it assume thy body, I allow,
> And fixe it self in thy lip, eye, and brow.

The "what thou wert" may perhaps correspond to a tendency of rational investigation; the mind, as Donne says in his *Essays in Divinity*, is not satisfied with effects but seeks causes.[29] The "what," however, is not developed at all, and for good reason: only at the end of the poem are we ready to consider the "what" of love. It is the "who" that most nearly opposes the transcendent movement of the mind by attracting interest to the details of the physical self.

An implied image of the first stanza is that of balancing two extremes. The second stanza opens by admitting that the purpose was "to ballast love." A swifter exposition now is possible, for within six lines Donne exhausts the physical approach to love, recognizes that he has gone too far, and declares that a "fitter" solution "must be sought." The body of love is transformed into the image of a "pinnace," and the purpose of the basic reversal in attitude is now explained as the hope "so more steddily to have gone." "Steady" is a word of favorable connotations when it refers to an intellectual or moral virtue between two extremes; but in the context the word refers to a single extreme, that of weighing down the immaterial lightness of spirit, and for what purpose? Although there is an honorable purpose implied, that of loving intelligently, by bringing one's knowledge of the beloved into a closer accord with the truth, the image of the ship also inevitably suggests the female body and a material destination for love's progress. Yet even in this countermovement the impulse to idealize love maintains itself:

> With wares which would sinke admiration,
> I saw, I had loves pinnace overfraught.

The material image is very effective, as the weight of physical detail threatens not only to balance immaterial lightness but to "sinke" it. The word "admiration," however, dominates the image — not by its ordinary meaning, which could express the love for physical beauty, but by its abstract sense, in which "admiration" naturally expresses the movement of the mind upward toward the inconceivable, "since all Divinity / Is love or wonder."

Something not quite visible in the initial terms prevents an equal contest, in spite of the formal presentation of opposing positions. The intellectual extreme intellectualizes itself out of its exclusively transcendent direction and accepts as its expressive purpose the need to act. Similarly, the physical extreme exhibits its impossibility by a physical demonstration (its equivalent of thinking). Though we may surmise a destination for the ship, the image itself serves more as a "convenient type" of beauty, a figure for the heaven of mind "where love doth sit." (This discrimination, borrowed from the quoted stanza of "A Valediction: Of the Booke," though a laughing witticism in that context, will bear an exact application in this context.) No physical purpose or goal is directly advanced; one may extend Donne's imaginative logic by saying that this ship seems to take its bearings from above.[30]

Intellect, by examining itself, may discover and accept its need to act through the body, but the action it contemplates will express the mind. To the body action is natural. But in this poem purpose and direction are not natural: they derive from the heaven of mind. It is the abstract, intellectual sense of "admiration" that dominates the physical purpose, which is otherwise unexpressed. In other words, the two extremes may yearn toward each other, but it is the intellectual and idealizing purpose which is granted the chief privilege of language and expression. When Donne drops the ship image to underscore the impossibility of the physical direction, the new image is wonderfully sensuous in its materials and action, but it suggests a familiar type of logical reduction. Intellect formally takes over the task of expressing the body's logic:

> Ev'ry thy haire for love to worke upon
> Is much too much, some fitter must be sought.

And so the final octave undertakes that search. The first step is to summarize and focus upon the dilemma:

> For, nor in nothing, nor in things
> Extreme, and scatt'ring bright, can love inhere.

Each attempted solution has proved, by itself, inadequate. The mind discovered its own inadequacy; the body demonstrated it, and by the formal assistance of the mind expressed it. The mind seeks its expression downward, and the body seeks its expression upward: a middle ground has been indicated but no way to reach it. At this point the crucial second step is made. We return to the first reference to the angel and find that, if we look more closely at this authentic symbol for ideal love, we may see an inherent solution that reconciles the extremes:

> Then as an Angell, face and wings
> Of aire, not pure as it, yet pure doth weare,
> So thy love may be my loves spheare.

The solution is not obvious to a modern reader. It is a specialized application of the kind of thinking by which the mind discovered its own inadequacy. Pure as the mind is, and aspires to be in the motion that attracts its thoughts upward toward the single and immaterial principle of things — in order to act on earth the mind must take on the impurity of a body. Human love, which derives from the soul, stands between the mind and the body, not between the mind and its aspiration upward. Even when love is to be converted to the movement upward — as it is in this poem — that conversion requires a process of doing, and on earth, and it must express man's "middle nature," which lies between that of the angels and that of the beasts. The doctrine of angelic substance, as Grierson notes, is entirely traditional. In their spiritual nature angels do not possess bodies, but when they would appear to men they must assume a shape — composed, by common agreement, of the light but impressionable element of air. By earthly standards that air is pure, but it cannot be as pure as the spiritual nature of the angel which clothes itself in an airy shape. The angelic doctrine is conventional, and so is the Neoplatonic reasoning which concerns the mind and some of these relations between the mind and love. What is personal is Donne's imaginative emphasis on the interrelationship of body and soul in love, and his emphasis on the middle way, which derives from his full belief that neither man nor angel can pass from one extreme to another directly. "Thou hast, O God, denyed even to Angells, the ability of arriving from one Extreme to another, without passing the mean way between." [31] And so the angel provides by analogy a solution to the human predicament, a solution which confirms the necessity of accepting these limitations imposed even upon spirit. The answer is that the mind, in order to express love on earth, must take on impurity; but it is a rare and delicate impurity, like that of an angel's face and wings. The human mind derives its nature from heaven and aspires to return, but it must perform its office of human love on earth; and the ways, though airy, must be visible to human sight.

Yet as that answer emerges it brings with it what seems to be a further question: "So thy love may be my loves sphaere." This reintroduces the "what thou wert," which was lost from sight when the effort to understand love was transferred to the body and the "who." The third and concluding step of the octave is to define the love between the sexes in those terms which have at last been brought forward.

> Just such disparitie
> As is twixt Aire and Angells puritie,
> 'Twixt womens love, and mens will ever bee.

As in all efforts to define the relations of the sexes, the presence of a certain voluntary leverage of wit is difficult to exclude. We may think that Donne has welcomed his opportunity, but as a by-product of his main enterprise. The unexpected development at the end is based upon a concealed term; it is a maneuver which reminds us of the epigrammatic reversals and simple inversions. Yet nothing is really reversed or altered; the conclusion lifts into high relief a subject which has been continuous, the effort of the mind to understand love and to understand its own nature as that responds to the influence of love. The reintroduction of the angel solves the apparent dilemma by defining the middle nature of love as delivering on earth its messages from on high. Now the definition is extended to include the relations of man and woman in love. Man's love is all spirit, like an angel; woman's love is the sphere in which the celestial body of man's love may reside; or like the angel's face and wings of air, woman's love provides the medium through which man's spiritual love may express itself on earth. If we think only of the he and she of it, we see a witticism, though a rare and complimentary one. Seldom has the body of love, as object, received so delicate a compliment from the mind of love contemplating the high subject of itself. Yet the body of love, as "who," has now been related to the "what," and the reconciliation of extremes has been given the fullest expression of the poem.

The details of the poem are finely drawn and admirable, like the hairs which love would work upon, and it is hard to resist working too much. Let us now step back to look again at the form, which is our chief subject. One clear inference to be drawn from our detailed study is that the poem does not reconcile two extremes which are granted equal voice and force. The commanding lyric which creates the scene and attitude of the first six lines presents an extreme which dominates the poem. It goes too far and must be countered; but in the opposing case physical love is never presented as a positive experience which expresses joy and is, at least in its moment of expression, complete and self-sufficient. The body meets the intellect more than halfway, and the result is less a synthesis of opposites than a reconciliation drawn up in favor of the intellect. The conclusion is not an arbitrary piece of wit, but confirms in a final definition a truth which has been demonstrated by the imaginative action of the poem: that it is chiefly the mind which seeks satisfaction in love, and as far as possible in accordance with the mind's understanding of its own nature.

We have marked the movements by which the ternary form tempers and resolves its theme. It remains to say a word about Donne's use of that theme. Man's tendency to idealize his love is treated as a stable and simple fact. That is, the poem not only accepts this fact as if it were the familiar product of observation; the poem also builds upon this, as upon a trusted base of unquestionable truth. It would be absurd to assume that Donne was unaware of certain objections that could be raised against this unchallenged attitude; indeed, not the least effective of these objections could be borrowed from other of his poems. But within "Aire and Angels" this attitude is allowed to maintain itself consistently and without check.

Does it seem surprising to refer to the idealizing of love as a simple fact? After all, we have just seen in the poem what an imposing superstructure of thought is invoked by the mind of love. But what of the intimate movements within the mind, which may be marshaled by thought, but which may also give thought a first impetus? Donne seems to be isolating such a movement, and attributing to it the simplicity of feeling. But the poem never acknowledges what it has done. And so we see Donne treating a movement of the mind as a simple emotional truth, or perhaps as a passion of the mind, at the heart of the mind's famous power to construct its grand architecture.[32]

In "Aire and Angels" the issue between intellectual and physical love is resolved by tempering, without full challenge, the pure, transcendent motive of intellectual love. The poem is a contemplation of love presented as a narrative of the mind's experience. "Loves Growth" may be considered a companion piece in spite of certain emphatic differences. Here the mind unfolds its experience with the effect of narrative immediacy, though there is no suggestion of scene or even of local situation. There is, however, a "thee" whose presence is felt no less strongly, at a crucial moment, than that of the lady in "Aire and Angels." Most important, the mind's experience, though formally an argument, evolves as an excited monologue in which reasons are made to seem events, and in which vivid images and physical details (*pace* Professor Tuve) create effects which serve artistic purposes not unlike those answered by the illusion of scene and action. But this poem, unlike "Aire and Angels," is a contemplation of love that chiefly denies the intellectual status of love. In its version of the conflict between the mind and body the poem concentrates mostly on one traditional form of that dualism, the ancient war between the life of thought and the life of action. One further observation helps establish a kind of external relationship between the two poems. Both are composed of two stanzas which employ (though differently in each poem) a similar basic variation of the sonnet — that is, a sestet followed by an octave.

The poet begins by adopting an attitude of disillusionment, which allows him the rhetorical advantage of directing his ironic doubt at full speed and without preliminaries upon himself and his acknowledged error:

> I scarce beleeve my love to be so pure
> As I had thought it was,
> Because it doth endure
> Vicissitude, and season, as the grasse;
> Me thinkes I lyed all winter, when I swore,
> My love was infinite, if spring make'it more.

The tentativeness, as if the poet were reluctant to acknowledge an intellectual scandal, turns into the open mischief of the fourth line with its progression from the resounding general term for change, "Vicissitude," to that common symbol of flesh and ephemerality, "grasse." The admission of personal error then brings the mischief to a further stage. Love's purity and love's infinity are brought together as two ideas proved false by experience. Love is not a changeless essence, and its finiteness is discovered — not by the usual disenchantment which marks its decrease and registers that proof in the familiar images of winter and death, but by the unexpected results of springtime.

With the octave the speaker drops the pretense and deals more directly with the implications of his idea and its rhetorical development. With himself no longer included in his attack, he adopts a harsh and disillusioned tone not unlike that of "Loves Alchymie." Love is a homeopathic medicine "which cures all sorrow / With more." If it is not only no quintessence, but a mixture of all the elements which pain the soul or sense, and if like other terrestrial things it *borrows* from the sun its "working vigour," then the poetry textbooks are wrong:

> Love's not so pure, and abstract, as they use
> To say, which have no Mistresse but their Muse.

The concept of purity here is on a deliberately lower plane. The poets are called in because they have a reputation as expert witnesses, but their illusions are entirely the product of their own idealizing contemplation. (Their illusions will remain, as a kind of touchstone, between the directly observed *and* contemplated illusions of the second stanza and the illusions that are observed in the first stanza, but contemplated only enough to reject them.) Then, in the final couplet of the first stanza, a clarifying definition of love is advanced which completes this stage of the poem with a positive emphasis:

> But as all else, being elemented too,
> Love sometimes would contemplate, sometimes do.

Love is like other terrestrial things, impure and "elemented," but this is disillusioning only to those who have set their minds on purity. Love has a double nature and is committed (at least alternately, in terms of time) to both the world of thought and the world of action. How this definition applies to the problem of love's increase is not immediately apparent.

Then in the second stanza we return to our contemplation of love from the perspective of spring and growth. We are made to see that the changes are not actual: they are registered by a mind contemplating, not timeless objects of thought, but intermediate objects that relate both to thought and to action. The increase is not ultimately real. Spring does not make love "greater, but more eminent." The increase is part of the inevitable illusion of appearances, the illusion, we may interpolate, that the life of action reveals when measured from the perspective of eternity. At sunrise the stars appear to be magnified but they are not so. The optical illusion is a lesson to the mind. Another "illusion" follows:

> Gentle love deeds, as blossomes on a bough,
> From loves awakened root do bud out now.

This provides a more comprehensive lesson, to both mind and senses. The phenomenon has the full confirmation of our experience, and we respond to it with feeling and with thought. The blossoms express an action that is irrepressible in its immediacy; yet a full sense of the delicate and the transitory is also expressed. The blossoms come and go, as an image of earthly time — a pulsating reflection of eternity.

They unite an image of time with an image of action and express by their appearance and increase the hidden root of the tree and the hidden source of "Gentle love deeds." In this brief view of a garden of Platonic love the presence of sex fulfills its part in the harmony.

Then we have our final image in the series, another optical example:

> If, as in water stir'd more circles bee
> Produc'd by one, love such additions take,
> Those like so many spheares, but one heaven make,
> For, they are all concentrique unto thee.

Like the blossoms, the circles which are produced in the water emerge from the transitory world of appearances and action. They are seen in that world by a mind which is capable of recognizing them as images that have a double aspect. In their motion and multiplicity they represent the immediate world of change; in their meaning, as the mind contemplates them, they are images of timeless ideas and unity. The mind so contemplating is not idealizing naively, with no more than a scant glance at the object. The object is being looked at steadily, both for itself and for the satisfaction of the mind's conscious purpose; and that is to seek images that may explain apparent growth and multiplicity in terms able to satisfy the mind's commitment to the unified and the changeless. The originating force of love takes all apparent additions to itself; its multiple world of addition is nevertheless one, as the heaven is one. What is changeable may be attributed to the immediate life of action, and to the effects of time, and to the responses of the mind mediating between the worlds of pure thought and impure action.

The end of the poem turns upon an image drawn from the familiar experience of political life. The tone is in part a reversion to the tough skepticism with which the poem began.

> And though each spring doe adde to love new heate,
> As princes doe in times of action get
> New taxes, and remit them not in peace,
> No winter shall abate the springs encrease.

The times of action, whether in public affairs of state or in private love affairs, are times of increase. But taxes are not like blossoms or circles in water, nor even like love in springtime. One cannot think that taxes have grown "no greater, but more eminent." The image offered to the mind is that of an object which draws its positive principle from the action of change. Unlike other objects in the poem, it owes nothing to the responses of the mind interpreting between the world of thought and the world of action.[33] The most public and authenticated experience of the poem is directed toward a phenomenon of growth which is no ordinary illusion, but challenges and can withstand the inspection of both direct observation and contemplative thought.

It is not only the tone of tough skepticism which seems to have reappeared. The epigrammatic texture of the beginning, with its nimble play of surprise and reversal, seems consolidated into one baffling final thrust, which does not promise entertainment and the pleasures of the unforeseen, but confronts and contradicts. But does it contradict? We have seen little evidence that Donne enjoys a willful discontinuity; rather, he is a great and proud master of an imaginative logic able to reveal continuity emerging from apparent discontinuity.

If we consider the poem an intellectual drama it is because it develops as a statement which argues with itself, and — in apparent defiance of its underlying control — exhibits a freedom and flexibility of movement which creates the artistic illusion (one that Donne prized) of spontaneity. The mind which acts out the poem does not do so according to the usual prescriptions of the dramatic monologue. That is, we do not have projected a *character* whose inconsistencies are held together by the unifying concept of an individual personality. Instead we have individual attitudes and ideas projected by a representative mind. What unifies is not an idea of personality but an idea, a view of human experience that unites the free opposition and variety of the parts into a whole. We shall return to this subject at the end.

After the initial mockery of the claims that love is a pure essence untouchable by change, we have images that confront in a more complicated imaginative way the facts of change and the facts of illusion. Nature and human nature are not separated, as they are in that ridiculed purity of the poetic abstraction, which arbitrarily detaches literary love from experience. Spring, the buds, the circles in the water appear, increase, disappear, and promise to reappear. They are objects that exist in time, and are characterized by action and change; but they are intermediate objects, as it were; they are accurately observed in nature, but they can be translated by the contemplative mind into meanings which express the mind's deep commitment to timeless thoughts. A certain honest precariousness of balance is maintained, and the possibility of illusion and self-deception is not eliminated — in spite of the warm and tender earnestness of tone. What is transitory in the objects is not denied; only in their interpreted meaning do they demonstrate a permanence by which human feelings may orient themselves. The argument is an imaginative argument, and is protected from assertive claim by the conscious tact and modesty of images offered without insistence to our understanding. In the sensuous immediacy of its appearance love seems greater, as it flowers from the hidden root or as it radiates from the still point of an unmoved mover.

But in the final image the still point is related, as it were, to a moved mover; each spring will, like princes, levy new taxes of love upon the poet. Part of our surprise is due to the fact that the imaginative argument, before the new image, seemed to offer a satisfactory solution to the poem. It is a wrench to have the persuasive eloquence dropped and a version of the earlier tone and manner renewed. Yet there is a structural, or musical, sense which the revival of the earlier tone satisfies, for Donne is also reviving his first theme — that observation of love's seasonal increase which was the formal beginning of disillusionment. He returns to accept the fact of love's increase, but not as a cause for pretended disillusionment, and not as an aspect of appearance which may be translated into an image of reality; instead he produces an image that demonstrates increase as a standard and governing principle in certain human affairs.

This last image is a kind of parody, played out on a human, social plane, of the mind's devotion to modes of thought which derive from concepts of changelessness. But the mockery is not destructive. Once wit has torn down the false pretenses, it can, and does, begin to rebuild. By themselves the illusions of the mind may be hateful; but the imaginative efforts of the mind to establish relations between object and subject, between the life of thought and the life of action – these efforts have a dignity which, though not exempt from laughter, is free from the self-deceit of a willful idealism. The high, pretentious claims of love are disallowed, and then the imaginative claims of love are tactfully re-established by the central images of the poem. These claims, which center on a "thee" and an actual human relationship, are not destroyed by the mockery at the end of the poem, for that mockery is gentle and affectionate, and grants no large exemption to the mind which creates such poems. In its earthly manifestation love must endure increase, gentle love deeds, illusions, and the laughter these provoke; love must endure in a world where taxes also must be. As in "Aire and Angels" the form does not so much reconcile opposites as temper one of them.

The final effect is a difficult balance not unlike that in some of the poems which maintain a binary form. The errors and extremes have tempered themselves, but the result is not quite a seesaw or stand-off. It goes without saying that the result is not a triumphant resolution; what we get finally we may recognize as a modest solution that expresses and accepts fully the human complications. In the poem experience and the abstract means of understanding experience achieve a significant truce – with a minimum of sacrifice or compromise and with a maximum of cheerful good will. We may indeed wonder whether this truce ought not be one definition of the secular and individual wholeness which many wise men have sought in art.

And so we may say that a variety of parts, including a free and unsuppressed opposition, is unified into a whole. That whole may be dynamic and precarious, a delicate balance achieved in movement rather than a still point which is the fixed and governing locus for extraneous movement. The human advantage (which the strict philosopher may scorn as disastrous to his art) is that movement and human experience do not need to be rejected as extraneous, or neglected as a kind of second-class reality.

As in "Aire and Angels," the passion of the mind to abstract and idealize is accepted as a simple fact which it is the business of poetic consciousness to temper. The individual details by which the specific balance is achieved differ, as they may be expected to do. But some of the basic materials themselves, and their imaginative use, are more similar than different. In "The Good-morrow," "Aire and Angels," "Loves Growth" (and "Lovers Infinitenesse," as we shall see) the nature of the balance reflects a central vision of the poet: that vision strives to hold the restless, the multiple, the inventively difficult, in a *satisfied* relationship with the humanly modest and simple.

A quotation from Sir Thomas Browne may serve as commentary on "Lovers Infinitenesse," the example which concludes this chapter.

There are wonders in true affection: it is a body of enigmas, mysteries, and riddles; wherein two so become one, as they both become two. I love my friend before myself, and yet methinks I do not love him enough: some few months hence my multiplied affection will make me believe that I have not loved him at all. . . . United souls are not satisfied with embraces, but desire to be truly each other; which being impossible, their desires are infinite, and must proceed without a possibility of satisfaction.[34]

Like Browne, Donne was also drawn by "a body of enigmas, mysteries, and riddles," and would contemplate that "body" with an eye instructed by the detailed study of his own inner experience. In "Aire and Angels" we noted the determined effort of the mind to understand love and to understand its own nature as that responds to the influence of love. We recognized that Donne was treating an intimate movement within the mind as a simple emotional truth, as "a passion of the mind." In "The Good-morrow" the stubborn refusal to annihilate the past and the external is another example of such "passion," one which opposes the mind's traditional commitment to transcendence only to justify that commitment more fully, and without sacrificing any of the conditions of individual human experience. In "Loves Growth" the mind's desire for purity is crossed by the heart's firm knowledge that love increases, and the solution of the poem must come to terms with that intimate evidence.

Belief in the expanding economy of love is another passion, whether of heart or of mind, summed up in the epigram which concludes "A Lecture upon the Shadow":

> Love is a growing, or full constant light;
> And his first minute, after noone, is night.

Here we may note that Donne appoints an intellectual escape from the infinity of desire which Browne declares to be a fixed and impossible condition of human love. Donne's passionate interest in the "enigmas, mysteries, and riddles" is not willing to accept the impossible for long, or to contemplate it with Browne's ironic detachment. And so the "full constant light" is one lesson which may be derived from a lecture "in loves philosophy." In "Lovers Infinitenesse," however, as in "The Good-morrow," the solution of the impossible is not to be derived as a detachable lesson, but must work its way through a fuller participation in the "body of enigmas."

The opening lines of this poem were discussed earlier as an example of lyric simplicity and the partnership of sound and sense. Though our attention was limited to a specific problem, certain matters which are now of direct interest to us did present themselves in a way which we now can more fully use.

> If yet I have not all thy love,
> Deare, I shall never have it all,
> I cannot breath one other sigh, to move;
> Nor can intreat one other teare to fall.

Our first impression, we noted, is that argument and feeling seem identical. The lover is expressing the lyric desire to possess love completely, and this desire is heightened by the declaration of personal failure. The voice of love rings true and we are not immediately disposed to raise any questions. That the expressed gestures of inadequacy are the conventional ones of a literary lover does not for the moment concern us. We may reasonably think, for the moment, that where the feelings are presented as universally familiar the expression may willingly forgo the lesser advantages of novelty. What does concern us at once is that the confessed sense of limits and inadequacy in love, though its first effect is to intensify the singleness of the lyric desire, also marks a slower motion that will begin to develop what is incomplete and disparate in the lover's desire.

The conventional gestures of the literary lover (the sighs, tears, oaths, letters) assume a sharper focus, and are made into the materials of a leading imaginative idea which is to govern the first two stanzas and is to be transformed in the third. The language of the idea is that of commerce, and here I must enter a prompt caveat. The quality of Donne's wit owes little to any unusualness of the imagery; the commercial references are witty, but they do not signify what they would if this were a modern poem. Their particular contribution will concern us, but we may postpone the matter for a little while. The lover has "spent" all the "treasure, which should purchase thee." He is troubled by the thought that no more can be "due" him than was intended when the "bargaine" was first made. Then the lyric tone of longing for impossibility returns, and the stanza ends on a note similar to that of the beginning:

> If then thy gift of love were partiall,
> That some to mee, some should to others fall,
> Deare, I shall never have Thee All.

The second stanza opens with a kind of lyric which seems most characteristic of Donne:

> Or if then thou gavest mee all,
> All was but All, which thou hadst then.

We need not confront those formidable pronouncements which concern "passionate ratiocination," or "a direct sensuous apprehension of thought, or recreation of thought into feeling." The individual quality of these lines, recognizable anywhere as Donne's, expresses a fleeting and lyrical gift which cannot be fixed by any absolute description or ambitious generalization. We hear an individual voice of great charm and power, a voice we have learned to recognize and admire in many singing and speaking roles, but the art of immediacy in these lines is one for which there are no adequate textbook rules or directions. In the first stanza we heard a voice of love, universally familiar but made individual by the created sense that these feelings were being expressed by an actual speaking voice: "I cannot breath one other sigh, to move." The voice that opens the second stanza is no universally familiar voice of love; its message is direct and personal; the inflections are those of an individual voice addressing an actual person. What is individual in this voice cannot be identified with a movement of the verse by which the feelings are made to seem immediately present, as if acted out by the physical sound of the verse. Instead the imaginative authority of Donne's fiction is both swift and absolute. A general situation and human problem are transformed into a *personal* immediacy by the full and intimate pressure of the speaking voice.

Very well, we have lingered on a special effect which is common to the art of poetry though mysterious to the art of criticism. Now we must return to the formal part of the argument as that contemplates the "enigmas" of love. If the mistress did indeed give all her love, nevertheless the lover can still think of causes for worry. Other men, now or in the future, may create new love in her heart. He has already done his utmost, but they will be able to deal from "stocks intire," and in the familiar commodities of love (tears, sighs, oaths, letters) they will be able to "outbid" him. This new love, not having been "vowed" to him, will create new fears in addition to the general fear expressed in the first stanza. The lyric note then returns, and the business imagery changes into a related but more basic image of possession, that of real estate on which valuable things grow. He reverses himself on the new love that was not "vowed":

> And yet it was, thy gift being generall,
> The ground, thy heart is mine, what ever shall
> Grow there, deare, I should have it all.

The first stanza ended much as it began, on a lyric note of longing for the impossible. Donne chooses to vary the pattern, so that the lyric ending now counters the argument of doubt and advances an affirmative claim.

The last stanza converts the whole argument into a lyrical counterstatement:

> Yet I would not have all yet,
> Hee that hath all can have no more,
> And since my love doth every day admit
> New growth, thou shouldst have new rewards in store;
> Thou canst not every day give me thy heart,
> If thou canst give it, then thou never gavest it:
> Loves riddles are, that though thy heart depart,
> It stayes at home, and thou with losing savest it:

But wee will have a way more liberall,
Then changing hearts, to joyne them, so wee shall
Be one, and one anothers All.

The first step seems to contradict the new affirmative movement begun at the end of the second stanza. One might say that the logic is
denied — indeed, the whole basis of the reasoning — while the affirmative feeling moves ahead without interruption, even though it is attached to other objects and another train of reasoning. This will be
clearer in a moment. From the point of view of this chapter what is
most interesting about the form is the way the solution of the dilemma is reached. Opposites are not reconciled. Instead, the whole
basis of the dilemma, including the special restrictive terms which
have been used to develop it, is rejected in favor of a more fundamental human feeling. The familiar pain of impossibility, "I shall
never have Thee All," was answered by the poet's assertion that his
mistress' heart is his, and therefore whatever may "Grow" there, "I
should have it all." But the desire to "have Thee All" transfers the
traditionally acknowledged infiniteness of love (and its enigmas) to
the finite lover and his projected desire, while at the same time attempting to translate love itself into terms which are finite. The wit
of the image that ends the second stanza enjoys a brief success, but
reveals only its own dead end. No logical transition or superstructure
seems necessary. Donne simply rejects the argument, and contradicts
the specific terms, while renewing the true basis of the feeling: the
love of the finite for the infinite.

"Yet I would not have all yet." Feeling had got on the wrong mental track and up to a point had permitted itself to be governed and
directed by the mind's attachment to the logic of legality, as in "Aire
and Angels" and "Loves Growth" the mind's loyalties had been
partly misdirected and in need of tempering. "And since my love
doth every day admit / New growth"— the "since" does not express
a measured step in logic but the absolute conclusion of feeling, and it
casually relegates the exhaustion claimed in the first stanza to the
status of an illusory feeling. The "new love" created by other men,
which "may beget new feares"— that incidental fecundity is quite
ignored, as if it were simply the result of a misdirection, an irrele-

vance produced by worrying too precisely on the wrong point. The worries which concern time — when the covenant was made, what the intentions were, what the future probabilities and rights will be — these are undermined by accelerating the worry over time until it reaches an impossible absurdity: "Thou canst not every day give me thy heart." The lover's misplaced infinity of desire is fittingly answered by the "every day." The next line concludes this stage of the contradiction by advancing another impossibility: "If thou canst give it, then thou never gavest it." Infinity translated into the manifestations of "every day" is absurd in a way that is partly physical, but the present translation comes from a deeper level of the imagination; if it is absurd it is nevertheless entirely free of the physical. It underlines a psychological truth involving a contrast between ordinary time, when love may think its actions voluntary, and the true time of the heart, which cannot be measured and is not subject to individual will. That truth is in one sense personal and intimate, drawn from the experience of self-knowledge in love; yet, once pronounced, it is recognizable as public truth. The following two lines turn on this pivot. Their truths are drawn from the traditions of experience; they are public religious paradoxes but are equally relevant to the private experience of secular love and its riddling mysteries. They complete the bafflement of love's exchanges, whether by contract or gift. For the heart which remains by departing and is saved by being lost cannot solve its desire for infinity by exchanges — nor even by admitting new growth and expecting new rewards.

And so we may see that though the third stanza contradicted the old basis of the first two stanzas, it involved new contradictions, and these have now been run into the ground. Previously the basis of the reasoning was abandoned, but now the reasoning seems to have denied itself. The paradoxes both mark an end and point the way to a new beginning. It is one which has been potential in the feeling and in the language of the stanza.

As the language of growth succeeded that of exchange, but also proved finally inadequate to express the love of the finite for the infinite, it too must be succeeded. We have a new metaphorical dispensation which is modeled on a pattern of religious experience. The commercial imagery of the first two stanzas is a "sacred parody" [35] of the language of covenant — immediately recognizable to witty contemporaries as a translation of the Old Law into the terms of human love. But love is unsuccessful in trying to interpret the letter of the law, what the intentions were, what the gift meant, the threat of new love inseparable from new fears. There is a deliberate emphasis on material terms, though they are those of literary convention. Only once does Donne import the language of the new dispensation: "And all my treasure, which should purchase thee." Contemporaries, I think, would have noticed that language, familiar in sermons — as, for instance, in the sermon Donne preached in commemoration of Lady Danvers: "in that *kingdome*, which . . . *our* Saviour, hath purchac't for us all, with the inestimable price, of his incorruptible bloud." [36] They should have noticed also that the language remains bound, as it were, by the sighs, oaths, tears, letters of the Old Law. Perhaps the best brief illustration of the issue may be found in Donne's Holy Sonnet XVI. God has made two wills:

> Yet such are thy laws, that men argue yet
> Whether a man those statutes can fulfill;
> None doth; but all-healing grace and spirit
> Revive againe what law and letter kill.
> Thy lawes abridgement, and thy last command
> Is all but love; O let this last Will stand!

The language of the third stanza is the language of revived spirit. It is still a translated language, depending on reference, and though still frustrated it has turned in the right direction. (Only once does the language come close to dropping its veiled translation: "and thou with losing savest it.") But the final emphasis of the poem is not religious, and this honored paradox of the New Testament also serves as the last stage of bafflement. The "way more liberall" maintains its imaginative reference to the revived freedom of spirit in a religion of love; so also does the new metaphor of union by joining. Even being "one, and one anothers All" does not break with the metaphorical language of religious love. Nevertheless, we must make one kind of choice. If the poem has employed the experiences of human love in order to express divine love, then the human base is unwontedly thin and contributes little. However, if a recognizable pattern of divine love has been employed in order to express human love, the references are then rich and gain in reciprocal significance. The universe of poetry does not demand the strict "either / or" decisions familiar in other kinds of discourse. But poetry has its own hard laws and cannot be indifferent to matters which concern the life of its form, the integrity of its proportions, or its essential economy. In this poem neither the psychological experience of the individual lover, nor even the cumulative credit of literary convention, is endowed with a rich public treasury of convertible mythologies and symbols. But the underlying pattern of religious experience is thus endowed, and artistic intention is not likely, in such a case, to falter in the wise management of its affairs.

We do not need to remind ourselves that Donne and his contemporaries did not shrink shyly from witty comparisons between human and divine love. The "way more liberall" and the final image of union can bear both their religious and their sexual references. The sexual references, however, are dominant. If the poem has been primarily concerned with the infiniteness, not of love but of lovers, then the terms of the solution must remain content with the human reference. There is wit in the idea of sexual oneness, and in the paradigm of infiniteness figured in the universe of love. But the wit is not mocking or destructive. It offers a conclusion that is plausible and modest, though smiling and conscious of itself as an imaginative act. The lovers who strive to express their love for the infinite in quantitative terms, in possessing and acting by the measure of time, are baffled. But if they give up their pretentious claims, they can find a large enough paradise of infiniteness within them, "happier far."

There has, after all, been a kind of tempering, by which the conscious mind, subtle to plague itself, has been induced to accept a simple and modest solution. We may infer that Donne uses the old patterns of the mind's experience as other poets use myths, to be built upon, varied, and revealed by art. In "The Good-morrow" a simplicity of feeling achieves its modest victory with the resistance and assistance of imaginative consciousness. In "Aire and Angels" the passion of the mind to idealize its love is accepted as a simple truth, though the passion is one that imaginative consciousness must temper. "Loves Growth," in spite of its mockery, does not dishonor but again only modifies the mind's commitment to abstract means of understanding experience.

In "Lovers Infinitenesse" the speaker arrogates to the lover the infiniteness traditionally belonging to love. He suffers and strives to understand his nature in love, and is thwarted by the enigmas. But the passion of his mind persists; its honor and dignity outlast the personal errors which fall by the way. The end of the poem does not pinch off the lover's desire for infiniteness in love, but that desire has been turned from quantitative extent to qualitative depth. The last lines express a kind of secular and individual humility, which triumphs; they deny both the pessimistic passivity of the first two stanzas and the cheerful initiative that begins the third stanza. They proclaim a solving infiniteness of love, and incorporate the deeper paradoxes of losing and saving, and transform an uncertain contract of partners into a union where the otherness of each confirms joy.[37]

The lovers can encompass the infinite, not as a fact but as an imaginative act, as a microcosmic "pattern" of the macrocosmic universe. Love "makes one little roome, an every where," without needing to think that it has made an everywhere one little room. "Harmless lovers" can accept the miracles of modest conclusions; at least they will not mistake "halfe-acre tombes" for infinity, but can be content with "a well wrought urne." Love, which can endure in a world of taxes, and can accept the angelic embarrassment of "mean ways" and impure wings, can be content with the humble infiniteness of the enclosed moment and the triumphant wit of simplicity.

CHAPTER III

THE BURDEN OF *Consciousness*

"MEANES BLESSE," Donne says with conviction, and, "I hate extreames." [1] A man may love the blessing he does not possess but seeks. He may also hate a part of himself, and for a vast variety of reasons and nonreasons — even when that part of himself gives pleasure, and is exercised with great distinction, and is a proved means to the end he seeks.

Whatever may be new in this study of the forms of Donne's wit, one basic and familiar fact is no more than reconfirmed: that a characteristic movement of his mind is the energetic pursuit of a limited theme. The most persistent form, therefore, is the witty inversion, but as form it is most significant in the ways by which it is transformed. As method the inversion leads directly to an extreme, though it may reach a mean by many indirect ways: for instance, by setting off in the wrong direction and then circling back; by exhausting the possibilities of a position, or the perversities of a native inclination, in order to return with new hope to the old point of departure; by reconciling extremes; by tempering one extreme; by opposing to the mind's imaginative self-consciousness of alternatives a single passionate attachment. These are but suggestive samples and do not nearly cover the possibilities. Almost every poem we have considered at length can provide a detailed study of these and other methods of developing explicit or implicit oppositions.

"Oh, to vex me, contraryes meet in one." That is a cry of anguish, before God. Yet the course of the sonnet [2] confirms Donne's conviction that the contraries are not part of his individual bad luck or

just punishment, but a settled part of God's law for man, which it
is man's good luck to endure. The scope of the present study does
not permit a full treatment of the religious poems, but we shall need
to consult them in order to see some of our problems in the lyrics
more clearly. First, however, we must remind ourselves of the active
presence of contrariety in those poems which we have studied and
in some which the exposition has had to neglect.

When we look at Donne's poems as a whole, we find that the
religious poems, to be sure, have a few special forms of contrariety
and their own distinctive urgency, but that these differences do not
entirely displace the kinds of opposition that are shared by a large
number of his poems. A formal inventory would include most of the
dueling pairs which have been prominent in religious and secular
thought. It should be enough to think of the master conflict between
body and soul; or, to vary the names, between passion and reason,
or multiplicity and oneness, or appearance and reality, or the life
of action and the life of thought. But there is no need to draw up an
inventory. All of the major conflicts which need concern us are
centered in problems of consciousness — in the mind's questioning
of itself and its ways of knowing.

Let us begin with some fresh materials.

> Nothing but man of all invenom'd things
> Doth worke upon itselfe, with inborne stings.

This thought, from Donne's "Elegie on the Lady Marckham," reveals a constant source of one kind of conflict. The gift of reason is
the burden of consciousness. For man is a responsible agent; and
knowledge of his motives and intentions, what they pretend to be
and what they are, and whether they express themselves truly in
his actions, he cannot avoid and would not avoid. Reason is a fearful
gift which makes the concept of man as the microcosm of the universe a pretty image, but one wholly inadequate to express the monstrous talent which man has.

> Greater then due, no forme we can bestow
> On him; for Man into himselfe can draw
> All; All his faith can swallow, 'or reason chaw.

> All that is fill'd, and all that which doth fill,
> All the round world, to man is but a pill.[3]

Man is a responsible agent who must satisfy God, and himself, and also "wise, and good lookers on."[4] But he is also a monster because the power which makes him responsible has no sure power over itself. His talents for diagnosis are subtle, energetic, and radical; they can penetrate with alarming clarity and finality to

> faults in inward parts,
> Corruptions in our braines, or in our hearts,
> Poysoning the fountaines, whence our actions spring.[5]

But what man so clearly sees he cannot by seeing cure. Reason, which freely and actively seeks out causes, can become strangely passive before effects, or can exercise its major responsibility as a minor agent acting mostly against itself.

> So, to the punishments which God doth fling,
> Our apprehension contributes the sting.
> To us, as to his chickins, he doth cast
> Hemlocke, and wee as men, his hemlocke taste.[6]

But the precious gift of consciousness is one which man must maintain though the upkeep is costly — yet still, being a gift, man may do with it what he freely chooses. He may wear his burden lightly upon occasion and may entertain friends and himself with all the mental agility he can exercise. So important a gift could hardly have been entrusted to man if it were not also intended for his pleasure. Use itself is a pleasure, and skillful use may be thought the most significant human game, one which combines a profound delight with the gayest of instruction. Only by exercising his talent can man learn its nature and its range. Only by pitting it against external obstacles and against itself can he learn what it may do and what it may not do; and only by measuring his talent against his discovered needs may he examine both his talent and his needs in conjunction, so that he may learn the nature and the degree of satisfaction for which he may hope. Only consciousness can clearly separate error from truth and fully understand its own capacity to deceive itself.

There is then a gay use and a grim one. These may alternate, or lead one to the other, or they may join together in patterns as various as the imagination of the poet who shapes them. Our background study emphasized the concept of wit as an intellectual pleasure, as the play of the mind which also had a recognized value as an educational discipline. We noted that this concept of wit enjoyed great flexibility and comprehensiveness, that its advantages lay in the breadth and depth of its tolerance of the imaginative, and in its willingness to entertain fictions as an expression of the joyous energy of the serious mind. But such wit also involved accepting the dangers of a strenuous freedom that required a man to be both beholder and partaker of human affairs. No interpreter of Donne, however sympathetic, can escape occasional difficulties in maintaining his own accepted role as beholder and partaker of the experiences presented — even when, in certain poems, he knows that he should know better than to lose his balance. But the difficulty is not a matter of clever tricks which Donne can manage. It is not a self-contained product of individual accomplishment. There is a kind of genuine difficulty that is essential in Donne; out of it he makes an art which speaks of man to men, an art which Donne can control magnificently as a poet though he cannot control it as a man.

We have touched on this problem and we shall need to return. Every poem considered at length has provided some demonstration of Donne's imaginative art of consciousness. The accomplishment is perhaps the most distinguished in our language. Certainly no other lyric poet has used the subject of his own mind so consistently as an object, as an end, of art redirected and reshaped by the disciplined means of art. Few poets who convince us that they are fully present in their poems are at the same time so impersonal. The result is that the lyrics achieve a great variety both in the kind and the degree of consciousness. To summarize that variety may do more harm than good, and though we cannot avoid trying to make some general sense of Donne's art of consciousness, we shall be more prudent if we stop short of definition.

Let us continue by first reminding ourselves of Donne's gay use of consciousness, and here it may be useful to recall a single example, that happy freedom of consciousness demonstrated in "The

Sunne Rising." There, we noted, the world of love, through the office of wit, does not deny or exclude the reality of the external world,
but manages to include the imperfect representation of the world's
body in love's own perfect model of reality. By a delicate and complex balance love is allowed to possess and enjoy the natural illusion that it is superior to time, and that it is composed of the best
moments and materials of the outside world. The imaginative art of
the poem demonstrates a secure knowledge of the ordinary external
world, and of the authoritative experiences of the interior world of
love and contemplation; the imaginative art is able to combine and
balance both worlds with sure mastery of them and of its own form
and status as fiction. The art of consciousness makes its invisible
presence felt but escapes direct observation and questioning. Yet it
is there in the manifest pleasure of the doing, and in the untouched
center around which the poem turns — that happy extravagance by
which the lovers look out on other illusions from their own privileged
and unexamined position. The mind of the poet is at once engaged
in its imagining and detached in its knowledge of what it is doing; it
is both beholder and partaker as it acts and contemplates itself acting.

And so Donne can rattle the links in the chain of being and make
a merry music. He can challenge the laws of nature and the laws of
custom, and the laws of his own nature and his effective knowledge
of those laws. He can rejoice in his powers and convert the familiar
defeats of known weakness into strange victories. The gay use of
consciousness and the grim use are not always kept apart; they join
together and make their own unpredictable discoveries. "I have a
ridling disposition," Donne wrote in a letter to Sir Henry Wotton,
asking him not to have copies made of the work he sent. For the
satires he felt some justifiable fear, and for his paradoxes and certain
elegies a little shame — "Against both which affections although I be
tough enough, yet I have a ridling disposition to bee ashamed of
feare and afrayd of shame." [7] Taken by itself this kind of remark,
depending as it does on verbal transposition, might seem typical of
the polite wit by which friends entertain each other in letters — if we
did not recognize its true and familiar ring.

Time after time Donne draws the old conflicts into new lines of opposition. He melts old metal and mints current coin. He is an absolute master of the public paradoxes and antinomies; he turns to them naturally, whether for pleasure, or exercise, or profit. He contemplates the ironic reflections they cast on human affairs. He can use them in their traditional forms, whether to consolidate or challenge or explode a situation; or, since he knows them all by heart, he can freely rearrange or vary them in surprising combinations.

> How witty's ruine! how importunate
> Upon mankinde! it labour'd to frustrate
> Even Gods purpose; and made woman, sent
> For mans reliefe, cause of his languishment.
>
> .   .   .   .
>
> For that first marriage was our funerall:
> One woman at one blow, then kill'd us all,
> And singly, one by one, they kill us now.
> We do delightfully our selves allow
> To that consumption; and profusely blinde,
> Wee kill our selves to propagate our kinde.
> And yet we do not that; we are not men.

"Oft from new proofes, and new phrase, new doubts grow."

> lesse is their gaine
> Then hazard still, to meditate on ill,
> Though with good minde . . .
>
> .   .   .   .
>
> Arguing is heretiques game, and Exercise
> As wrastlers, perfects them; Not liberties
> Of speech, but silence; hands, not tongues,
> end heresies.

And yet:

> Vertue hath some, but wise degrees of vice.
>
> .   .   .   .
>
> And ignorance of vice, makes vertue lesse,
> Quenching compassion of our wretchednesse.
>
> .   .   .   .
>
> Statesmen purge vice with vice, and may corrode
> The bad with bad, a spider with a toad:
> For so, ill thralls not them, but they tame ill
> And make her do much good against her will.

And further:

> doubt wisely; in strange way
> To stand inquiring right, is not to stray;
> To sleepe, or runne wrong, is. . . .
>
> . . . .
>
> Is not this excuse for mere contraries,
> Equally strong? cannot both sides say so?
> That thou mayest rightly obey power, her bounds know.

And finally, one may conclude these random samplings:

> So may a selfe-dispising, get self-love,
>
> . . . .
>
> For if the 'eye seeke good objects, and will take
> No crosse from bad, wee cannot scape a snake.
>
> . . . .
>
> But most the eye needs crossing, that can rome,
> And move; To th'other th'objects must come home.
> And crosse thy heart: for that in man alone
> Points downewards, and hath palpitation.
> Crosse those dejections, when it downewards tends,
> And when it to forbidden heights pretends.
>
> . . . .
>
> So when thy braine workes, ere thou utter it,
> Crosse and correct concupiscence of witt.
> Be covetous of Crosses, let none fall.
> Crosse no man else, but crosse thy selfe in all.[8]

Donne is indeed a master of the public paradoxes and antinomies.
He mines and refines them for the public purposes of sermons and
for the semipublic purposes of letters and poems which speak to
friends. But the most important purpose of his mastery, the one at
the root of all others, is private: "crosse thy selfe in all." The themes
of his art vary, but the distinguishing cause, insofar as one can identify it with a principal effect which is the distinguishing mark of his
poetic achievement, is the drive for consciousness. Heart and mind
cross each other, and the mind crosses itself. It is an earnest game,
though the stakes vary. It continues through many encounters, no
single one of which may be named as climacteric, and no score can
be kept. Yet the game is as serious as its record is distinguished.

And so the gift and burden of consciousness can be gay, or grim, or gay and grim. As an instrument it is faulty; yet it can never be abandoned except by itself. Though it can be crossed by the heart, or by faith, or by an external illumination, though it may be confronted by its own faults and errors, it alone can inspect those faults and acknowledge them. The other side of Donne's drive for consciousness, as we noted earlier, is the longing to escape from its burden, to go beyond it and shake off the "pedantry" of being taught by sense. But nevertheless he is a tireless explorer of what he can know, and he accepts, however reluctantly, the discipline and the limits of consciousness. One might vary what he says of power and apply it to his own pursuits: that thou mayest rightly obey thought, her bounds know.

Not that we should mistake Donne for a bold philosopher. As theologian he is in general surprisingly unspeculative. It is not thought which Donne explores, but his own thought, and mind, and experience. To a poet, or preacher, of authoritative imaginative power and sensitivity, who can *see*, discriminate, and express, his own mind is an intellectual field quite large enough to command a permanent audience.

And so Donne explores and experiments. Sometimes the oppositions are within the single poem and sometimes they confront each other in different poems and from different contexts. Since he is not a philosopher but a poet, the conflicts are attached to specific situations and to contexts which pulse with life, in which ideas move as dramatis personae in the creation of an actual scene. These remarks of course apply chiefly to the lyric poems, and most certainly to those upon which his reputation rests. But Donne is more than one kind of poet. The one constant which needs emphasizing is the fact of experimentation and opposition. In order to introduce some further remarks on that subject, it is convenient to quote from a didactic essay in verse, the letter to Sir Edward Herbert:

> Man is a lumpe, where all beasts kneaded bee,
> Wisdome makes him an Arke where all agree;
> The foole, in whom these beasts do live at jarre,
> Is sport to others, and a Theater,

Nor scapes hee so, but is himselfe their prey;
   All which was man in him, is eate away,
   And now his beasts on one another feed,
   Yet couple'in anger, and new monsters breed.
How happy'is hee, which hath due place assign'd
   To'his beasts, and disaforested his minde!

Donne seems to be saying that man, through wisdom, can live in harmony with the beasts of his passion, as he lived with the creatures in the ark. There is good precedent for that opening announcement, but it is not a theme which engages Donne, even in this poem, and least of all in the lyrics. The grotesque actions of the passions do interest him, though less in their merely monstrous activities than in their protean manifestations within the temple of reason. The passions, as in good Renaissance Platonism, are not to be banished out of the ark but are to be put in their proper stalls by wisdom, which then can occupy the master suite of the mind. How the inhabitants will "agree" is not Donne's usual subject, but the "disaforesting" of the mind is very much his subject.

   Yet he seldom is interested in following the moral blueprint of the passage just quoted. As a matter of fact, he seems far less imaginatively engaged in the secular poems by the grotesque but predictable inventions of the passions than by the subtler deceits and poses of the mind. In "The Canonization" we can recognize a kind of "disaforesting"—that movement away from external disparateness and false appearances toward the simplicity of an inner world. But Donne is not willing to stop there, and the movement turns back on itself until the external world is included again, epitomized by the lovers. The "disaforesting" is a traditional purgative technique, the first step by which contemplation rejects what is external to its ultimate concerns. Yet Donne is not often willing to chain his mind to that bargain. He can despise the external world with his whole heart from time to time, but not with his whole mind, which has its own reasons and feelings, of which the heart knows nothing, or next to nothing. And so the contempt which wholly rejects the external world is for the most part an extreme, a desperate thrust in a single direction for special purposes, which include the possibility of releasing counter-forces. When Donne "empties" himself of "the world" and its external concerns according to the prescribed techniques of contemplation, he is not likely to maintain this detachment for longer than a poem, even when it is a long poem. The most impressive successes of that uneven masterpiece, the two "Anniversaries," are those passages in which his imaginative mastery of the external world expresses itself with full concern — both stimulated and instructed by his own relations, reflexive, as it were, to what is at once outside and inside himself. Donne is no poet of mysticism or ecstasy. To anticipate a later turn of the argument, as a religious poet he is distinguished not by success but by significant failure, not by the desired triumphs of arrival but by the moving struggle to arrive — a struggle which, we may hope, divine criticism confirms and approves, but which human criticism surely ought to admire and value.

If man's monstrous talent of consciousness can draw all into himself, "All his faith can swallow, 'or reason chaw," then the passions that feed and breed upon themselves are by comparison a more limited and predictable object for the mind to contemplate. The mind watching itself in creative motion cannot be fixed either as object or as subject; nor can it separate itself, except by the imposition of a rigorous discipline, from imaginative acknowledgments of past and present experience in the world. Donne has, as we know, some firm intellectual beliefs in the limits as well as the responsibilities of consciousness. He is not willing to solve his imaginative problems by accepting arbitrary divisions between the inside world and the outside world. He knows the traditional plans for that ark which wisdom is to occupy and command; but he knows too that the plans do not envisage the full circumstances of individual voyages, which may have to be launched on "What sea soever," and — the calm speculations of the drafting board left behind, and with them the admiring confidence of the dry dock — "In what torne ship soever I embarke." [9]

Donne's most distinguished lyric achievements are those poems in which the difficult oppositions of consciousness clarify themselves in conflict and realize a rare and precious balance. But the riddles which belong to the art of imaginative integration are profound, and not accessible to rule and prediction, whether of beholder or partaker. Donne might have applied the words of his ambitious lover to himself as poet:

> Thou canst not every day give me thy heart,
> If thou canst give it, then thou never gavest it.

And so he experiments and explores. Though the most valuable conflicts are within himself and are expressed in single poems, much of the significant refining and "disaforesting" takes place in poems which contradict each other because they are trying the extreme "bounds" of a particular set of oppositions. Every poem is not a full-scale effort to reconcile extremes. The point is at least as obvious as the realization that Donne is not trying to express himself wholly and sincerely in every poem. Yet we cannot afford to neglect what is obvious if it has troubled good critics of Donne.

Consider for a moment "Loves Alchymie." It is the kind of poem which easily lends itself to biographical solutions, to chronologies of Donne's psyche in love's progress. But such efforts, however attractive, are surely misdirected. The poem is a lyric satire that purges the mind by making two extremes destroy each other. The main enemy being attacked is idealized love and its affected pretension to be angelically all mind. The mystery is a manufactured one in which the mind deceives itself and would, like the alchemist, impose its deceptions upon others. Intellectual ridicule runs this extreme into the ground. The other extreme, that of a completely sensual love, is countered indirectly but in its own terms by the specific disgust which the poem engenders. The poem is not conclusive; the purging of error is not likely to satisfy us either intellectually or esthetically. We are never happy to have an ending undo its own beginning or ours, and then leave us more deprived than improved. Yet this, we remember, was one of the acknowledged offices of wit, to clear the ground for proper building. Though we may prefer the more amiable exercises, and especially those which are spiced with gaiety and are willing to turn some of their laughter upon themselves, we should at least see that what Donne is doing here with single-minded concentration is not unlike the process which governs many of his poems. He is "disaforesting" the mind of certain specific deceptions by revealing them in their naked hatefulness. As a complex human relationship love is treated by Donne with all the complexity due the subject — at least all the complexity that his own deep fascination and ranging mind can bring to bear. But not in every poem. For poems may oppose each other in limited skirmishes which are preparations for the great encounters within the single poem. When one extreme is pursued Donne is hardly unaware of alternatives. For instance, man's tendency to idealize love, far from being demolished, is the working basis of "Aire and Angels," but it would be naive to infer that Donne has had a change of mind or heart between poems.

Nor should the reader flatter himself and his own fastidious judgment of decorum by dreaming that Donne's intention was to please and instruct him in one metrical package — until some compulsive breach of taste, or flaw of psyche, seized control and wrote "Loves Alchymie." No rhetorician, or fellow poet, would so underestimate the skill and superb control of these two stanzas. Such speculations are even more idle than wondering whether Donne wrote the poem with his wife in mind or with his imminent marriage in mind; but none of these can compare with the speculation that he had his mother ("Mummy") in the darker and therefore most interesting rooms of his mind.[10] The poem is a stunning piece of satire; neither literal truth nor personal truth, it answers in permanent form a limited and recurrent truth of masculine attitude and feeling.

Donne's poetic refusal to separate the body and soul of love has been famous and influential in the twentieth century. In the course of this study we have also seen how Donne refuses to annihilate the past and the external. We have seen him exclude and then readmit certain passions of the mind — such as the mind's desire to idealize love, or the apparently opposing stubborn desire to ratify the truth of growth in love, or the desire to find an allowable kind of infiniteness in the lover. These are attitudes which we (as modern readers) have come to associate with Donne's poetic vision. Most modern readers are likely to find these attitudes characteristic and attractive. They speak a language of poetry which we have learned to understand and admire. They may be thought to articulate certain needs which we have come to recognize. I review these items, not to assess

their historical accuracy or relevance, but to introduce another characteristic attitude of Donne's poetic consciousness which expresses
itself in similar ways, but is protected by a kind of historical sterility.
That is, it involves intellectual and poetic problems like the ones we
have been considering, but it is not an attitude the modern reader of
poetry is likely to recognize as attractive or relevant to his own
needs. I refer to Donne's attitude toward so-called negative theology.
(Under this term I include a number of loosely related beliefs and
techniques which mark the difference between man and God by rec-
ommending methods of withdrawal from the human, and by coun-
tenancing only negative statements concerning the nature of God.)
Let us for the next few pages consider this particular subject in order
to see whether it alters our view of Donne's mind.

Donne's formal positions as theologian have little sympathy with
the negative approach to God. His own skepticism does not turn
into that path. For though his private relations with God are anguished and radical, his public relations are conservative and emphasize the simple and the certain. At one deep level of his faith Donne
is profoundly convinced of his own nothingness, but it is a nothingness informed (like the creation of the world) by God; and this conviction, although he cannot control it steadily, is anchored to his
belief in the goodness of creation.[11] A few passages from the elo-
quent prayer which ends Book I of the *Essays in Divinity* best illustrate some of the balanced views which underlie Donne's opposition
to negative theology. Since this prayer also provides a comment (useful later) on the doctrine that "meanes blesse," I shall quote more
than serves the immediate and limited point.

as thou did'st so make Heaven, as thou did'st not neglect Earth, and
madest them answerable and agreeable to one another, so let my
Soul's Creatures have that temper and Harmony, that they be not by
a misdevout consideration of the next life, stupidly and treacherously
negligent of the offices and duties which thou enjoynest amongst us
in this life; nor so anxious in these, that the other (which is our better
business, though this also must be attended) be the less endeavoured.
Thou hast, O God, denied even to Angells, the ability of arriving
from one Extreme to another, without passing the mean way between. . . . Yet since my soul is sent immediately from thee, let me

(for her return) rely, not principally, but wholly upon thee and thy word. . . . And that for fame, which is a mean Nature between them [soul and body], I so esteem opinion, that I despise not others thoughts of me, since most men are such, as most men think they be: nor so reverence it, that I make it alwayes the rule of my Actions. And because in this world my Body was first made, and then my Soul, but in the next my soul shall be first, and then my body, In my Exterior and morall conversation let my first and presentest care be to give them satisfaction with whom I am mingled, because they may be scandaliz'd, but thou, which seest hearts, canst not: But for my faith, let my first relation be to thee, because of that thou art justly jealous, which they cannot be.[12]

Donne's convictions as here expressed are simple and substantial, but in their personal management, as in translating the mysteries of faith, or the decisions of thought, into the problems of action, these clear principles enjoy no sweet exemption from difficulties. Even when they unite the decisions of thought with the sincerity of prayer, the solutions will not have surrendered all of their potential enigmas; the beautifully balanced principles, under the pressure of private crisis, may come apart and oppose each other like the materials of paradox. In private Donne has a "ridling disposition"; he is complicated and struggles to understand how the vexatious "contraryes meet in one." But as public theologian he can announce: "because all which can be said hereof is cloudy, and therefore apt to be misimagined, and ill interpreted, for, *obscurum loquitur quisque suo periculo*, I will turn to certain and evident things." [13] The "evident things" are often not unparadoxical, as in the passage that follows this quotation; but one can make some distinctions between Donne's public paradoxes which are chiefly intended to reinforce clear doctrine and the private ones which try his soul, and are chiefly intended to discover what in the agony of conscience *he* can truly hold in hope.

It is the public position, however, which most concerns us for the moment, and this is opposed to the attractions of negative theology.

Canst thou rely and leane upon so infirm a knowledge, as is delivered by negations? And because a devout speculative man [the Pseudo-Dionysius] hath said, *Negationes de Deo sunt verae, affirmationes autem sunt inconvenientes*, will it serve thy turn to hear, that God is that which cannot be named, cannot be comprehended,

or which is nothing else? When every negation implyes some priva-
tion, which cannot be safely enough admitted in God; and is, besides,
so inconsiderable a kind of proofe, that in civill and judiciall practice, no man is bound by it, nor bound to prove it.[14]

Yet even the public position has another side. Donne concludes his
brief sketch of the concepts of God by an act of toleration:

Thou shalt not then, O my faithfull soul, despise any of these errone-
ous pictures, thou shalt not destroy, nor demolish their buildings;
but thou shalt not make them thy foundation. For thou beleevest
more then they pretend to teach, and art assured of more then thou
canst utter.[15]

We recognize an authentic voice of Donne: audible in certain
secular poems, of which Satire III is the most notable document, and
in personal letters, and in semipublic religious poems like "The
Litanie," or in a private religious poem like the sonnet "Show me
deare Christ, thy spouse, so bright and clear," and in the many instances of public preaching when the famous convert suppresses the
obvious temptations and speaks for tolerance, for the essentials in
religion, and for the *via media* of the visible church. This voice may
in part be attributed to Donne's own skeptical awareness of the alternatives potential in human thought, and to his own practiced consciousness of the weaknesses and limits of the human intellect. It
suggests an alert and creative skepticism which, like Bacon's, recognizes the force of negative instances and the need to suspend judgment. Or, to make a modern parallel, Donne like Jaspers also learns
intellectual lessons from the "encompassing," from the abyss of
what he does not know. But he does know enough of the oddities
possible in thought for this knowledge to reinforce his allegiance to
a reasonable middle way, and it is the sober rationalist who dislikes
negative theology. One must also add, to fill out this brief sketch, that
Donne displays an evident generosity of mind — at least toward the
doubts of others. Toward himself generosity would be irrelevant.
His personal relations with God are anguished and not subject to
the laws of limits. He reserves his passionate inwardness for his own
religious experience.

And so it is to *himself* that Donne transfers arguments and attitudes from negative theology. One should of course discount a charming and casual game like that played in "Negative Love," but the persistent and searching intensity of his interest in these ideas cannot be misunderstood by any careful reader. I have emphasized his unwillingness to follow the purgative path of mystic contemplation further than its initial stage. He lacks talent or genius, and if I interpret his mind correctly he lacks conviction; he is not, however, without desire. He is moved by his desire as by a passion of mind, not constant but recurrent — it is an extreme which seeks to oppose his constant drive for consciousness.

Where salvation is the issue it is plain enough why Donne should need to oppose consciousness. What may be less expected, however, is the presence of this attitude in the love poems, and I can best conclude the point by referring to them. But since much of the scope of the religious problem can be illustrated by two brief quotations, let me at least mention these. The first is from the noble "Hymne to God My God, in My Sicknesse." In his rare calm and resignation Donne carries his burden of consciousness once more as a gay gift; and as he approaches "that Holy roome" where he is to join the choir of saints and become God's music, he pauses in a characteristic gesture:

> I tune the Instrument here at the dore,
> And what I must doe then, thinke here before.

The other example, which opposes consciousness, concludes "A Hymne to Christ, at the Authors Last Going into Germany":

> Churches are best for Prayer, that have least light:
> To see God only, I goe out of sight:
> And to scape stormy dayes, I chuse
> An Everlasting night.

The one full-scale lyric exercise in self-annihilation is "A Nocturnall upon S. Lucies Day, Being the Shortest Day." It is a strange poem, one of a kind, and cannot be classified or briefly described. It is fully and profoundly a masterpiece of Donne's individual poetic imagination, but he never wrote anything else quite like it. If we wish to entertain a comparison, the most instructive one is "Loves Alchymie," which is also unique. They resemble each other only in being the single-minded pursuit of an extreme which does not oppose itself but opposes other poems and their extremes. Both poems might be considered witty inversions, though "A Nocturnall" also takes a further step and, like other poems we have studied, but less clearly and more privately, intimates at the end the possibility of a new beginning. The poem devotes its emotional tone and imaginative power to the "last things," as if the subject were Christian death and not the death of love. Against the surface rhythms of the ordinary world of love, which go about their cyclical business, the poet places the slow, deep, resolute movement of his own rhythm. He has been *preparing* toward the mysterious *her* and "her long nights festivall" by concentrating on a negative path of withdrawal, fixing his mind on what he and his love are *not*, and by doing so entering into "her Vigill, and her Eve." It is a kind of ritual (and that in itself is most rare in Donne) through which he empties himself, and his love, of concern with self and love.[16]

In poetic and religious thought human love and divine love, though intellectually distinct, are imaginatively reciprocal. Whether human love be a training ground for divine love, or an elementary lesson leading to advanced knowledge of the idea of beauty, or whether it be an instructive image of the higher reality — the imaginative opportunities of understanding the unknown by the known have seemed too valuable to neglect. Nor has the reciprocality of the relationship been altogether single in its emphasis and orientation. Human love is not so inconsiderable a mystery that those who would speak of it cannot learn much from a similar but different range of experience and knowledge. One cannot read Donne or near-contemporaries without remembering these elementary facts and realizing what a rich imaginative exchange they make possible. (The case is altered in modern literature, where many of the traditional attributes of divine love have been engrossed by human love, and where the sensuous core of love's experience often is translated into a kind of transcendent lechery, or even into the inventions of a solipsistic mysticism. Nor has modern politics neglected to draw upon this rich source both in imagining the love of citizens for each other, and for the state, and in imagining the grand love, immanent or transcendent according to the inscrutable turn of circumstance, of the state for the citizen.)

So we may consider, for the immediate point, that Donne's negative path in "A Nocturnall" is a transfer to human love of attitudes generally perfected in preparing for divine love. We know that Donne is fascinated by the problems of nothingness. It may be less evident that he is also fascinated by the related problems of mystical unknowing, with which he crosses the passionate scrupulousness of his energy to know. We can recall, for instance, the ironies of "Loves Exchange," in which the strength of consciousness demonstrates itself as a weakness in love. Because the poet failed to trust the "first motions" of love, he must make full and painful reparations, one item of which is the prayer, "Love, let me never know that this / Is love." The underlying problem is far from negligible to Donne, in spite of the laughter. The same is to be said of his witty description of that sect of love whose clergymen favor abstract spiritual love: "Their Soules exhal'd with what they do not see." [17] In "Aire and Angels" the laughter is much muted and more delicate as it considers the alternatives between seeing "Some lovely glorious nothing" and seeking to know "what thou wert, and who." In "A Valediction: Forbidding Mourning" the superior lovers are decorated with a compliment intended to make mourning difficult:

> But we by a love, so much refin'd,
>   That our selves know not what it is,
> Inter-assured of the mind,
>   Care lesse, eyes, lips, and hands to misse.

The compliment is not without some playful reserve, as the context makes apparent by its delicate mixture of practical shrewdness and imaginative grace. But if we insist on discrediting those attitudes toward which Donne maintains the imaginative flexibility of contingent belief, we shall have to tear great holes in his poems. Nor could many poets endure more than a very small application of the test of literality.

It would seem wiser to credit Donne with being honestly attracted to some of the doctrines of unknowing. He can be more playful when he deals with the extreme chiefly in its public emphasis than when he expresses his own deep longing to be released from the burden of consciousness. So the tone is gay in "The Relique" as the central miracle of the lovers is revealed: "Yet knew not what wee lov'd, nor why." It is in "The Extasie," however, that we can see Donne's normal balance of attitude. As in "The Good-morrow" the awakening in love reveals the former state of ignorance:

> Wee see by this, it was not sexe,
> Wee see, we saw not what did move:
> But as all severall soules containe
> Mixture of things, they know not what . . .

Here not-knowing carries its usual meaning in ordinary human affairs: it is a sign that one has gone wrong or not far enough. This poem expresses the main emphasis of the best love lyrics, which put their hope in knowledge, though they are wise enough to cross and temper the extremes of consciousness.[18]

One may conclude, therefore, that attitudes associated with negative theology, though they inspire one splendid poem, "A Nocturnall," do not engage Donne's mind so deeply as other problems of consciousness. The ways of "learned ignorance," as the ways of mysticism and ecstasy, do not lead to a simplicity toward which Donne can concentrate the chief talents and resources of his consciousness.[19] Yet it is significant that, in spite of his formal diffidence, he does not neglect his opportunity to cross consciousness with this extreme; and we should note with interest the differences between his public and private emphasis.

We are not likely to find a single explanation that will cover all of Donne's various kinds of extremes, and there is no reason why we should feel an equal responsibility toward all his poems. Besides, it is time to question a little more seriously what kind of blessing is supposed to emerge from what kind of mean. "The Litanie" is Donne's most fully developed argument for moderation. The basic technique is to oppose extremes, to build up an extraordinarily varied and intense world of paradoxes and antitheses which glitter and clash — and do so all in order to justify and illuminate the desirability of "mean ways." The reader familiar with Donne's thought is not likely to question many of the details of the poem, for neither the method nor the desire to reconcile these particular extremes is in any important way unusual. Yet one kind of discrimination is made possible here because of the extent and the systematic nature of Donne's treatment.

In his effort to advance a reconciling mean for every pair of divisive extremes Donne cultivates a detachment appropriate more to a public survey than to a private inventory. His own personal conflicts are not particularly distinguished in the general run but merely serve with the rest. Issues that reverberate through some of the best lyrics are reduced to a brief incisiveness: "From thinking us all soule . . . deliver us"; "That our affections kill us not, nor dye / Heare us." On the other hand, some of the issues equally or more emphatically advanced here have no deep hold on Donne's imagination. We know that he is not himself very much interested in contemplating God in the "creatures," but he still is interested in drawing the convenient parallel: "What in thy booke, thou dost, or creatures say." Perhaps it is not entirely fair to remark that the Elizabethan satirist appears as the Jacobean apologist, going out of his way to include "great courts" as a type of this world's good, and kings as representatives of "majestie divine." We may in part attribute these items to the theme and purpose of his discourse, but nevertheless we can be quite clear on the fact that such items do not characteristically engage his imagination.

These remarks are introductory to a more important distinction. What shall we say of the hope expressed in these lines?

> That wee may change to evennesse
> This intermitting aguish Pietie.

Perhaps the most decisive thing to say is that "evennesse" is not a mean which stirs Donne's religious imagination. It is desirable certainly, but other blessings, though more painful and radical, do more deeply draw and excite his religious hopes. For the most part the evenness of piety represents a kind of religious experience concerning which Donne has little of significance to say. That this is a limit or defect in Donne has been and may be argued; but it is a kind of argument hard to control, and it ought to be introduced by some reminder that Donne's company is rather distinguished in this matter.

My point, however, concerns the fact that evenness in piety should represent the ideal mean, the mean of means. When we do not find Donne deeply stirred by this thought, we may reasonably question the wholeheartedness of his devotion to mean ways.

We may carry our doubt a step further when we consider that the deepest paradox in the poem utterly abandons moderation in favor of an extreme of extremes, one which has no opposite and cannot be reconciled with anything else. The central statement comes in the twenty-third stanza:

> Heare us, for till thou heare us, Lord
> We know not what to say.

The next four stanzas end with brief variations:

> That we may heare, Lord heare us, when wee pray.

> That we may locke our eares, Lord open thine.

> That we may open our eares, Lord lock thine.

> Heare us, weake ecchoes, O thou eare, and cry.

These variations and the stanzas which they conclude profit a great deal from the central paradox, but they add almost nothing to it, and one may well think that the last line quoted detracts. The central paradox is our main concern, and it seems unquestionably to penetrate beyond the normal range where concern for equilibrium and mean could possess any relevance.

Everything depends on God and the immediate experience of relationship with Him. In the long quotation from the prayer which ends Book I of the *Essays in Divinity* I pointed out the emphasis on formal balance. Earth and heaven were answerable to each other, and the proper harmony of the soul required due consideration of its double duty to both kingdoms. What I did not emphasize at the time is the fact that two statements, balanced as if illustrating the esthetic possibilities of the mean, quite undercut the apparent balance and cancel its value. At least this will be true in any moment of crisis, and both statements, since they concern salvation and faith, touch on parts of the religious experience where crisis may be expected. "Yet since my soul is sent immediately from thee, let me (for her return) rely, not principally, but wholly upon thee and thy word. . . . But for my faith, let my first relation be to thee." These are pronouncements which, we know, can justify one extreme of human response to salvation. They can authorize a terrible exclusiveness and cutting certainty turned against others — but that is an attitude entirely antipathetic to Donne. For it is the opposite extreme to which he is most vulnerable — the inner doubt which rises to fill the silences of God, when "We know not what to say." And it is not only this extreme of extremes to which he most profoundly reacts. He also commits himself to lesser extremes; and as religious man, struggling to reconcile his immediate experience with his detached and abstract understanding of that experience, he finds himself directly trusting the wisdom potential in the extreme and preferring it above the established wisdom of mean ways.[20]

> I durst not view heaven yesterday; and to day
> In prayers, and flattering speaches I court God:
> To morrow I quake with true feare of his rod.
> So my devout fitts come and go away
> Like a fantastique Ague: save that here
> Those are my best dayes, when I shake with feare.[21]

Let us return to the paradox that man does not know what to say until God hears him. Two of several problems are particularly relevant to our consideration of Donne, for they involve matters which also bear on the secular lyrics. The first problem is that of consciousness. The poet listening to God presumably has in hand what is knowable in himself, but beyond that lies the unknowable in himself, and what it chooses, or can be coaxed or forced, to reveal of itself; and on the other side the relationship is with a mysterious, unknowable God Who is not the God "of the philosophers and scholars."

A further stress is the standing necessity of bringing as closely together as possible the *immediacy* of the religious experience and the consciousness of participating in it. The problems of Donne as a religious poet, though not altogether different from those of the secular poet, are nevertheless more specialized and fixed. For the religious poet consciousness, which characteristically separates and detaches, must also assume the responsibility of integrating the whole man, who must act. The poet must hope, in the moment of happening, to draw the advocate, the witnesses of fact and fiction, and the detached judge, into the simple unity of one participant who has fully inherited his moment. Consciousness must be satisfied — up to the instant in which it loses its own identity; and unless it is both satisfied and lost the difficult conditions remain unfulfilled.

A further difficulty is that the moment of happening is a lyric moment, and there are no adequate symbols or translations which can stand for that lyric parenthesis. Even when fully achieved, the knowledge of that moment, unlike other kinds of knowledge, cannot be held or repeated by memory without the loss of its inner life. It has to be renewed, performed all over again. The unfulfilled moment, however, when consciousness realizes its failure, is a moment that the poet is used to understanding and expressing. One such realization is that "In prayers, and flattering speaches I court God." In comparison, the failure signalized by shaking "with feare" is the kind of lesser extreme which may be convertible to hope.

Religious literature is articulate and exact in describing the vast variety of failure; success does not have the same motive to speak for itself. Perhaps we could take as one standard of success Donne's pronouncement in a letter to the Countess of Bedford:

nor must wit
Be colleague to religion, but be it.[22]

There is, however, much that is inscrutable in this. We cannot learn from so absolute an integrity anything of its methods and degrees of attainment — nor anything of the familiar anguish in the conflict between consciousness and spontaneity. It is better to rely on our detailed knowledge of Donne's ways and to conclude that consciousness in practice must, while recognizing what it does not know, also assume the responsibility of what it does know. If consciousness is to be assimilated or transcended, it must preside at its own dismissal.

We can convert some of these materials to a problem of secular poetry if we turn to a matter which concerns Donne's modern career. In the dominant power and tenacity of Donne's consciousness we may mark one kind of antithesis to the mythic imagination, which characteristically moves below the level of conscious thought and by renewing old forms and gestures recovers the established patterns of past wisdom. Donne turns from the externals of myth even more positively than from ecstasy and mysticism. He may be discontent with merely new knowledge and yearn deeply for better knowledge, but his most prominent actions as poet are individual and experimental: no one has ever regarded his poetic aim as the recovery of past wisdom. Yet we must recognize that as a term and concept "myth" has become intricate and ambitiously dynamic. Besides, we know too little concerning the basic forms which poetic imagination follows and varies to be comfortable with a surgical distinction. So, for example, though a logical and rhetorical poet, Donne is not therefore an antimusical poet. Even without attempting either a hard definition or a final assessment, it would seem wiser not to call him an antimythic poet simply on the grounds that he rejects the externals of myth.

In studying the ternary forms I ventured the suggestion that Donne possessed an imaginative sensitivity to certain ancient patterns of the mind's experience, and that these patterns were to him what myths are to other poets. It was not my concern to present a case — nor is it now, since the elected problems and emphasis have other commitments — but in following some of the deeper movements of Donne's wit I noted, as a kind of evidence, ways in which the intimate and simple motions of the mind influenced and resolved surface perplexities. The fidelity in the mind's experience of itself, the reconciliations and temperings, the surprises and returns, the delicate sense of the most inward motions of the mind, those even which seem to precede the mind's awareness of its own activity — these may not correspond to a poetic deployment of public myths, but neither are they to be excluded arbitrarily from the scope and practices of the mythic imagination.

Donne does not, it is true, satisfy the modern appetite for the mythic. But even here something ought to be said. A renewed interest in myth, collaborating with discoveries and rediscoveries concerning the individual psyche and the history of the psyche, has deepened the modern awareness of forms which are familiar in myth but are not the exclusive property of myth. Nor do these forms contradict or supplant, though they may influence, the conventional forms of plot, argument, and rhetorical organization. Or to make another point, the freshness of Donne, and the coincidence of his poetic revival at a time when poets were turning from a tradition felt to be exhausted, had some of the initial effect of disclosing a lost poetic vein of rich potentiality. Some of that experience has by now been assimilated and transformed. But in his first impact during the 1920's and 1930's Donne helped teach modern poets how to convert some old artistic resources into the poetry of a new age. Donne did not make any old myths available, though he helped sponsor a few critical myths. But he did make available poetic forms and attitudes which offered the kind of stability that poets value since it allows them to turn the old materials of poetry into new and individual purposes of expression.

Our age values the common and stable language provided by myth and also values the revelation of deeper forms and patterns of meaning in art — some of which are to be associated with myth, but not all. By general critical agreement Donne has been a powerful force in sharpening both the precision of modern readers and their sensitivity to the subtler forms potential in poetic language. Three brief illustrations will clarify my point. First a quotation from H. B. Charlton's *Shakespearian Comedy*:

The appreciation of Donne is distorting the valuation of Shakespeare. . . . To our most modern coteries, drama is poetry or it is nothing; and by poetry they mean some sort of allegorical arabesque in which the images of Shakespeare's plays are far more important than their men and women.[23]

It is an interesting complaint and, whether just or not, the attribution of the damage to Donne is significant. The charge is summed up by saying that to "our most modern coteries" only "form" counts.

The second quotation is from S. L. Bethell's *Shakespeare and the Popular Dramatic Tradition*:

The pleasure apparently aroused in the Elizabethan theatre by a concurrence of seeming incompatibles is obviously related to the vogue of 'conceited' writing, especially as practised by the so-called 'metaphysical' poets; it is worth remembering that the important works of Shakespeare were contemporary with the secular poetry of John Donne.[24]

Finally, let us take note of a recent defense of Shelley, whose poetic reputation has been severely challenged by the metaphysical revival. Earl R. Wasserman's *The Subtler Language* interprets Shelley's method as a kind of dialectical drama, by which the poet creates his poetic form through an ironic process of redefining his imagistic arguments. The "subtler language" is one that creates and reveals imaginative patterns of poetic structure emerging from the images. Before the revival of Donne the need for such an argument, as the means for making it, did not exist. We do not have to give Donne all of the credit, or blame, but we cannot escape acknowledging the force of his influence and example on modern readers.

There is another point at which Donne touches on modern attitudes that surround the mythic. Since there is no longer a valid common language of myth and symbol which poets may use with confidence, part of their creative energy must always go into extensive refining of what is generally available. Even more demanding, and no doubt often exhausting, is the frequent effort to invent a partly private language and raise it to the level of general validity. The point is that no major artist can accept any longer the general validity of the poetic language he has inherited. He must instead expend on means much of the creative energy which luckier poets, we may suppose, were able to devote to ends. It is in this respect that Donne has provided a valuable example for modern poets. His own effective use of the resources of consciousness made him a major instructor of poets who had come to feel that their own problems of expression were basically similar to his. Donne also had inherited beliefs and ideas which he could not build on directly, whether he wished to or not. He also had doubted the stability of his language and what it represented. Yet while expressing his imaginative consciousness of alternatives, and his awareness that the poetic materials were imaginatively tentative and fictional, he was able to create poems of great penetration and power.

Such poems are always their own esthetic justification; however achieved, once recognized they assert their own accomplishment. The materials may have been tentative, lightly held and perhaps dubious; the results may even be unsettling: but once we recognize the authentic power of a poem we have also admitted the inner stability of its achievement. We may wonder at, or envy, or even deplore both means and end. Such responses have, and make, their own significant histories. Perhaps it is worth adding that it is always easier to doubt separate esthetic "facts" than their composite existence in an esthetic achievement. The main point I wish to emphasize, however, is that Donne did achieve a certain stability out of apparent instability, and that this example, though not always understood in its historical context, did seem relevant to the problems and needs of modern poets.

Not all of the inaccuracies are to be charged to the poets, who, whatever they have said, have proved themselves by their practice not unable to learn from Donne's diction, his rhythm, his firm sense of structure. That they made him too modern in some respects we may acknowledge — without wishing to occupy the other extreme, and to prove him a minor poet entrenched in the seventeenth century, able to say very little to us, and that little requiring the mediation of learned guides and custodians. The scholars have made their errors too. But this book, though attempting to profit from both disciplines and to speak only the truth, is not confident enough in its purity to publish a final score. Donne's quarrel with himself may not be so deep and sustained, nor so radical in challenging the accepted regulations of individual and social existence, as the private quarrels out of which modern poets have attempted to make some of their poetry. But modern poets have not been entirely wrong in feeling a kinship with Donne's imaginative effort to achieve a precious equilibrium between the most inward parts of the self and the same necessities of the external world which register themselves on ordinary citizens inhabiting a daylight world of logic and common experience.

Let us assume that Donne's accomplishment in poetic consciousness is clear enough by now so that we may safely draw a distinction that must be made in order not to overstate the relationship between

Donne and modern poetry. If we acknowledge that Eliot's use of myth and symbol represents a poetic success which overcomes the typical difficulties of the modern poet, then we may see where Donne both approaches a modern attitude toward myth and finally diverges. In his critical prose Eliot frequently describes the poet as being both more primitive and more civilized than his contemporaries; the good poet will be conscious or unconscious "where he ought to be"— according to the stage and level of the poetic assignment.[25] The description is not without problems, but let us accept the apparent import without trying to worry it. At this point we can see the unmistakable relevance of Donne, who is highly civilized and conscious in his deployment of materials, but who is, in the famous operations of his "undissociated" sensibility, in his power of feeling, and in his being "expert beyond experience," also primitive. The divergence may be marked by the development of Eliot's own poetic practice. The circular movement of the *Four Quartets*, the ritualized uniting of ends and beginnings — these represent a "mythic return," a recovery of past wisdom by submitting the discipline and the quick immediacies of consciousness to purposes which are "primitive." Presumably Eliot is conscious "where he ought to be," though admirers of his poem will not easily enter into the more delicate discriminations between conscious and unconscious writing, but will instead face the familiar stability of integrated poetic achievement. There is, however, one significant public role which Eliot sets for consciousness. The reward of returning, of arriving where you are, is that then you may know the place for the first time. It is a reward of consciousness which cannot be entirely different from rewards posited or achieved by Donne — not if consciousness is conceived of as having depth as well as breadth. The difference is that in Donne the return is not often so clearly set as the goal — though in the ternary forms we often return, as if by a spontaneous or inspired logic, to the old beginning redefined by experience. But when this happens the efforts of arriving are likely to yield the new knowledge that the place is preciously, if painfully, different from where one started. If we measure Donne by Eliot's accomplishment, Donne is most certainly not a mythic poet.

When Donne uses the imaginative materials of poetic thought he consciously does so in ways that emphasize their fictional status. He makes these materials compete, as it were, with other materials and with other elements of consciousness. He may long to reduce, to resolve the image into the idea; but as poet he has a disciplined consciousness of the knowledge to be won by controlling the subtle differences between the image and what it imaginatively represents. It is a lesson learned in the school of wit and it involves the simultaneous practice of judgment and fancy. In effect it is a poetic process of discovery rather than of recovery.[26]

One may draw a similar conclusion from Donne's use of sensuous immediacy. He is less often interested in the standard rhetorical aims of perspicuity, by which the idea is made to shine through the flesh, than he is in endowing the parts of a competitive argument with energy and life. His purpose is not to identify himself or a leading idea with a commanding immediacy of expression. Nor does he cultivate the assimilative powers of symbol. Instead he practices an art of metaphor and creates his imaginative harmonies out of similarities and differences, without either suppressing or quite assimilating the differences. If we wish to mark the range and quality of his poetic accomplishment, we may do so without believing in his (or any poet's) absolute fusion of thought and feeling. We shall have enough to do in recognizing his complex art of nonfusion, the fine degrees of immediacy and detachment he can control.

The best of the secular lyrics are characterized by the sureness with which they balance their complex materials and by the powers which they release in motion. Donne valued and cultivated spontaneity, not as an easy appearance or whimsical freakishness, but as a genuine effect and end of his art. His most profound mastery lies in the inventions of heart and mind which in their quick circumstances and local trials yet fulfill the imaginative logic and form of a poetic argument. We have studied some of the freshness and gaiety in the witty inversions, and some of the complex balances created and maintained by the binary forms. Though I implied that Donne was a dissatisfied master of binary forms, we did not find his ternary forms lacking in mastery of balance. When, in the greatest lyrics, full imaginative resolution is achieved, it is never at the expense of consciousness; instead, the quantity and quality of elements controlled by consciousness would seem to increase. Donne is a restless genius, but he is marvelously patient, modest, and tactful — not in specific propositions, or the logic of their development, which is often mischievous, but in the larger scrupulousness of his discrimination between imaginative and literal truth, and between experience and the abstract means of understanding experience.

If we glance, for one final time, at the religious lyrics, we cannot mistake one difference in their commitments. The fictions are fiercer and are driven harder: "At the round earths imagin'd corners"; "What if this present were the worlds last night?" The balance of opposites no longer can express joy, but is more nearly an art of painful necessity and a driving toward crisis beyond which release may be hoped for. I have noted that Donne the man is also troubled by the freedom the poet exercises, by the forms which art creates as marvelous answers which balance and forestall, which deflect or defy — answers which are imaginative acts against questions that, to the man, have a literal and permanent side. In the religious lyrics the literal is more insistent, and would, as it were, convert the fictions.

Donne's passionate drive to resign himself in God does not find its characteristic expression in purifying the present in order to recover past wisdom. As Christian influenced by Platonic thought and imagination, he must of course think in these or similar ways. One may recall the prayer quoted from the *Essays in Divinity*: "Yet since my soul is sent immediately from thee, let me (for her return) rely, not principally, but wholly upon thee and thy word." But his religious expression does not endeavor to unite end and beginning in the imaginative form of a "mythic return." [27] In "Goodfriday, 1613. Riding Westward," he concludes:

> O Saviour, as thou hang'st upon the tree;
> I turne my backe to thee, but to receive
> Corrections, till thy mercies bid thee leave.
> O thinke mee worth thine anger, punish mee,
> Burne off my rusts, and my deformity,
> Restore thine Image, so much, by thy grace,
> That thou may'st know mee, and I'll turne my face.

God's word is immediate and individual, and Donne's characteristic expression is influenced by this belief. He does not seek known paths, or ensure his progress by practicing a poetic devotion of gesture and ritual. Donne has faith in the ultimate beginning but not in any beginning which he may make. To turn into the troubled self with enough confidence to convert obstacles and terrors into the familiar comforts of a known path to a known destination — this requires a kind of initial assurance that Donne as a poet seldom possessed. In comparison beginnings are easy for Milton, who is a great but different religious poet. As for George Herbert, whose anguish may not be less than Donne's, and whose poetic method can bear close comparison with Donne's, his beginnings demonstrate a profound faith in the underlying order of their consequences. With Donne the anger, punishment, and burning are less metaphorical than actual; and the violence of the necessary means, whether the same ultimate "image" be "restored" or not, must proceed by unfamiliar paths to an uncertain destination.

> Yet grace, if thou repent, thou canst not lacke;
> But who shall give thee that grace to beginne? [28]

So long as that question can be raised it is unanswerable.

There is one major exception to these remarks on the religious lyrics. It is a beautiful poem which we have glanced at before, and it significantly underlines differences in Donne's general poetic practice. That the "Hymne to God My God, in My Sicknesse" is a poem which expresses religious "success" rather than "failure" we may note in passing; our immediate interest, however, lies in its tone and manner. Though the circumstances are grim, the poem is an example of Donne's gay consciousness. The calm confidence of the beginning is apparent at once, as Donne tunes his "Instrument" at the door of death, "And what I must doe then, thinke here before." He begins where most of his other religious poems aspire to end; the path and the destination are assured, and wit can embrace its benevolent ironies without violence. By their love his physicians have become cosmographers and he their map.

> I joy, that in these straits, I see my West;
> For, though theire currants yeeld returne to none,

What shall my West hurt me? As West and East
In all flatt Maps (and I am one) are one,
So death doth touch the Resurrection.

Notice how easily, without need for a second look, these fictions accept themselves. The gap between the image and what it represents, which it is one of Donne's great achievements to maintain and richly explore, does not concern him now. He knows that he is constructing a fiction by the use of images; but the images are such, and his attitude (somehow, by whatever grace) is such, that the difference between image and idea is a bridge to be swiftly crossed, with great advantage, rather than a marvelous lookout for surveying both sides and the significant possibilities of relationship. Consciousness, we could say, has achieved spontaneity.

The graceful transition from metaphor to symbol is accomplished with authority in the last two stanzas:

We thinke that *Paradise* and *Calvarie*,
    Christs Crosse, and *Adams* tree, stood in one place;
Looke Lord, and finde both *Adams* met in me;
    As the first *Adams* sweat surrounds my face,
    May the last *Adams* blood my soule embrace.

So, in his purple wrapp'd receive mee Lord,
    By these his thornes give me his other Crowne;
And as to other soules I preach'd thy word,
    Be this my Text, my Sermon to mine owne,
    Therfore that he may raise the Lord throws down.

"We thinke" marks the conscious fiction, as Donne refers, though not as to a dogma, to one version of a Christian cyclical myth. The legend that the cross was made of the original forbidden tree may be an esthetic indulgence or extravagance by which folk art improves on history — as Donne's contemporary and fellow skeptic, Bacon, might have said. But Donne's detached sense of an imagined story is entirely assimilated into the feeling sense of believed truth when God is invoked as witness that the Adams of sweat and blood are "met in me." And the throwing down, in this "Sermon" at least, is accomplished without violence or anguish; for Donne begins the poem assured of its end, the raising up.

Though the process of the poem is not simple, the final effect is one of calm simplicity. Part of the reason for pressing this example is the fact that, though its harmony is perhaps unique in Donne, the poem does not stand by itself as an isolated triumph over an isolated problem. Attached to religious simplicity, that integration of consciousness into spontaneous thought and action, there are severe conditions, which are well known; and the goal is, however difficult, also very specific. We can mark, and learn from, the parallel; for in the course of our study of Donne's wit we became increasingly aware that underneath the dazzling complexities of the secular lyrics there is a significant concern for simplicity — if the right conditions can be fulfilled.[29] A balanced view of Donne's constitution as a poet requires recognizing his capacity for intense and simple feeling, and his deep desire, though it is not continuous or systematic, to resolve the problems of consciousness.

The older critics were justly impressed with Donne's tenderness as a lover, and though this conviction prompted sentimental distinctions between the poems Donne must have written to his wife and those other poems, nevertheless these critics did have one grasp of a substantial esthetic truth which is missed if we think only of Donne's iconoclastic wit and brilliant constructions. Donne is brilliant and individual — we need to see this; but he is no merely ingenious transformer of commonplaces (as if he scorned or feared them), no inveterate producer of exotic conundrums and complications. He is also the poet who conducts his imaginative explorations from this home port:

> Fill'd with her love, may I be rather grown
> Mad with much *heart*, then *ideott* with none.[30]

And he is the poet of no idle epigram,

> And learn'st thus much by our Anatomie,
> The heart being perish'd, no part can be free.[31]

The center of "A Valediction: Forbidding Mourning," as of "Sweetest love, I do not goe," is a simple one of human feeling in a common, inescapable situation. The intellectual indirectness of the poems, their excesses and conscious fictions, are the necessary means of expressing with tact and imaginative delicacy a basic pattern of human relationship. In "A Valediction: Of Weeping" his mistress is the lover's heaven, whence tears originate — a commonplace that springs alive by its astonishing literalness and by its imaginative precision. Under the steady flow of inventions he can express the delicate logic of a real grief and a real need to suppress it. He shifts not only from "me" to "thee" (and to his concern for her grief), but from the image of minting to a deeper source of grief, the mutual dangers of oneness. Though his arguments develop indirectly and subtly, what they express is capable of endless human repetition and engagement because the experience is widely familiar — as fact essentially simple, but as experience infinitely complex.

The complexity of Donne's consciousness, and the dazzling structures it creates, can obscure for us one essential and defining effort of his intellect. We admire the way his mind explores its own limits for the sake of pleasure and understanding, the way it can oppose itself and laugh at an impasse or the beautifully concealed trap of a dead end. Such activities were, and still deserve to be, admired — so long as the old idea of wit as intellectual pleasure can exert any claim. For Donne still is, in this good old-fashioned sense, the wittiest poet in the English language. But he is also a poet deeply eager to break through the intellectual complexities, and to use them against themselves as a means of discovering, or rediscovering, the simple truths which the mind complicates. For in these matters mind is both ally and opponent, and finally judge. Donne's efforts and ways are certainly individual to himself but his goal is hardly unfamiliar. Two quotations from philosophers who are both different and individual in their ways may serve to illustrate the basic point. The first is from Plotinus:

Withdraw within yourself, and examine yourself. If you do not yet therein discover beauty, do as the artist, who cuts off, polishes, purifies until he has adorned his statue with all the marks of beauty. Remove from your soul, therefore, all that is superfluous, straighten out all that is crooked, purify and illuminate what is obscure, and do not cease perfecting your statue . . .[32]

The second quotation is from Ludwig Wittgenstein:

Why is philosophy so complicated? It ought to be *entirely* simple. Philosophy unties the knots in our thinking that we have, in a senseless way, put there. To do this it must make movements as complicated as these knots are. Although the *result* of philosophy is simple its method cannot be, if it is to succeed. . . . The complexity of philosophy is not its subject matter, but our knotted understanding.[33]

To conclude I may use Donne's own firm statement once more and now apply it to the struggles of consciousness and simplicity in the *Songs and Sonets*: "*Knowledge* cannot save us, but we cannot be saved without Knowledge; Faith is not on this side Knowledge, but beyond it." One mark of his greatness as a poet, and his endurance as a man, is how seriously and patiently he held to these hard terms.[34] Even as a love poet spinning marvelous fancies in and out of truth, he displays an exactness of discrimination and a refusal to cut his knots without having mastered them. The imaginative power, the intensity of feeling, and the mastery of discipline — in Donne these may bear comparison with the urgent relations of knowledge and faith.

But I do not want to end on the note of strenuousness. I wish to remind the reader that Donne's most impressive reconciliations and truces are marked by a cheerful good will, by a rare and amiable austerity of comic spirit. He is a love poet without peer in expressing that masculine love which protects and assures by the sincere compliment of shared laughter. The best performances are carried through with an unmistakable gaiety and high instructive delight.

ON DONNE'S *Modern Career*

OF ALL the qualities which engage our interest in a writer, his newness is the one most inevitably subject to extension, consolidation, and loss. It cannot remain as it first was. Once the experience has been widely shared, and given a rational explanation, its capacity to produce excitement will be countered by the rigid scholasticism it also promotes, and by the gradual exposing of inadequacies and faults. These are troubles which always beset the most ambitious and disciplined products of the mind.

Yet the sense that a writer is in some way different and new commands our interest, and cannot be quite separated from our desire to understand him in his wholeness. (The motive is not less powerful even when a writer seems new because he has been misunderstood, or because the times have carelessly forgotten what once was more generally known.) We guard against arbitrary and factitious claims, we correct, we redress balances; but not many students of literature consciously oppose the right of the sense of novelty to affect our experience of literature. The arguments are more likely to concern the accuracy of claims and their conformity with the knowable facts.

Time, and the students of time, are sure to cooperate in disabusing us of errors. We should not be surprised, however, if the effectively disenchanting accounts appear well after the first sense of freshness has lost its creative charm. Indeed, as with other human constructions, the walls may be entered, the inadequacy of their position and their very structure exposed in detail — long after the true builders have decamped. Not seldom what we learn is why what is no longer defended was indefensible.

I am not thinking, at the moment, of criticism that may be regarded as hostile to Donne or to his modern sponsors; what I have in mind are two sober, modest, and persuasive accounts of nineteenth- and early twentieth-century critical response to Donne — Joseph E. Duncan's *The Revival of Metaphysical Poetry* and Kathleen Tillotson's "Donne's Poetry in the Nineteenth Century." No one is likely ever again to think that informed appreciation of Donne began only in the second decade of the twentieth century. And yet, granted that there is an older history behind the modern sense of Donne's newness, that modern sense does create its own history, for which there is no precedent. The decisive difference is this: in the twentieth century Donne was not a minor influence in a critical crosscurrent but entered a mainstream. Critical response became an active partner of creative response, a partner of the best of the new poetry being written. For instance, Yeats and Eliot make critical comments on Donne and, besides, refer to him in their poetry. The references are complimentary; but more than that, they exhibit and create admiration and understanding; most important of all, they imply that there is an angle at which modern imaginative creation coincides with the poetry of Donne.

What is constant here is the prestige that accrues to Donne. It is a general prestige of great value. In one sense it is fixed and even measurable if we knew how to measure such things. But in another sense the prestige is dynamic. It enters the world of poetry and alters established relations, and it may release unpredictable energy in new directions. Furthermore, the prestige of the sponsors must be taken into account. If Yeats and Eliot, when they praise Donne, have not reached the peak of their own prestige, and do not make their pronouncements as the honored representatives of a cultural order which looks back on its best accomplishments; if, instead, their prestige is growing and their accomplishments point the way to further accomplishments, both by themselves and others, and to further recognitions of the worth and meaning of their accomplishments, then we have a situation that produces great force. The increase in Donne's prestige will have immense weight and power, which are terms of measure, though we cannot translate them accurately.

When Yeats and Eliot implied that there were angles at which their own imaginative creation coincided with that of Donne, they stimulated other poets to find *their* individual angles of relationship. This is a fact we had better grasp firmly, for it is a key to the problem of influence. At its best literary influence liberates, though not necessarily all at once. It first imposes a point of view (sometimes in the shape of an intimidating achievement), and the advantage of that point of view can seldom be gained without some initial discipline in imitation. But if the new form of knowledge is genuinely creative, it acts by freeing the individual poet and by helping him to realize his own full powers.

What a poet needs most he is most likely to get from a contemporary or near contemporary. And yet the closer poets are in time the more immediate are the personal tensions. The first effects of influence may be to constrict more than to liberate, and these effects are sure to be resented — not without reason, for they may permanently misdirect or disable the young writer. On the other hand, the poet of an earlier age, no matter how close he may seem to be to the real interest of the later poet, is also different. What is the same can safely inspire, and what is different may be thought one kind of historical protection for the identity of the modern poet. A poet can hardly avoid being interested in the individual ways his predecessors met and solved their own defining problems. He is accustomed to looking for oblique hints. We may therefore expect an unusual excitement when an old poet, who can offer no threat to the identity of the living poet, is elevated to a kind of honorary citizenship among the moderns.

When Eliot, in 1947, explains his earlier attitude toward Milton, and in the course of that explanation describes the program of his own poetic generation, he admits, not without some evident embarrassment at the results, that the preference for Donne fostered some excessive opposition to Milton. The program he describes, however, unmistakably leads to Donne:

It was one of our tenets that verse should have the virtues of prose, that diction should become assimilated to cultivated contemporary speech, before aspiring to the elevation of poetry. Another tenet was that the subject-matter and the imagery of poetry should be extended to topics and objects related to the life of a modern man or woman; that we were to seek the non-poetic, to seek even material refractory to transmutation into poetry, and words and phrases which had not been used in poetry before.[1]

Eliot's analysis of the poetic situation seems clear and self-evident. We may let that stand while we seek to supplement it with other reasons for the poetic influence of Donne. When Eliot remarked that Donne "enlarged the possibilities of lyric verse as no other English poet has done,"[2] he was not making a statement of absolute accomplishment which put Donne's poetry in the balance against all the other cooperative achievements in the English lyric. The emphasis falls on Donne's originality, and even more on the *possibilities* which Donne made available. To literary men of the twentieth century, distrustful of "absolutes," Donne's apparent ability to get along without abstractions, or to endow those abstractions he used with a freshness of physical, dramatic immediacy, commanded attention. Furthermore, models for the use of ideas and attitudes, not as a fixed foundation on which to build, but as part of the structure of conflict itself, were less available in poetry than in fiction. James and Conrad, to mention only two modern masters, had shown how ideas could be put into active jeopardy, and thus made to participate in the very body of the imaginative action. But models available in the more economical art of poetry were wanting — at least until Donne's practice helped instruct a generation of critics, and made them more alert to the subtle motions within the poetry of others.

If we set Donne against Browning, whose influence on modern poetry cannot be dismissed, the comparison serves chiefly to emphasize the superior brevity and concentration of Donne's verse. In Donne the suppressions and gaps are less *posed*; they do not suggest character and action as on an external stage. Rather, they suggest the action of thought, and the audience is involved by its participating in the motions of logical and imaginative understanding. Donne gives us a drama in which the most important action is internal, whereas the usual dramatic monologue, like Drayton's most famous sonnet, gives us a drama of situation, a conflict externally staged. Donne's drama is therefore barer, more stripped away — as if to demonstrate one of the tenets of the symbolist esthetic. In Donne the physical is conveyed less by stationing characters and forming a scene than by the constant press of feeling detail, produced, as it were, from the very heart of the conflict.

If we look at Donne in his age — even after we have attended the lessons by modern students of Renaissance rhetoric — we may see that some of Donne's differences from his contemporaries can be attributed to his pressing harder than they, and specializing, the general rules of fitness and logical exactness. The effects of differences in the emphasis or combination of poetic materials may be radical enough, even when the old laws of rhetoric have not been subverted. This made for less richness, range, and amplitude, but for harder rules, and surprising rewards, within a narrower circuit. He put more drive, more intensity, more tension, in the *difference* between the image and what it stood for. Wit (the recognition of similarity) and judgment (the recognition of difference), which later critics were to separate into two distinct faculties, he drove closer together, in order to achieve more significance, more surprise, more shock — and all within a tighter form. What he sacrificed in literary range did not concern the poets of the 1920's, who were interested less in what Donne did not, or could not, do than in what he showed the way to do.

The chief lesson to modern poets was the demonstration of self-consciousness, not as an enemy to imaginative creation but as a potential ally. Donne's skepticism in a world of change, his fierce introspection, his powerful turning of recalcitrant or hostile materials into poetic triumphs — these were likely to interest poets who felt themselves at the end of one age and at the beginning of another, who felt themselves distressingly conscious of their consciousness that the new age was a difficult one in which to write poetry.

Consider Stephen Spender's statement that the central problem of the poet is "to be able to relate his talents to the life of his times, so that through them he can transform a wide experience of the life of that time into his poetry . . . [and] transmute the antipoetic material of modern life into transparent poetry." The poet must find a belief which will "put man at the centre of his poetry." [3] Whatever the personal distortions here, we may accept the degree of consciousness and the concern as facts of the times. And we may note that consciousness and such desire, in partnership, create difficulties. In certain sensitive areas, like art or religion, the price of consciousness may be high.

Our Renaissance poets, even the great and confident ones, thought often on the subject of the status of the poet. About matters of style and language even minor poets were probably more self-conscious than minor poets today. The rhetorical tradition was more alive and complete; contemporary fads had their day and their commentators; there were the familiar realities of patronage, and the hard box-office realities of the theater. What we may suppose the Renaissance poets did not have was a self-conscious problem of how to express their age and themselves in that age. This we may think to be new, along with the central problem of belief. The Renaissance poets did not need to worry about their belief in themselves as poets; nor did they need to confront as an obsessive individual problem the finding of subject matter and style to make that belief effective. And yet we may consider Donne, even if his own awareness did not extend as far as the recognizable implications of his practice, a model for the modern dilemma. If we think of Robert Frost and his admirable achievement, we see how fortunate he was to find his style early and to build his lifework on that style. But his achievement is not one which haunts the imagination of our time as does the work of Yeats, whose victories are built on the rejected parts of himself.

It is time to draw up a list of tangible stylistic elements in Donne which may be thought to have influenced modern poets. The advantage of such a list does not lie in its completeness, or in its performing the work of judgment for us, but in its bringing the problem of influence most clearly out into the open. The items on the list are by now familiar and obvious. One may begin with Eliot's pronouncement emphasizing the virtues of prose and the desirability of the "non-poetic." Donne's precedent here is a commanding one; he was the central figure in a stylistic revolution that brought to bear on poetry the new rationalism being developed in prose. We now call that prose anti-Ciceronian, or Senecan, and we note the probable effects of the new science upon it; but the general pattern is clear: it emphasized *matter*, broke with some of the traditional forms of *manner*, cultivated abrupt immediacy, and attempted to convey the very process of the thought. The problem is complicated historically by our knowledge of the frequent invasions of poetic elements into prose and vice versa. But from the viewpoint of twentieth-century poets the nature of Donne's achievement seemed clear and was unquestionably stimulating. Besides, the elements of formal prose style were less relevant than Donne's ability to *talk* in verse, to use a syntax, diction, and rhythm which seemed easily, naturally colloquial, and yet which created an authentic language of poetry. It was a language modern poets might well envy — none so often or so eloquently as Yeats.

The problem of language in poetry is a constant, and constantly changing, one. The modern concern may seem to be obsessive, but one cannot fail to recognize both the seriousness of the problem and its entanglement in other features of the times. The earliness of Yeats's concern (by the 1890's),[4] and the differences between his earlier and later poetry, should remind us how complicated the problem is. Every poet may talk about the *same* problem, as if it were one problem, but the actual solution has to be an individual one. Is this not what we must conclude in trying to gauge Donne's influence — that no single answer we can produce will account for the diction of both Yeats and Eliot, not to mention other poets of distinguished merit? And yet, though the conclusion may be a safe one to make, it does not eliminate the fact that Donne's example, once recognized, did provide a model which few would ignore. Imitators, whether in the seventeenth or in the twentieth century, might lift themes or phrases; but ambitious poets, while not mistaking themselves for another, would want to study the style for its inner secrets. They might envy the ease of Donne's language and conclude that it was an irretrievable gift of the times. It could not be reproduced by any modern poet without absurdity; but still, in its cultivated mastery of colloquial speech, it was closer to the real needs of ambitious modern poets than the prose of modern naturalism. It proved to be closer than the coarse, colloquial diction of the early Kipling or of Edgar Lee Masters, or than the slack, heavy rhetoric of the poetic Left.

And so the model was carefully studied. Of this there can be no doubt. But what our modern masters chiefly learned they transformed, and any honest description has to be very general — perhaps in terms of *direction,* or *emphasis,* or even *inspiration.* Other qualities of Donne's style, however, were more nearly common poetic property and lay readier at hand. His imaginative daring gave license to individual raids on modern experience. The satiric bent of his wit suited the temper of our times. The same can be said of his famous harshness and obscurity, of his cultivating the *strain* rather than the *vein* of poetry, of his writing for a small and select audience of connoisseurs, of his writing an urban poetry the main subject of which is the nature of man. Finally, the rich example of his uses of imagery fascinated our century and helped the better poets write better and the worse poets worse.

Other qualities engaged and stimulated fruitful admiration for a high standard of achievement, and so perhaps deserve to be listed as possible sources of influence. Donne's power to concentrate thought in language could serve, as it did for I. A. Richards and others, as a rebuke to the lazy habits of modern readers, and as a standard by which to measure the products of modern romanticism. Donne provided a perfect example for the "poetry of inclusion," and for the seriousness of wit and irony. Nor did the personality expressed in the poetry want modern admirers who could identify aspects of their own problems with his. Here we may note, in particular, the individualism of Donne, its brilliant maneuvers and tortured stresses. We may think also of his fundamental seriousness, the manifest agony of spirit underlying the great wit of his religious poetry and prose.

So much for the sources of probable influence. What one may no doubt say with assurance is that these items — familiar as they are, and huddled together with a minimum of differentiation — describe a kind of high-water mark of Donne's modern reputation and influence. In his decline there are two motions that can be observed. One is that of assimilation; the other is more difficult to name: it is characterized by a recognition of differences where chiefly similarities had been seen, and by a change in the times, a drifting away from one set of interests, from what no longer engages to what does engage. The terms are not happy ones, but the phenomena can hardly be unfamiliar. One may also note that the process of assimilation, in these matters as well as in many others, accelerates the speed of the drifting away. The final consideration of Donne's influence will concern itself with these two motions, and first with that of assimilation.

All the best modern poets have now read Donne, most of them closely. It would be as difficult to avoid the experience as to have had it fifty years ago, for Donne has become a standard part of the educational curriculum of modern poets. But they have read Donne with ears tuned to Yeats and Eliot and Auden, and to poets who have made their reputation since, and to older poets who still seem recent, like Hopkins and Emily Dickinson. There is no countering the force of a living or recently living poet who has shaped his triumphs out of contemporary language, out of an idiom of contemporary feeling and concern. We may perhaps agree that the figure of Donne stands behind some of the best early poems by Karl Shapiro, but we had better recognize that between Donne and Shapiro is the immediate figure of Auden. Robert Penn Warren is a master of the older metaphysical poetry and a creator of the new. In his dramatic lyrics the older poets, whom he had assimilated independently, leave him free. But in his "Ballad of Billie Potts," where he needed to meditate in verse, a voice of Eliot's *Four Quartets* may be heard occasionally to intervene. We may guess that Warren heard that voice too, for it disappeared from *Brother to Dragons*.

A poet's problem is to find his own center, his way of seeing his material, of turning language into style and of using his own voice. He must be dependent on external help, but no single item borrowed from others can do more than act as a spark to unite with what is already there and latent. No good poet coming into his strength will be unaware that he must resist his master, though he love him. The older masters will leave him freer, but it will take great efforts to avoid or go beyond the authority of a modern master's use of an older poet.

Modern poets, then, read Donne directly and were influenced by his practice; but they were also influenced by the practice of modern masters and, after a while, by the cooperative developments and changes through which Donne became assimilated into modern poetry. The poets did not wait for a scholarly appraisal, or even to see whether they had taken all they could use. Whatever was most successful in the poetic revival of Donne was successfully assimilated and changed.

Whether in extreme ways or in subtle ways, the materials poets are moved to be poetic about change with the times and with the poets — and not only with different poets but with the same ones, at different stages of their careers. A scholar may reasonably agree with the poets that their use of an earlier poet can be brilliantly perceptive, and can inspire new and challenging reappraisals which are of great benefit to the reputation of the earlier poet, to the institution of scholarship, and to the living culture itself. But the contribution of the poets, by the very nature of its creative function, is also necessarily partial. No poet, as poet, is going to devote his working life to the disciplined study of a great predecessor. Besides, why should a body of poetry, which in itself cannot directly offer a fixed and systematized program, even when one can be extracted — why should that poetry remain unchanged during a period of active use? That is, unchanged in influence; for a body of poetry is of course always unchanged in one sense, however changed in the interpretations of active poets, critics, and scholars. If we think of the influence of Freud, who did recently present the world with a body of systematized thought, we may see what is clearly not to be expected from a body of verse. Freud's insights have been borrowed freely, but new disciples usually bring changes, and no disciples bring oblivion. Plainly, we can see the unsuccessful influence in poetry far better than the successful, which is likely to be drawn into the many influences, new and old, which are always working in a significant poet. Unsuccessful influence may leave a popular poet even more sharply exposed to the reversals of reputation; and this has probably been true, for instance, of Rupert Brooke, Edna Millay, and Elinor Wylie, whose relations with Donne were superficial and perhaps opportunistic.

But besides the normal process of assimilation which Donne has undergone, there has been a recognizable drift away. His place in the poetic curriculum, however, still remains assured, for the height of prestige he attained is not likely to drop below a certain point for a long time. It may take several revivals to counterbalance the relative obscurity of more than two centuries. Still, he is likely to maintain some place in the curriculum, even if the newer poets may not be doing their postgraduate work on Donne. No poet could have long supported all of the claims, all of the demands, made in the name of Donne. By one line he led to the Augustans and the achievement of intellectual concentration in poetry. By another line he led to the individualism, originality, and sensuous immediacy of the better Romantics. He represented a complex of desirable medieval and Renaissance intellectual and poetic virtues, previously thought to be lost but now rediscovered by the faithful. They were important virtues and needed to be re-emphasized in our world, and such circumstances both encourage and make understandable a necessary amount of overemphasis. We can look with tolerance and gratitude at the stimulating history that emphasis produced. Only laziness and complacency can claim to have suffered absolute losses.

For the attentive admiration accorded him, however, Donne had to pay the inevitable price, which exceeded the normal rate and terms of poetic assimilation. His poems were mercilessly racked and anatomized to see how they worked, and these discoveries were not only credited to his honor but busily applied and exploited elsewhere. Furthermore, his poems were charged with the formidable responsibility of providing shrines at which the modern dissociated sensibility could commune with the undissociated sensibility. Under the press of such a demand no mere poet could supply more than a diminishing satisfaction.

We may observe other conditions that are related to a movement away from Donne. The interest of his most important early sponsor, T. S. Eliot, has gone in directions that partly differ from those of his earlier stage. Eliot has indicated the area of his own dissatisfaction with Donne, and this no doubt has had its effect. One would guess it has encouraged some transfer of poetic interest to Herbert. But at any rate the negative force of Eliot's withdrawal of active interest represents a kind of landmark — in spite of cultural time lags, and the fact that it is impossible to control poetic prestige exactly, and the fact that even prophets of superior reputation may commit some errors.

But we must come back to the plain fact that the times have changed. They would have changed anyway, but they have changed faster and more than it may be comfortable to consider. The early enthusiasm for Donne was nourished and sharpened by a sense of the closeness and the similarities between the two ages. We have since become increasingly aware of differences, including some that were obscured by the early enthusiasm. All of these might not make Donne less attractive — as, for instance, our better realization of the stable realm of discourse and reference which permitted Donne to exercise and yet control the remarkable freedom of his wit. But the general effect of familiarity, revision, and the passage of time has tended to move Donne from the creative center which he once dominated. No single poet has taken his place; there have been, and will be, adjustments in the understanding and reputation of many poets whose positions were affected by the revival of Donne. That is a process which goes on anyway, but it is always accelerated by any sharp break, and consequent re-establishment of equilibrium, in the order of relationships.

One sign of the masterpiece is the apparent fact that its first appreciative audience will chiefly recognize their own authentic features, and subsequent audiences will recognize theirs. Perhaps we may read Donne's fate in his failure to keep up the game. Perhaps the future will say that what cost him most dearly in the 1950's was his neglect of myth, without which no poet could deeply interest the mythic-minded readers of that age.

There is a kind of stability, something we may call perennial, in art or religion or philosophy. But it is trite yet true that every generation attends to its cultural past, or to God, with senses, mind, and soul influenced by its own needs and surpluses, confidences and worries. Poet heroes, like ideas or causes, may have to die and return cyclically, in order to avoid being stabilized in a false facsimile. In order to live they must suffer their chances in the hearts and minds of living generations.

Appendixes

THE STANZA OF *"Lovers Infinitenesse"*

VERY little has been written on the stanzas Donne creates. Admirers profess to admire, but they are seldom concrete in their reasons. They tend, rather, to accept the descriptions of those who dislike Donne, declaring only that the alleged vices are virtues. J. E. V. Crofts is at least concrete, in an absolute kind of way: "having gone to the trouble of inventing these patterns, he persistently effaces and makes us forget them by allowing the natural rhythm of his language to pour over them, like a flood over a harrow, drowning them out of sight. . . . His verse is often definitely out of phase in the sense that the metrical shape and the rhythmical movement have no discernible relation. He seems to have regarded the pattern of verse (when he thought about it) not as an aid or an instrument of expression, but as a kind of obstacle" (*ESMEA*, XXII [1937], 138–39). One seems to recognize the revival of items, brought up to date, from the Johnsonian canon of taste. Mr. Crofts deserves the kind of answer he has not, to my knowledge, received; and he is most lively· "It is all in some measure a *tour de force*, and our sense of its poetic quality is liable to be surcharged with the kind of admiration which we give to the complete model of a frigate made out of mutton bones by a prisoner of war." Mr. Kermode's fine and measured judgment (elsewhere not so passive) seems to have been influenced by Mr. Crofts: "We are asked to *admire*, and that is why the poet creates difficulties for himself, choosing arbitrary and complex stanza forms, of which the main point often seems to be that they put tremendous obstacles in his way . . . they all offer this kind of pleasure — delight in a dazzling conjuring trick" (*John Donne*, pp. 18–19).

Donne's stanzas are not, I think, so perfectly integrated as the stanzas of George Herbert. But Herbert is, in this respect, a supreme master in English. Besides, Herbert does not need quite so much room and flexibility as Donne needs. Still, I do not see how any sympathetic and sensitive reading of Donne can mistake the high degree of skill with which he relates his thoughts and his rhythms and his syntax to the form of the stanza — in order to achieve something like full reciprocity in the movement of a whole unit.

Remarks on the formal structure of stanzas — the function, effects, and success of relationships — are likely to be more personal than most critical remarks. There are no clear principles to go by, and there have not been enough sustained analyses or experimental demonstrations. It was once my intention to make some such endeavors myself, but I have had to postpone the effort. Nor could I expect many readers to want more technical analysis in one book. I append an example, which does not aspire to treat all the features of Donne's stanza in "Lovers Infinitenesse," but will indicate, in part by omission, how many technical details of the form are functional in creating the meaning. I hope also to indicate how strictly and subtly Donne worked, and to remind the reader again that he is a poetic logician gifted with a musical sense and love of form.

The stanza Donne invents, and its triple development, may be considered as a small pattern of what the poem accomplishes. Its beauty of form does not lend itself easily to the art of printing. The first, second, seventh, eighth, and eleventh lines have four beats; the other lines have five. But the length of line does not match with the rhyme. Instead, except in the ninth and tenth lines, the poet alternately pairs the rhyme with four-beat and five-beat lines. A paradigm for the eye might be written so: *a*-4 *b*-4 *a*-5 *b*-5 / *c*-5 *d*-5 *c*-4 *d*-4 / *b*-5 *b*-5 *b*-4. The rhythmic structure makes its own pattern: first two lines of four beats, then two of five; then two of five and two of four; then two of five and a single line of four. The last line, however, has compensatory weight; for it is the concluding line of a rhyming triplet, and it also acts as a refrain which is repeated with variation throughout the poem. Furthermore, the last line significantly focuses the meaning of each stanza and in its variations signals the progressive development of the poem. Donne has been at some pains to construct a concealed esthetic form: five weighted lines of four beats against six lines of five beats, a balance of emphasis against an apparent imbalance of quantity, a symmetry of significance out of an apparent asymmetry of proportion.

We may look at the stanza from another point of view. Its internal structure is tight and continuous, but a further continuity between stanzas is derived from the refrain and from the fact that the final triplet uses the same rhyme in each stanza. Furthermore, the *b* rhyme of the first stanza becomes the *a* rhyme of the second. Only in the third stanza is the triplet felt as a separate, independent voice which is not answering a musical impulse already established within the stanza. Here it is given a free and special position from which to make the most important statement of the poem. We shall return to this third stanza, but first we may take another point of view.

Each stanza of the three develops in a triple movement. Our paradigm of the rhymes indicated a 4-4-3 division and relationship. In the first stanza this is also, liberally interpreted, the division into which the larger rhythms fall. In the third stanza the rhythms are less continuous and are composed of smaller units, but the rhythmical and logical periods tend to coincide in groups of 4-4-3. The second stanza varies both rhythmical and logical periods, which coincide, but in divisions of 2-6-3. In this, but not in the third stanza, the overt signs of the logical argument ("Or if," "But if," "And yet") are reliable guides to the divisions. In the first stanza the logical signs, and perhaps the logical divisions, are those of a 6-2-3 relationship. It is of course difficult to mark the exact divisions of imaginative logic; for its external signs may be clearer than its internal movements, which are swifter yet more lingering than the measured movements of prose discourse. Let us conclude this business by noting that there are significant variations among the stanzas, and that, as rhyme and length of line work against each other to create a balance out of an apparent imbalance, the periods of logic and / or rhythm can work against both to the same end. Only the final triplet is a stable unit, but that has its variation in the refrain, and in the independent difference we noted in the third stanza.

Let us turn to the third stanza, which not only concludes and resolves the poetic theme but does so by recapitulating, or re-enacting, formal elements in the two preceding stanzas. The confident declaration with which the stanza begins, the acceptance of growth in love and the transfer of hope from the past to the future — this new direction makes an ostensible break with the worries and longings of the first two stanzas. We begin again, looking forward with pleasure to conditions that were previously a source of worry. A new contract is drawn up, this time on the initiative of the speaker; he assumes a personal responsibility for the expansion he predicts, and moving from passive to active he wishes to bind his partner to the new obligation. The new contract may be right in the feelings it expresses but its terms are also wrong. They are quietly dropped as the paradoxes of love's exchanges reveal past error and future possibilities. The image of growth undermined the images of exchange, but the image of growth is rendered irrelevant by the progressively deeper enigmas of love: by the immaterial, involuntary nature of giving, and by the losing and saving of hearts. These last two lines before the final triplet carry more weight than any lines which precede them. They sum up everything that was wrongheaded in the poem. At the same time they stand on the threshold of what is right, the new and final beginning. Donne has broken his established form and risked another imbalance to endow these lines with added weight, for each has a fifth stress though the stanza provides for only four. The triplet, with its independent voice, answers and resolves the apparent dilemmas of the first two stanzas and of its own stanza. It begins in a casual, offhand way, then tightens after the caesura of the second line. The last line, beginning with its initial spondee, marvelously defies the technical enjambment and the licensed demands of syntax. It pauses as if in balance against the whole poem, and makes its four beats felt.

NOTES ON DONNE'S *Religious Thought*

CAREFUL tact, and more room for proper discrimination than I can spare, are desirable in applying cross references from Donne's religious prose to the secular poems. I trust, however, that the importance of the issue may excuse its peremptory handling in this appendix. A suitable treatment in the text proper would have seriously changed the proportions and emphasis of my chapter.

The sermons, no more than the poems, are occasions for the full and immediate "sincerity" of self-expression. Both have their own kinds of discipline and commitment, and their obligation to circumstance, purpose, and art as well as to the personal truth of the moment. (I am being heavy-handed, of course; for some comments of the same kind, see the *Sermons*, IV, 91–92.) I mean, it is not easy to say Donne always thought exactly thus and so on certain issues. For instance, the preacher is likely to bear down hard on the many forms of intellectual presumption. It is my considered belief, however, that these occasions do not define Donne's whole attitude, much less represent his own deepest conviction.

I do not think it misleading to say that the sermons, like the love poems, put their hope in knowledge — and not only in that ultimate knowledge that Donne passionately imagines, always a little conscious of his own temerity, and trembling with the disciplined wisdom of fear. Even in contemplating the beatific vision of God (in prospect), he can speak like a man who has learned the important lessons of human knowledge, and thus knows intimately what to hope for. In this world we do not see one another as we are: "we see but outsides." Here "I never saw my selfe, but in disguises: There, Then I shall see my selfe, and see God too." "In heaven I shall see God, and God essentially. . . . I shall love God. Now love presumes knowledge; for, *Amari nisi nota non possunt*, we can love nothing, but that which we do, or think we do understand. There, in heaven, I shall *know* God . . . I shall *love* God. But even love it selfe, as noble a passion as it is, is but a paine, except we enjoy that we love. . . . There then, in heaven, I shall have *continuitatem Intuendi*; It is not onely *vision*, but *Intuition*, not onely a seeing, but a beholding, a contemplating of God, and that *in Continuitate*, I shall have an un-interrupted, an un-intermitted, an un-discontinued sight of God; I shall looke, and never looke off; not looke, and looke againe, as here, but looke, and looke still. . . . There my soule shall have *Inconcussam quietem* . . . that peace, which is in it selfe; My soule shall be thoroughly awake, and thoroughly asleep too; still busie, active, diligent, and yet still at rest" (*Sermons*, IX, 127–29).

If we can believe that Donne meant these words, then we can also believe that he meant the aspiration for intelligence, love, and active peace which he expresses in many of the best secular poems, and that the religious and secular hopes differ more in degree than in kind.

I have argued that negative theology, ecstasy, and mysticism do not deeply engage Donne's mind. It follows, therefore, that I find unbelievable much of the central attitude in Itrat Husain's *The Dogmatic and Mystical Theology of John Donne* (New York: Macmillan, 1938) and *The Mystical Element in the Metaphysical Poets of the Seventeenth Century* (Edinburgh: Oliver and Boyd, 1948). Nor can I agree with the interpretation of Donne's sexual and religious mysticism by Masood-Ul-Hasan, in *Donne's Imagery* (Aligarh: Muslim University, 1957–58). Helen White soundly analyzes the problem and decides that Donne is no mystic: *The Metaphysical Poets* (New York: Macmillan, 1936), pp. 115–20. Helen Gardner, in her excellent edition of the *Divine Poems*, states: "There is an ecstasy of joy and an ecstasy of grief in his love poetry; in his divine poetry we are conscious almost always of an effort of will" (p. xxxv). This last echoes Miss White. Perhaps Miss Gardner has revised her opinion; more likely, she has used her words with greater care in "The Argument about 'The Ecstasy' " (p. 304): "I do not believe that Donne was very deeply moved by the conception of ecstasy. He too often in his sermons disparages the idea of ecstatic revelation for me to feel that it had ever had a strong hold on his imagination." I am in substantial agreement, and I note that Mrs. Simpson, in her second edition of *A Study of the Prose Works of John Donne* (pp. 91–96), modifies her earlier position and acknowledges a debt to Miss Gardner. I think M. M. Mahood (*Poetry and Humanism* [London: Jonathan Cape, 1950], pp. 121–22) muddies the waters. We might as well try to apply, for normal critical purposes, the esoteric profundity of Wittgenstein (*Tractatus Logico-Philosophicus* [New York: Harcourt, Brace, 1922], 6. 44–45): "Not *how* the world is, is the mystical, but *that* it is. . . . The feeling of the world as a limited whole is the mystical feeling." Donne, we should have to say, is a poet of the *how*; but he is also a poet and preacher who tries to bring the *how* toward an identity with "a limited whole." I stress that word "toward."

Some words of Whitehead are, I think, useful here, if we remember that Donne's thought as preacher cannot be simply identified with his thought as poet: "That we fail to find in experience any elements intrinsically incapable of exhibition as examples of general theory, is the hope of rationalism. This hope . . . is the faith which forms the motive for the pursuit of all sciences alike, including metaphysics. . . . But in itself the faith does not embody a premise from which the theory starts; it is an ideal which is seeking satisfaction. In so far as we believe that doctrine, we are rationalists" (*Process and Reality*, p. 67). As a poet Donne comes under this definition of rationalism. The definition cannot quite apply to a theologian, and it is even less suitable to a preacher. Still, the careful reader of Donne's sermons will not be unimpressed by the fervor with which faith seeks "satisfaction." Even when Donne fails, or surrenders, it is not wholly without a sense of the "degrees" of knowledge, and the preferability of present limits (compensated for by otherworldly hopes) to present irrationalism.

Let me try to illustrate. Donne must have felt an attraction in reading Pico della Mirandola, who was favored by the literary attention of Thomas More and recognized as a standard of youthful talent. (Walton recorded a complimentary comparison between Donne and Pico.) But in the *Essays in Divinity* (p. 13) Donne describes Pico as "a man of an incontinent wit, and subject to the concupiscence of inaccessible knowledges and transcendencies." There may seem to be a small element of self-description, when we recall Donne's own "voluptuousness, which is an Hydroptique immoderate desire of humane learning and languages." The difference, however, is more significant — even though the repulsion of "transcendencies" may be thought to exert a certain attraction. Donne characteristically sets limits. When we search after God's mysteries we testify our "liveliness" toward Him, and He is glorified by that, and by "our not finding them" (*Essays in Divinity*, p. 27).

Or consider Donne on "holy simplicity." This is a theme that necessitates the disparagement of earthly knowledge — yet in Donne only up to a point. I do not think that Donne would agree with Martz that Savonarola's doctrine "is not, then, a simplicity of abnegation" (*Poetry of Meditation*, p. 283; see especially the quotation on p. 285). In preaching on the conversion of St. Paul, Donne writes: "*Saul* was struck blinde, but it was a blindnesse contracted from light. . . . This blindnesse which we speak of, which is a sober and temperate abstinence from the immoderate study, and curious knowledges of this world, this holy simplicity of the soule, is not a darknesse, a dimnesse, a stupidity in the understanding, contracted by living in a corner, it is not an idle retiring into a Monastery, or into a Village, or a Country solitude, it is not a lazy affectation of ignorance; not darknesse, but a greater light, must make us blinde . . . must make us blinde to the world so, as that we look upon no face, no pleasure, no knowledge, with such an Affection, such an Ambition, such a Devotion, as upon God, and the wayes to him. *Saul* had such a blindnesse, as came from light; we must affect no other simplicity, then arises from the knowledge of God, and his Religion. . . . That powerfull light felled *Saul*; but after he was fallen, his owne sight was restored to him againe" (*Sermons*, VI, 215). What seems to me significant is the way Donne limits the inevitable asceticism and takes his stand in the world of intellectual action. He rounds out the above passage by affirming that in those who use their learning well God will increase "that learning, even in this world." It is an affirmation that Milton also shared.

I have said that Donne is reluctant to go the whole standard course of the purgative program. Let us watch him going rather far and see what happens. "And when . . . I come to such a melting and pouring out of my heart, that there be no spirit, that is, none of mine own spirit left in me; when I have so exhausted, so evacuated my self, that is, all confidence in my self, that I come into the hands of my God, as pliably, as ductily, as that first clod of earth, of which he made me in *Adam*, was in his hands, in which clod of earth, there was no kinde of reluctation against Gods purpose; this is a blessed nullification of the heart. . . . This is a blessed nullification, a glorious annihilation of thc heart." Contrition may serve the same end and give God "a *Vacuity*, a new place to create a new heart in." But when God has done so, and "re-enabled me," then if we "put this heart to nothing, to think nothing, to consider nothing; not to know our age, but by the Church-Book, and not by any action done in the course of our lives . . . this is such a nullification of the heart, such an annihilation, such an exinanition thereof, as reflects upon God himself" (*Sermons*, IX, 177–78). Perhaps it is not too strained to see in the passage a movement not unlike that in "The Extasie," where the unper-plexing is a process of purification that leads to a "re-enabling."

I have argued that Donne finds himself trusting extremes and pre-ferring them above the established wisdom of mean ways. I am con-vinced that, although Donne submits himself to standard religious disciplines, including those of "meditation," there is an essential spontaneity in his religious thought and feeling. I mean the kind of spontaneity which may not only express, but also resist or oppose, the forms of traditional wisdom which are signs of perfect inspiration in the true believer. To some the spontaneity will be subject to grave suspicion, and will seem the product of unregenerate individuality, a light out of the shadow of impure motive, a glitter from the self-indulgence of pulpit spellbinding. But modern critics are not likely to match Donne in the expressive art of religious accusation. As Ben Jonson would recommend reading "*Livy* before *Salust*, *Sydney* be-fore *Donne*," perhaps the critic of religious prose might need to find an exact place in the curriculum for Donne. But I wish only to insist on an element of spontaneity in Donne's religious expression, a spontaneity that is perhaps related to his cultivation of extremes. I might add, as my own judgment of the evidence, that this part of his appeal is an honorable one, though perhaps not safe for all witnesses. We see in Donne a powerful religious imagination by means of which he tries to bind himself wholly to a discipline in which he believes. To disparage the dilemma and all its results would be to entertain intellectual and spiritual presumption, against which Donne strove with unflagging effort and awareness. So complex may be thought the simple ways of God.

My interpretation of "The Litanie," it may be noted, differs from Helen Gardner's emphasis. I do not see "in the whole poem a habit of mind which has been shaped by the practice of systematic self-examination" (*Divine Poems*, p. xxvi). The central paradox is much too strong for that "habit" and "shape." I agree that the poem "tells us much, though indirectly, of its author's mind at the time when it was written": it tells us what he wants to think. "The ideal which is aspired to is simplicity of motive, 'evennesse' of piety, and a keeping of 'meane waies' " (p. xxiv).

It was Grierson, in *Criticism and Creation* (London: Chatto and Windus, 1949), who first made me see the importance of "mean ways" to Donne. Though I have come to disagree with his conclu-sions, my debt is not therefore any less. Helen White has written ex-cellently of Donne's "consciousness of his own instability, his changeableness, his incapacity for that steady equilibrium which is one of the great ideals of the spiritual life of his age." She observes with sympathetic perception "the most remarkable and moving thing of all": that Donne's "omniscient self-awareness" attains to the humility of confession. And she quotes, with telling effect, "that most candid confession of all": "And I have sinned *before thy face*, in my *hypocricies* in Prayer, in my *ostentation*, and the mingling a respect of *my self* in preaching thy Word" (*Metaphysical Poets*, pp. 131–32).

Yet something can be added to this account that is not unlike Donne's attitude toward knowledge or his attitude toward the annihilation of the self. The nullified heart must be "re-enabled." The irresolute and perplexed heart, which Donne knows from the inside, is no object for tolerance or sympathy. In the main it "is a sickly complexion of the soul, a dangerous impotencie. . . . Not to be able to con-centre those doubts, which arise in my self, in a resolution at last, whether in Moral or in Religious Actions, is rather a vertiginous giddiness, then a wise circumspection, or wariness." But what of the inconstant heart? The empty and the irresolute heart may often be overcome, but never the inconstant heart. That is, we may go "so far, as to bring holy Resolutions into Actions; yet never so far, as to bring holy Actions into Habits" (*Sermons*, IX, 179–80). Donne desired pious constancy, as he desired mean ways, but not with all his heart and all his mind.

Notes

NOTES

UNLESS otherwise noted, I have followed original spellings in quoting sources, except that I have used the modern *s* and the modern preferences for *u* and *v*. In certain obvious cases I have added accents or italics to illustrate my argument. For the most part I have quietly supplied end punctuation in quoting lines of poetry, except where doing so might be misleading.

Introduction

[1] Rosemond Tuve, *Elizabethan and Metaphysical Imagery* (Chicago: University of Chicago Press, 1947); Leonard Unger, *The Man in the Name* (Minneapolis: University of Minnesota Press, 1956); René Wellek, "The Criticism of T. S. Eliot," *Sewanee Review*, LXIV (1956), 398–443; Joseph Duncan, *The Revival of Metaphysical Poetry* (Minneapolis: University of Minnesota Press, 1959); Frank Kermode, "Dissociation of Sensibility," *Kenyon Review*, XIX (1957), 169–94. See also Kathleen Tillotson, "Donne's Poetry in the Nineteenth Century," *Elizabethan and Jacobean Studies Presented to F. P. Wilson* (Oxford: The Clarendon Press, 1959), pp. 307–26.

[2] "The Argument about 'The Ecstasy,' " *Elizabethan and Jacobean Studies Presented to F. P. Wilson*, p. 305.

[3] *ELH*, XXVIII (1961), 31–53. All students of Donne are in these matters indebted to the extensive contributions of Don Cameron Allen.

[4] The references are to Helen Gardner's *The Metaphysical Poets* (Penguin Books, 1957), p. 21, and *The Business of Criticism* (Oxford: The Clarendon Press, 1959), p. 70. Quotations from the sermons will be drawn from *The Sermons of John Donne*, ed. E. M. Simpson and G. R. Potter (Berkeley and Los Angeles: University of California Press, 1953–62).

[5] *The Complete Poetry and Selected Prose of John Donne* (New York: Random House, 1952), p. 403.

[6] *A Treatise of Human Nature*, I, iv, 6.

[7] *Coleridge on the Seventeenth Century*, ed. Roberta F. Brinkley (Durham: Duke University Press, 1955), p. 523.

[8] *Ibid.*, p. 192.

[9] *The Collected Works of Paul Valéry*, Vol. VII, ed. Jackson Mathews (New York: Pantheon Books, 1958), p. 107.

Chapter I. Questions of Style

[1] *Ben Jonson,* ed. C. H. Herford and Percy Simpson (Oxford: The Clarendon Press, 1925–52), I, 132. Drummond adds his own comment that Jonson at other times denied this.

[2] *Elizabethan Critical Essays,* ed. Gregory Smith (Oxford: The Clarendon Press, 1904), I, 157.

[3] *Ibid.,* pp. 47–48; Horace, *Ars Poetica,* l. 311.

[4] *Institutiones Oratoriae,* VIII, iii, 17.

[5] *Critical Essays of the Seventeenth Century,* ed. J. E. Spingarn (Oxford: The Clarendon Press, 1908–9), I, 123.

[6] *Ibid.,* p. 21.

[7] *The Poems of George Chapman,* ed. Phyllis B. Bartlett (New York: Modern Language Association of America, 1941), p. 384.

[8] Letter, "To Mr. S. B." All quotations of Donne's poetry are from *The Poems of John Donne,* ed. Herbert Grierson (London: Oxford University Press, 1945).

[9] *Lives of the Most Eminent English Poets,* ed. Cunningham (London, 1854): "Cowley," I, 22; "Waller," I, 259.

[10] Sonnet XLVI of *Delia,* in *Poems and a Defence of Ryme,* ed. A. C. Sprague (Cambridge: Harvard University Press, 1930).

[11] Prologue to Book I, 414–20, *Lydgate's Fall of Princes,* ed. Henry Berger (London: Early English Text Society, 1923–27), I, 12. *The Pastime of Pleasure by Stephen Hawes,* ed. W. E. Mead (London: Early English Text Society, 1928), p. 6.

[12] Quoted from T. H. Jamieson's edition, I, 144, by E. M. W. Tillyard, in *The Poetry of Sir Thomas Wyatt* (London: The Scholartis Press, 1949), p. 19. The comment below is from p. 18.

[13] *Ben Jonson,* I, 148.

[14] These quotations are from the poems numbered 4, 9, 31, 33, 37, in *Collected Poems,* ed. Kenneth Muir (London: Routledge and K. Paul, 1949).

[15] These preceding quotations come, respectively, from Sonnets 2 and 6 of "La Corona," and from Satire V, l. 7.

[16] *Troilus and Criseyde,* II, 421–24, *The Complete Works of Geoffrey Chaucer,* ed. F. N. Robinson (Boston: Houghton Mifflin, 1933).

[17] *The Collected Writings of Thomas De Quincey,* ed. Masson (London, 1896–97), X, 100–1.

[18] *Coleridge on the Seventeenth Century,* pp. 520–21. Cf. *Coleridge's Miscellaneous Criticism,* ed. T. M. Raysor (Cambridge: Harvard University Press, 1936), pp. 67, 131–45, 184.

[19] The studies of Donne's verse which I published in the early 1940's were all based upon this principle. It seemed necessary at the time to give some ordered account of Donne's characteristic range of metrical practice. Many of his admirers appeared insufficiently aware of the precise rhetorical effects he managed by means of the metrical basis of his language. Today meter seems to be the kind of elementary (or obsolescent) subject students do not need to learn; they may even hear that it is one of those fictions now proved not to exist. Many of Donne's admirers no doubt still read his verse as heightened prose. Nevertheless, I must dissent from a recent tendency to emphasize the metrical norm as if this alone explained almost everything in Donne. I am thinking of Catherine Ing, *Elizabethan Lyrics* (London: Chatto and Windus, 1951), pp. 234–36; C. S. Lewis, *English Literature in the Sixteenth Cen-*

tury (Oxford: The Clarendon Press, 1954), pp. 549–51; Helen Gardner, *The Divine Poems* (London: Oxford University Press, 1952), pp. 78–79. Perhaps it is overpersonal to wish that Miss Gardner had considered my "Donne's Prosody," *PMLA*, LIX (1944), 395, or that Mr. Lewis had considered more of my general position than the one item which he learned through Percy Simpson's article on the Elizabethan practices in rhyme. The quotation of Donne below is from "The Good-morrow."

²⁰ Elegy VII, l. 1; Elegy XVI, l. 31; "An Epithalamion, or Mariage Song on the Lady Elizabeth," l. 92.

²¹ It may be objected that "Us" in the fourth line quoted is also an exception. I must plead the rhetorical emphasis and the flow. In the other two examples the rhythm makes a forced pause; here it is not compelled to do so. Besides, "Us" comes under the immediate shadow of the greater emphasis to be released by "end," which completes the contrast with "meanes."

²² *Astrophel and Stella*, ed. Mona Wilson (London: The Nonesuch Press, 1931), pp. 2, 55.

²³ *Collected Poems*, nos. 37, 31.

²⁴ Elegy X, ll. 1–3; "Aire and Angels"; "The Good-morrow."

²⁵ The whole poem is analyzed as an example of Donne's "ternary form" at the end of Chapter II.

²⁶ "Poetry and Tradition," *Essays* (New York: Macmillan, 1924), p. 314.

²⁷ In my early studies of Donne, which drew heavily upon Croll's pioneer work, I tried to make out a case for Donne's relationship to Stoic style. Had I known at the time Ernst Cassirer's book, since translated and published as *The Platonic Renaissance in England* (Austin: University of Texas Press, 1953), I might have recognized the relevance of certain strands of Platonic thought.

²⁸ Elegy VIII, ll. 1–2, 27–28.

²⁹ Elegy VI, ll. 15–19.

³⁰ Satire IV, ll. 73–74.

³¹ Satire I, ll. 83–87, 71–76.

³² Holy Sonnet III.

³³ The following two passages and my analysis of them have been discussed by Seymour Chatman and John Crowe Ranson, in *Kenyon Review*, XVIII (1956), 443–51, 470–73.

³⁴ See, for instance, my "A Note on Meter," *Kenyon Review*, XVIII (1956), 451–60.

³⁵ *Coleridge on the Seventeenth Century*, p. 549. See also the opening pages of *Biographia Literaria*. Coleridge may have got from Boyer the distinction, later applied to Donne, between the meter appropriate to songs and the meter "in poems where the writer *thinks*, and expects the reader to do so" (p. 521). One is reminded of Ben Jonson's taste for nonsinging verse. It is remarkable also that Boyer, while insisting that in the great poets "there is a reason assignable, not only for every word, but for the position of every word," likewise insisted on the value of "truth and nativeness" in thoughts and diction.

³⁶ That I. A. Richards learned from the older rhetoric, by agreement as well as by disagreement, is plain enough in *The Philosophy of Rhetoric* (London: Oxford University Press, 1936).

³⁷ It is probably true, however, that a modern attitude contributed to the enthusiastic revival of Donne. I have in mind the rebellious attitude toward language widely current in the period after World War I. This took the shape of distrusting not only slogans, but abstractions, not only shopworn sensuous-

ness, but eloquence. I suggest three (different) examples: Hulme, Pound, and Hemingway.

[38] To be brief, the Church Fathers used and disparaged the arts of eloquence; so did philosophers.

[39] *Poems and Dramas of Fulke Greville*, ed. Geoffrey Bullough (New York: Oxford University Press, 1945), I, 180–82.

[40] There were lively changes and counterchanges occurring in our greatest age of literature, but the poets may hardly be considered partisans. They made choices and worked out their own solutions under stress. Presumably they did not worry too much about the consequences, whether immediate or ultimate, of Ascham's dire warning: "Ye know not what hurt ye do to learning that care not for wordes but for matter, and so make a devorse betwixt the tong and the hart." They might have understood the critical norm intended by the exaggeration of the metaphors, but as poets they would not have known how to go about demonstrating any real separation between words and matter. Not even Bacon could do that, and he was no poet.

[41] The quotations are, in the order of occurrence, from the section "Elegies upon the Author" in *Poems of John Donne*: Carew, l. 39, p. 347; Mayne, ll. 20–21, p. 352; Wilson, ll. 14–16, p. 354; Mayne, ll. 7–8, p. 351. The last quotation is from Jonson's epigram, p. 5.

[42] For further background see my "Donne's Obscurity and the Elizabethan Tradition," *ELH*, XIII (1946), 98–118; and A. Alvarez, *The School of Donne* (London: Chatto and Windus, 1961), pp. 17–44.

[43] It goes without saying that our knowledge of poetic language will be more exact if we know its local history, so that we can gauge its meaning by our developed sense of its difference and similarity in respect to the language of contemporaries and predecessors. But it is also true that our knowledge cannot ever be complete enough to dispense with informed guesswork; and even if it were complete, it could not wholly substitute for critical sensibility.

[44] In his elegy Carew appears to recognize the distinctive limits Donne set for himself: "thy strict lawes will be / Too hard for Libertines in Poetrie." Furthermore, Donne's bending of "Our stubborne language" is contrasted with "their soft melting Phrases"; and Carew is apparently identifying himself with Donne's attitude when he refers contemptuously to "the blinde fate of language, whose tun'd chime / More charmes the outward sense."

[45] These quotations are pieced together from pages 131, 132, 134, and 136, of the posthumous *Speculations*, ed. Herbert Read (London: Routledge and K. Paul, 1949). The best rebuttal I know is in Richards' *Philosophy of Rhetoric*, pp. 127ff. George Williamson relies on part of the quoted material as a standard for proving the excellence of Donne. See *The Donne Tradition* (Cambridge: Harvard University Press, 1930), p. 245. And elsewhere he extends the views of Hulme (and Eliot) rather dangerously. Some of this material, from another point of view and with far greater detail, is excellently treated by Leonard Unger, in *Man in the Name*.

[46] "The First Anniversary," l. 353.

[47] *Adventures of Ideas* (New York: Macmillan, 1933), III, 14, 1. The inserted quotation is from the same work, III, 15, 6. These remarks of Whitehead have a definite place in the larger structure of his thought and are not without confirmation in the thought of others. Father Walter J. Ong, in his *Ramus: Method, and the Decay of Dialogue* (Cambridge: Harvard University Press, 1958), provides a lengthy account of the development of Renaissance

"visualism." T. S. Eliot's coinage, "the dissociation of sensibility," may also be considered as relevant here.

⁴⁸ "Song," from *Cynthia's Revels.*

⁴⁹ *Paradise Lost*, XI, 835. There are further examples, with extended analyses, in my *Answerable Style* (Minneapolis: University of Minnesota Press, 1953), pp. 145ff.

⁵⁰ Ll. 296–98. The next line quoted is l. 191.

⁵¹ "The First Anniversary," ll. 429–34.

⁵² "Hymne to God My God, in My Sicknesse."

⁵³ *Sermons*, III, 359. I take this to be a central statement — one which proves itself so not only by Donne's powerful demonstrations and extensions, but also by the brilliant moments of resistance which pay unwilling homage to his conviction.

⁵⁴ *Collected Works*, VII, 60.

⁵⁵ Clay Hunt, in his book *Donne's Poetry* (New Haven: Yale University Press, 1954), assumes that his technique of close reading will provide him with sufficient and reliable objectivity. It is a false hope, in criticism and elsewhere, that our good instruments and techniques can be trusted to think for us. In spite of intellectual vigor and acute perception, his book is shot through with the intrusive hostilities of his acquired expectations.

⁵⁶ *Critical Essays of the Seventeenth Century*, I, 211, 212, 214.

Chapter II. Forms of Wit

¹ *Huntington Library Bulletin*, VIII (1935), 103–31. The quotations, from Pope's letter to Henry Cromwell, Dec. 17, 1710, are cited on p. 103.

² *Critical Essays of the Seventeenth Century*, II, 59.

³ Book II, Chapter XI, Section 2. I have used A. C. Fraser's edition (New York: Dover Publications, 1959), I, 203.

⁴ *Critical Essays of the Seventeenth Century*, II, 23.

⁵ See *The Monarch of Wit* (London: Hutchinson, 1951), p. 120. Pope's definition is quoted from *An Essay on Criticism*, l. 300.

⁶ Introduction to *The Art of Poetry*, *Collected Works*, VII, xxiii.

⁷ Whitehead, in Chapter III of *Science and the Modern World* (New York: Macmillan, 1925), illuminates these matters under "the fallacy of misplaced concreteness," which occurs when the observer neglects the degree of abstraction involved in his perception. A dry piece of wit in *Process and Reality* (New York: Macmillan, 1929) makes a remarkable point against the doctrine of difference: "We habitually observe by the method of difference. Sometimes we see an elephant, and sometimes we do not. The result is that an elephant, when present, is noticed" (p. 6).

⁸ Quoted by Edward Surtz, *The Praise of Pleasure* (Cambridge: Harvard University Press, 1957), p. 11. See also *The Book of the Courtier*, trans. Charles S. Singleton (New York: Doubleday, 1959), pp. 144–45: "For laughter is found only in man, and it is nearly always a sign of a certain hilarity inwardly felt in the mind . . . whatever moves to laughter restores the spirit, gives pleasure." I am consciously neglecting a certain uneasiness inherited from classical attitudes toward laughter.

⁹ Robert Klein, "L'imagination chez Ficin et chez Bruno," *Revue de Métaphysique et de Morale*, LXI (1956), 39.

¹⁰ *The Advancement of Learning and The New Atlantis* (London: Oxford University Press, 1929), p. 273.

[11] Both of these letters are quoted by Evelyn M. Simpson, *A Study of the Prose Works of John Donne* (Oxford: The Clarendon Press, 1948), pp. 160–61.

[12] *Advancement of Learning*, in *The Works of Francis Bacon*, ed. Spedding, Ellis, and Heath (London, 1857–59), III, 438.

[13] *Ibid.*, p. 279.

[14] The edition I have used is *The English Philosophers from Bacon to Mill*, ed. E. A. Burtt (New York: Random House, 1939).

[15] *English Literature in the Earlier Seventeenth Century* (Oxford: The Clarendon Press, 1945), p. 184.

[16] *Works*, III, 405.

[17] The purpose Bacon is proposing is one sometimes described in classical rhetoric under *irony*, considered more as a pervasive figure than as a trope, and derived mainly from the impressive example of Socratic irony. A certain self-flattering complacency is always possible, and Quintilian describes a listener who "rejoices in merely being able to understand; he compliments his own intellectual gifts and applauds himself for the subtlety of another man's eloquence" (*Institutiones Oratoriae*, IX, ii, 78). Something of this attitude may be seen in a remark in Jaspar Mayne's elegy:

> Indeed so farre above its Reader, good,
> That wee are thought wits, when 'tis understood.

That for some this will always be true, I do not deny; but I take Mayne's remark as a serious report of one effect Donne had on his best contemporary readers: that of exacting a strenuous collaboration, without which his wit could not be realized. Jonson, in one of his epigrams to Donne, may be understood as making the same point: "Longer a knowing, then most wits doe live." The pressure put upon the reader is that of a stimulating challenge, not only to see what is done, and how, but "to inquire farther." Horatian irony often presents a similar challenge, and is mockingly explicit when the poet dares the reader to try his hand, sure to sweat and fail, at turning such commonplace materials into verse:

> Ex noto fictum carmen sequar, ut sibi quivis,
> Speret idem, sudet multum, frustraque laboret
> Ausus idem.   (*Ars Poetica*, ll. 240–42)

[18] Preface, *Wisdom of the Ancients.*

[19] *Critical Essays of the Seventeenth Century*, I, 38.

[20] Frank Kermode makes brief, penetrating remarks on the special effects of the poem. *John Donne* (London: Longmans, Green, 1957), pp. 20–21.

[21] The ship is of course intended to suggest sexual traffic. See below note 30 on "Aire and Angels."

[22] In his paradox, "A Defence of Womens Constancy," Donne asked: "Are not your wits pleased with those jests, which cozen your expectation?" It is a familiar criterion, as evidenced in *The Book of the Courtier*: "the main thing is to cheat expectation" (p. 178). But it is more appropriate to what the Italians called *arguzie* than to the sustained irony of urbane wit. For the classical background see, for example, Mary A. Grant, *The Ancient Rhetorical Theories of the Laughable* (Madison: University of Wisconsin Press, 1924), pp. 103ff., for distinctions between *dicax* and *facetus*. Urbanity and irony, which depend upon a whole effect, seem more characteristic of the wit called *facetus*; brilliance, brevity, and verbal sharpness characterize *dicacitas*. Donne's wit cultivated both extremes, and sometimes in the same poem. Nev-

ertheless, without denying his *dicacitas* (*arguzie*), I wish to emphasize his greater commitment to continuity and the whole effect. In my phrase "unexpected inevitability" it is the second word that assures the distinction of the wit. Some of the grounds for my emphasis, here and in pages to follow, beyond those deriving from observation, are discussed in the Introduction.

²³ It is not unlike the crosscurrent of modern fashion that produced mink-lined cloth coats. The sermons contain many observations of this sort.

²⁴ I agree here, at least, with Hunt, *Donne's Poetry*, p. 4.

²⁵ "The Crosse," ll. 59–60, 14.

²⁶ It may be useful by way of illustration to indicate some further examples of binary form. In "Twicknam Garden," for instance, we have a kind of stand-off, a poem deliberately unresolved in spite of its final epigrammatic flourish. For one thing, the poem seems to be partly private in its reserve of statement; some of the situation is kept in shadow, not only as it involves the woman but as it involves the man as well. "The Primrose" rejects two opposing extremes and elects a middle solution. Then an epigrammatic joke is produced which elaborately pretends to solve the problem, but only pretends. There is an interesting analysis of the poem and its relevance to Donne's mind by R. A. Durr, *JEGP*, LIX (1960), 218–22. A more finely wrought, more deeply imagined poem is "The Blossome." But if we consider it as a binary form we can see that its proffered solution does not settle all of the issues raised by the poem. For though the ending expresses Donne's personal commitment to both the body and the mind, and though the woman is nicely tried *in absentia*, the gay and arbitrary solution does not satisfy the real enemy in the dialogue: the "naked thinking heart" which has its own reasons and talents "to plague" itself, its own unanswerable argument of simple fidelity. The poem pretends to persuade the heart, but it exhibits also the mistress and the cleft lover, and the desirable solution is possible only if all parties agree. "A Valediction: Of the Booke" presents us with a further example. The poem begins as a challenge to fate, which parts the lovers. First we have a systematic praise of the learning their book of love establishes and secures. Then we move on to an apparently systematic exposition of what their book will in practice teach. But we move, with sly mischief, from lovers to lawyers to statesmen, and the mysteries of love come in for their share of all the incidental ridicule. In the last stanza everything which has been said is unexpectedly attributed to the mistress, and the lover abruptly announces that he will study *her*, from "abroad." His reasons, which are practical in a mad way, drop the whole fiction of "the booke" and its teasing but complimentary extravagance. The real theme is that of lovers parting, but it is a theme too serious for anything but indirect expression. The real theme and the apparent theme simply play against each other and remain unresolved. In a personal poem, however (as this would seem to be), we may postulate another principle of unity. The extravagant praise which partly mocks, the brilliant rationalization that is part of a bland *non sequitur*, the charming entertainment that diverts the mind from any of its practical concerns and worries — these all draw together to form a single expression: that of a teasing but protective masculine love.

²⁷ Stanley Archer, "Meditation and the Structure of Donne's 'Holy Sonnets,'" *ELH*, XXVIII (1961), 137–47, arrives at a different sum: "There are eighteen to be exact." Counting is no talent of mine, so perhaps I had better simply list the poems I have in mind: "The Good-morrow," "Goe, and catche a falling starre," "The Sunne Rising," "The Indifferent," "Loves Usury,"

"Lovers Infinitenesse," "The Legacie," "Breake of Day," "The Anniversarie," "Twicknam Garden," "Confined Love," "The Dreame," "A Valediction: Of Weeping," "The Flea," "The Message," "The Funeral," "The Primrose," "The Relique," "The Dampe," "A Jeat Ring Sent," "The Prohibition." I might mention that this chapter was written about a year before I read Mr. Archer's article; I am glad to have his independent confirmation that ternary form is important for understanding Donne. I have some hesitation in agreeing that "the structure of the 'Holy Sonnets' derives from Donne the poet rather than Donne the religious." "Derives" would seem to be too inflexible a word, and is no doubt inspired by Mr. Archer's effort to counter the rigor of Louis Martz's argument in *The Poetry of Meditation* (New Haven: Yale University Press, 1954). Mr. Martz does tend to stretch his definitions rather far, as in the recent *"Paradise Regained*: The Meditative Combat," *ELH*, XXVII (1960), 223–47. Theories of meditation antedated Christian practice, and these theories, particularly in the Platonic extensions of Plotinus and Proclus, would seem to have been the frequent object of some independent, or semi-independent, interest. Besides, the familiar movements of the mind in meditation, like the mysterious attractions of ternary form itself, are not likely to yield up their nativity; and though they can be learned, and stimulated, they can also be rediscovered by the powerful mind intent on its own exploration. Ternary form seems to me the larger source, and spiritual exercises only one specialized adaptation. I might also add that Mr. Martz has not been able to accommodate — it would be very difficult to manage in his exposition — the features held in common by traditional rhetoric and religious meditation. But all these questions are intended as tribute to a challenging new addition to critical knowledge.

[28] See J. A. Levine, " 'The Dissolution': Donne's Twofold Elegy," *ELH*, XXVIII (1961), 301–15, for a persuasive interpretation of the poem. Levine assumes that "dissolution" means orgasm and that Donne is therefore combining the funereal with the erotic elegy. The covert argument of the sexual experience, then, would in my terms be still another difficult theme simultaneously developed as part of an inversion.

[29] *Essays in Divinity*, ed. Evelyn M. Simpson (Oxford: The Clarendon Press, 1952), p. 21.

[30] D. C. Allen has written a brief, heavily fraught history of Donne's image: "Donne and the Ship Metaphor," *MLN*, LXXVI (1961), 308–12. There can be no doubt of the popularity of "the ship of love" as a theme for bawdy variations. These variations have a wide range. Juliet's Nurse can shift from her sentimentalizing "when 'twas a little prating thing" to a graphic vulgarity: "O, there is a nobleman in town, one Paris, that would fain lay knife aboard." And Lear's Fool can refer the metaphor for the body to a specialized part, as when he answers Edgar's "Come o'er the bourn, Bessy, to me":

> Her boat hath a leak,
> And she must not speak
> Why she dares not come over to thee.

But I must argue, in defense of my interpretation, for another range of the image. We know what to think when Shakespeare's Troilus declares that Pandar is his ship and the destination India: "Her bed is India." But "Our worser thoughts heavens mend" if we draw the same immediate conclusion when is young Romeo speaking:

> I am no pilot; yet, wert thou as far

> As that vast shore wash'd with the farthest sea,
> I should adventure for such merchandise.

Furthermore, there is a serious, nonerotic, significance to the ship image — a variation of one that Allen records. I quote Romeo again, in a different mood:

> Thou desperate pilot, now at once run on
> The dashing rocks thy sea-sick weary bark.

After Plotinus the pilot guiding a ship was one inevitable way to prefigure the soul in its relations with the body. Less than a century ago Lotze, in *Microcosmus*, was analyzing the philosophical inadequacies of the image. If we have license to relate macrocosm and microcosm, and if we overlook the possibility of a late sophistication of the text, the image may go back to Heraclitus: "Wisdom is one thing. It is to know the thought by which all things are steered through all things." *Early Greek Philosophy*, ed. and trans. John Burnet, 4th ed. (London: A. and C. Black, 1930), p. 135Y.

Allen notes that in *Samson Agonistes* Dalila makes her formal entrance as a ship of love. But there is also an indirect entrance, in which the ship of love and the body-soul freely exchange their parts in the image:

> What pilot so expert but needs must wreck
> Embarked with such a steers-mate at the helm?

And yet the vessel of love can be entirely excluded when Samson fuses the ship of the body and the ship of salvation:

> How could I once look up, or heave the head,
> Who like a foolish pilot have shipwrecked
> My vessel trusted to me from above,
> Gloriously rigged. . . .

Now Donne's pinnace is not "gloriously rigged," but "overfraught." The female body of love sails into the poem, but its potential range of suggestion is held in check and a kind of ballast is maintained. Donne's wit would, I think, be recognized by contemporaries as managing a very difficult maneuver; that of turning a known bawdy image into a delicate compliment refined for mixed company. *Honi soit qui mal y pense* — perhaps. But after we think our naughty thoughts we must also think that they have less than a customary justification. The poem proceeds without much benefit from them; soul and body continue their high dispute about love, and the ship of sex, like a phantom ship without crew or pilot, disappears. I do not want to suppress the ambiguity, which is present also in that weighty but elusive word "admiration," and in the conclusion of the poem, about which there has been energetic disagreement. Rather, I want to keep the ambiguity, but keep it subordinate, as a smile; as a laugh it would dominate and spoil things much finer than itself.

[31] *Essays in Divinity*, p. 37.

[32] In addition to the earlier analyses by Leonard Unger and Doniphan Louthan, the poem has recently received some close attention. I refer the reader particularly to the essays by A. J. Smith, in *MLR*, LI (1956), and in *Littérature Moderne*, VII (1957), to the extended comments by William Empson, "Donne the Space Man," *Kenyon Review*, XIX (1957), especially pp. 381–89, and to Helen Gardner, *Business of Criticism*, pp. 64–75.

[33] Perhaps one may say of the image what has been said of the new philo-

sophical analysis of language: that it makes possible a study of the mind's experience without the usual collaboration of the mind.

[34] *Religio Medici*, ed. Ernest Rhys (New York: Dutton, 1909), p. 74. I have modernized the spelling in a couple of places.

[35] I take this term from Martz, *Poetry of Meditation*. Rosemond Tuve has recently questioned the proper meaning of the term: "Sacred 'Parody' of Love Poetry, and Herbert," *Studies in the Renaissance*, VIII (1961), 249–88.

[36] *Sermons*, VIII, 93.

[37] F. H. Bradley's model argument for the concept of infinity, in the second essay of *Ethical Studies*, 2nd ed. (Oxford: The Clarendon Press, 1927), was not, but could have been, to a large extent based upon this poem. I mean, of course, the underlying structure of moral thought in the poem, which the poem plays upon and advances in the form of a seriously witty fiction, not a literal argument. For instance, Bradley writes of the false infinite: " 'Increase the quantity forever' means, 'Have forever a finite quantity, and forever say that it is not finite.' " "The finite was determined from the outside, so that everywhere to characterize and distinguish it was in fact to divide it . . . because the negative, required for distinction, was an outside other." But in the true infinite "you can distinguish without dividing . . . the whole is so present in each, that each has its own being in its opposite, and depends on that relation for its own life. . . . The simplest symbol of it is the circle, the line which returns into itself, not the straight line produced indefinitely." The conclusion is only a somewhat larger, nonsexual, version of Donne's. Bradley writes: " 'Realize yourself as an infinite whole' means, 'Realize yourself as the self-conscious member of an infinite whole, by realizing that whole in yourself.' "

I record this parallel as an interesting coincidence, one that I came upon after completing my interpretation of the poem. It helps reassure me that I have discovered rather than invented the import of certain moral arguments. One ought to be able to assume that neither Donne nor Bradley can be credited with having invented this moral logic.

I take this occasion to record another coincidence. I have read, since completing my manuscript, an illuminating chapter on Whitehead in Albert W. Levi, *Philosophy and the Modern World* (Bloomington: Indiana University Press, 1959). I offer the following quotation for its relevance to the movement of Donne's mind in the ternary forms: "The dialectical opposition of thesis and antithesis which always in Hegel receives its logical resolution in such a way as to override and therefore nullify the discrepancy, in Whitehead is completely different. In Hegel, opposition disappears in mid-air by an act of dialectical magic. Whitehead is too existentially oriented for such theatrical illusion. His opposites are elements in the nature of things. They are incorrigibly *there*" (pp. 530–31). I seem to have been fumbling for a similar notion when I spoke of Donne's imaginative refusal to annihilate the external. Donne's Platonism, like Whitehead's, can treat the diversity of experience with generous respect.

Chapter III. The Burden of Consciousness

[1] Satire II, l. 107; Elegy IX, l. 45.

[2] Holy Sonnet XIX.

[3] Letter "To Sir Edward Herbert," ll. 36–40.

[4] "The First Anniversary," l. 334; cf. *Essays in Divinity*, p. 38, which makes

it clear that the following line —"(Since most men be such as most thinke they bee)"— is no common piece of skepticism.

⁵ "The First Anniversary," ll. 329–31.

⁶ Letter "To Sir Edward Herbert," ll. 21–24.

⁷ *Complete Poetry and Selected Prose*, p. 364.

⁸ "The First Anniversary," ll. 99–102, 105–11; letter "To the Countesse of Bedford" ("You have refin'd mee"), l. 65; "The Progresse of the Soule," ll. 112–14, 118–20; letter "To the Countesse of Bedford" ("T'have written then, when you writ"), ll. 76, 79–80, 83–86; Satire III, ll. 77–79, 98–100; "The Crosse," ll. 38, 45–46, 49–54, 57–60.

⁹ "A Hymne to Christ, at the Authors Last Going into Germany."

¹⁰ Leslie Fiedler, "Archetype and Signature," *Sewanee Review*, LX (1952), 265–66.

¹¹ Helen Gardner suggests that Donne "as a poet of Love" was "inspired in part" by the *Dialoghi d'Amore* of Leone Ebreo (Don Judah Abrabanel), and in the context she seems to imply that Donne's doctrine of the creation drew on the same source: "The Argument about 'The Ecstasy,' " *Elizabethan and Jacobean Studies Presented to F. P. Wilson*, pp. 305–6. It is an interesting idea, and answers her admirable desire to recover the "events and circumstances" of historical immediacy in order to oppose that modern trend which "substitutes for historical reality a kind of Golden Age of the Mind" (*Business of Criticism*, p. 135). I hope I do not lack sympathy with her motive or misunderstand the "suggestion" referred to above. But a powerful reader like Donne had available a wide range of historical sources for his intellectual conviction. Milton held the same belief, though more steadily and more pervasively than Donne; I do not think we shall locate his particular source.

¹² *Essays in Divinity*, pp. 37–38.

¹³ *Ibid.*, pp. 29–30.

¹⁴ *Ibid.*, p. 21. An interesting attempt to relate Donne's metaphorical practice to the influence of Dionysius may be found in Isamu Muraoka's "The Historical Background of Metaphysical Poetry," *Studies in English Literature*, XXXVII (The English Literary Society of Japan, 1960), 49–64. I am indebted to Margaret Schlauch for calling my attention to the article.

¹⁵ *Essays in Divinity*, p. 22.

¹⁶ The most ambitious and detailed study of the poem is that by Richard Sleight, in *Interpretations*, ed. John Wain (London: Routledge and K. Paul, 1956). Kermode (*John Donne*, p. 21) also comments on two rhythms of the poem: "superficially slow in movement, but with a contrapuntal velocity of thought."

¹⁷ "A Valediction: Of the Booke."

¹⁸ For further discussion, see Appendix 2, pp. 217–18.

¹⁹ See Appendix 2, pp. 218–21.

²⁰ See Appendix 2, pp. 221–22.

²¹ Holy Sonnet XIX.

²² "Honour is so sublime perfection," ll. 44–45.

²³ *Shakesperian Comedy* (London: Methuen, 1938), p. 11. A list of the studies Mr. Charlton might have in mind would fill many pages and would even include a semihistorical work like Patrick Cruttwell's *The Shakespearean Moment* (London: Chatto and Windus, 1954).

²⁴ *Shakespeare and the Popular Dramatic Tradition* (Durham: Duke University Press, 1944), 26. Donne's "medievalism," which used to be associated

chiefly with scholastic philosophy, here benefits from an interpretation which brings it up to date with a modern critical development. For by implication Donne's art, like Shakespeare's, may be thought to have important roots in folk art. This kind of investigation has not, to my knowledge, been applied to Donne, as it has to Shakespeare — notably by Bethell and the late A. P. Rossiter.

[25] The quotation is from "Tradition and the Individual Talent." In trying to check the first reference I found at least a dozen statements to this effect, but none that satisfied my memory until I rediscovered an obscure quotation from an early review of Eliot's in F. O. Matthiessen's *The Achievement of T. S. Eliot*, 2nd ed. (New York: Oxford University Press, 1947), p. 94: "The artist, I believe, is more *primitive*, as well as more civilized, than his contemporaries, his experience is deeper than civilization, and he only uses the phenomena of civilization in expressing it."

[26] Up to a point Donne's characteristic method may be referred to rhetorical concepts of irony as a pervasive figure. But there are not, I think, precedents for Donne's kind of dynamic omission. There are, of course, precedents for saying the truth in jest, and for carrying a jest toward a known truth, but not for carrying the jest toward a truth not yet quite discovered. There certainly are not, for better or worse, critical precedents for the intimate and reciprocal relations between a man and what he is trying by art to say. Here we must frankly rely on post-Kantian attitudes toward the creative mind and take our critical risk that everything in the past is not to be explained by the past and its past. Even here, however, we may claim some distinguished historical support in the studies of seventeenth-century thought by Cassirer and Whitehead.

[27] It is true that he expresses pleasure in the circular form by which the Psalms turn back on themselves, and he likes to quote Seneca, the moral man, on the end as the true beginning. It is true that he can end a sermon: "This is the last word of our Text: but we make up our Circle by returning to the first word; the first word is, *For*; for the Text is a reason of that which is in the Verse immediately before the Text" (*Sermons*, IV, 130). I do not think, however, that this kind of pleasure is quite the same as that which went into the constructing of poems.

[28] Holy Sonnet IV.

[29] I am reminded of Whitehead's aphorism: "The aim of science is to seek the simplest explanations of complex facts. We are apt to fall into the error of thinking that the facts are simple because simplicity is the goal of our quest. The guiding motto in the life of every natural philosopher should be, Seek simplicity and distrust it." *The Concept of Nature* (Cambridge: The University Press, 1920), p. 163. One thinks most immediately, perhaps, of "Loves Growth."

[30] Elegy X, ll. 25–26.

[31] "The First Anniversary," ll. 185–86. D. C. Allen first called my attention to the just weight of these lines in his article, "The Double Journey of John Donne," *A Tribute to George Coffin Taylor*, ed. A. Williams (Chapel Hill: University of North Carolina Press, 1952), pp. 83–99. The nature of the evidence did not permit a continuous exposition of Donne's concern for simplicity, and repetition would now be tedious. For the reader who would review the discussion at leisure, the examples on which a set argument would depend are to be found in the studies of "The Good-morrow," "The Will," "Aire and Angels," "Loves Growth," and "Lovers Infinitenesse."

[32] *Enneads*, I, vi, 9. The influence of Plotinus, as Cassirer and others demonstrate, is pervasive but not simple in the seventeenth century. One has only to think of Plotinus against the Gnostics, and of his own emphasis on the rational effort required to achieve simplicity. His esthetic doctrine at once supports the older concept of imitation, reveals its inadequacies, and breaks important ground for a new concept. Milton was remembering Plotinus when he wrote, "The very essence of Truth is plainness, and brightness; the darkness and crookedness is our own" (Columbia *Milton*, III, 33). I suppose Plotinus is back of Donne's "disaforesting" of the mind. He certainly is back of those lines in "The Crosse" (ll. 33–34), as he also is back of the sonnet by Michelangelo that Mario Praz quotes as a "curious coincidence." "Donne's Relation to the Poetry of his Time," reprinted in *The Flaming Heart* (Garden City, N.Y.: Doubleday, 1958), p. 203.

[33] Quoted from an unpublished manuscript by Norman Malcolm, "Ludwig Wittgenstein: A Symposium," *Listener*, LXII (Feb. 4, 1960), 207.

[34] I have in mind the wise wit of Unger's conclusion to his case on "Fusion and Experience": "It is not easy to be patient in the search for unity, for patience is itself a kind of unity, a reconciling, perhaps a fusing, of thought and feeling" (*Man in the Name*, p. 140).

Postscript. On Donne's Modern Career

[1] "Milton," *Sewanee Review*, LVI (1948), 208.

[2] *A Garland for John Donne*, ed. Theodore Spencer (Cambridge: Harvard University Press, 1931), p. 14.

[3] Quoted by Roy Fuller, "Poetry: Tradition and Belief," *The Craft of Letters in England*, ed. John Lehmann (Boston: Houghton Mifflin, 1957), p. 90.

[4] See for instance *Letters to the New Island*, ed. Horace Reynolds (Cambridge: Harvard University Press, 1934), especially the remarks on Arthur Symons and John Davidson, pp. 144–46: "In both writers one finds that search for new subject matter, new emotions, which so clearly marks the reaction from that search for new forms merely, which distinguished the generation now going out. . . . The cultivated man has begun a somewhat hectic search for the common pleasures of common men and for the rough accidents of life. The typical young poet of our day is an aesthete with a surfeit . . . his heart full of an unsatisfied hunger for the commonplace." The problems of language, however, cannot be solved by new materials. Yeats comments on Davidson's style: "I find my enjoyment checked continually by some crudity of phrase."

Index

INDEX